Regulating Islam

Many countries in the Arab world have incorporated Islam into their state- and nation-building projects, naming it the 'religion of the state'. *Regulating Islam* offers an empirically rich account of how and why two contemporary Arab states, Morocco and Tunisia, have sought to regulate religious institutions and discourse. Drawing on a range of previously unexamined sources, Sarah J. Feuer traces and analyzes the efforts of Moroccan and Tunisian policymakers to regulate Islamic education as part of the respective regimes' broader survival strategies since their independence from French rule in 1956. Out of the comparative case study emerges a compelling theory to account for the complexities of religion-state dynamics across the Arab world today, highlighting the combined effect of ideological, political, and institutional factors on religious regulation in North Africa and the Middle East. The book makes an important and timely contribution to the on-going scholarly and policy debates concerning religion, politics, and authoritarian governance in the post-uprisings Arab landscape.

Sarah J. Feuer is a Soref Fellow at The Washington Institute for Near East Policy. She holds a PhD from the Department of Politics and the Crown Center for Middle East Studies at Brandeis University.

Regulating Islam

Religion and the State in
Contemporary Morocco and Tunisia

SARAH J. FEUER

CAMBRIDGE
UNIVERSITY PRESS

CAMBRIDGE
UNIVERSITY PRESS

University Printing House, Cambridge CB2 8BS, United Kingdom

One Liberty Plaza, 20th Floor, New York, NY 10006, USA

477 Williamstown Road, Port Melbourne, VIC 3207, Australia

314-321, 3rd Floor, Plot 3, Splendor Forum, Jasola District Centre, New Delhi - 110025, India

79 Anson Road, #06-04/06, Singapore 079906

Cambridge University Press is part of the University of Cambridge.

It furthers the University's mission by disseminating knowledge in the pursuit of
education, learning and research at the highest international levels of excellence.

www.cambridge.org
Information on this title: www.cambridge.org/9781108413213
DOI: 10.1017/9781108332859

First published 2018
First paperback edition 2020

A catalogue record for this publication is available from the British Library

Library of Congress Cataloging in Publication data
NAMES: Feuer, Sarah J., author.
TITLE: Regulating Islam : religion and the state in contemporary Morocco and
  Tunisia / Sarah J. Feuer.
DESCRIPTION: New York, NY : Cambridge University Press, 2017. | Includes
  bibliographical references and index.
IDENTIFIERS: LCCN 2017035940 | ISBN 9781108420204 (hardback)
SUBJECTS: LCSH: Islam and state—Morocco. | Islam and state—Tunisia. | Islam
  and state—Africa, North. | BISAC: POLITICAL SCIENCE / Government /
  International.
CLASSIFICATION: LCC BP64.A34 F48 2017 | DDC 322/.109611—dc23 LC record
  available at https://lccn.loc.gov/2017035940

ISBN 978-1-108-42020-4 Hardback
ISBN 978-1-108-41321-3 Paperback

To my parents

Contents

Figures

Tables

Acknowledgments

The work for this book began roughly seven years ago, and in that time I have benefited tremendously from the guidance, wisdom, and generosity of many people. The research that would ultimately form the nucleus of the study began while I was a PhD student in politics at Brandeis University's Crown Center for Middle East Studies. Shai Feldman has built an outstanding research center, one I was lucky to call home for six years. I am deeply grateful to Shai for his analytical rigor, his support, and his friendship throughout and since my doctoral studies. He is perhaps the primary reason this book exists. While at the Crown Center, I was also lucky enough to study under Eva Bellin, who as a stellar thesis advisor pushed me to pursue the comparative exercise at the heart of this book. Eva has remained a trusted mentor and friend of whom I am exceedingly appreciative. Two other first-rate scholars I came to know while at Brandeis, Chris Soper and Mounira Charrad, advised me on the dissertation and later offered invaluable suggestions aimed at sharpening the ideas and concepts contained in this book.

Those ideas and concepts came to life through my time in Morocco and Tunisia, where many individuals offered their insights into the research. In Morocco, I was indebted to Ahmed Abbadi, Samir Abu Kacem, Hassan Al Zahir, Mokhtar Benabdallaoui, Abdelwahab Bendaoud, Mohamed Boutarboush, Aziz Chbani, Mohsine Elahmadi, Imad Elarbi, Rached Elamrani, Abdelkader Ezzaki, Lahcen Haddad, Abdelali Hami el-Din, Jaafar Kansoussi, Hssein Khtou, Brahim Machrouh, Mohamed Melouk, Nizar Messari, Connell Monette, Nour-Eddine Quouar, Sadik Rddad, Mohamed Ramh, Abderrahmane Rami, Khalid Saqi, Fouad Shafiki, the group of students who hosted me at the Muhammad VI Institute for the Training of Imams, and Bilal Talidi for sharing their views and experiences with me. In Tunisia, Rafik Abdessalem, Houssein al-Abidi, Alaya Allani, Chiraz Arbi, Mokhtar Ayachi, Bochra Belhaj Hmida, Moncef Ben Abdeljelil, Hatem Ben Salem, Faouzia Charfi, Hamadi Ben Jaballah, Mahmoud Ben Romdhane, Hmida Ennaifer, Ridha Ferchiou, Said Ferjani, Iqbal Gharbi, Habib Kazdaghli, Riadh Moakhar, Asma Nouira, Hamadi Redissi, Habib Sayah, Oussama Sghaier, Mongea Suwaihi, Munir Tlili, Sami Triki, and Amira Yahyaoui graciously lent me their time, impressions, and expertise. I would also like to thank Laryssa Chomiak, who directs the American Institute for Maghreb Studies' research center in Tunis, for her assistance and hospitality during my time in Tunisia.

If the research and travel for the book began while at Brandeis, it continued and came to fruition during my time as a Soref fellow at the Washington Institute for Near East Policy. I have been incredibly lucky to call the Washington Institute my intellectual and professional home these past three years. I would especially like to thank Robert Satloff, the Institute's executive director, for supporting, steering, and refining my research. While at the Institute, I also benefited from a fantastic group of research assistants and interns, namely: Oula Alrifai, James Bowker, Gavi Barnhard, Nour Chaaban, Gabrielle Chefitz, Rachel Furlow, Eric Rosen, Patrick Schmidt, Alex Schnapp, Liza Tumen, Erica Wenig, and Matthew Wheeler.

Turning the manuscript into its current form was possible thanks to the care and kindness of Maria Marsh and James Gregory at Cambridge University Press. I would also like to thank two anonymous reviewers for offering excellent suggestions on how to improve an earlier draft. Along the way, Anne Wainscott and Lawrence Rubin also offered very helpful feedback on earlier iterations of the arguments contained in the manuscript. And at various stages of the editing and publication process, Caroline Chauncey, a friend and editor at Harvard Education Press, lent me her wisdom and perspective, for which I am deeply grateful.

Finally, I would like to thank my mother and father, Regine and Michael Feuer, and my brother, Jonathan, for their love and support.

A Note on Conventions

Arabic words are transliterated according to a simplified version of the *International Journal of Middle East Studies'* system (no diacritic marks, long vowels, or special characters). Arabic words that appear in English language dictionaries are not italicized. All other Arabic words are italicized in the first instance. Unless otherwise noted, translations from Arabic and French are my own.

NAMES

Arabic names are transcribed according to a simplified version of the *International Journal of Middle East Studies'* system, unless a different transcription is dominant in English-language texts (e.g., Alaouite, not ʿAlawite; Mohammed VI, not Muhammad VI).

PREVIOUSLY PUBLISHED MATERIAL

Short sections of the book previously appeared in a Washington Institute monograph, entitled *State Islam in the Battle against Extremism: Emerging Trends in Morocco and Tunisia*, published by the author in June 2016.

Introduction

This book investigates the political factors fueling state regulation of religion in the Arab Middle East, as played out in the realm of education. Recent scholarship has explored global variation in the relationship between religion and state, but an overarching theory to explain why and how governments regulate religion remains elusive. In the Arab world, most countries emerging from colonial rule in the twentieth century incorporated formal state establishment of Islam into their state- and nation-building projects, reflected in constitutional stipulations that Islam was "the religion of the state." But there has been considerable variation – both between states and within states over time – in the way this religious establishment has translated into state policies regulating religious interpretation and practice. State regulation of religious life in Saudi Arabia is quite unlike its counterparts in, say, Egypt or Morocco or Tunisia, despite the fact that all these countries have declared Islam to be the official state religion. The varying nature and degree of regulations touching on the religious realm across the Arab world have been evident in any number of policy domains, not least in education. What explains such variation?

To answer this question, I examine the evolving politics of religious regulation in the education systems of two Arab countries – Morocco and Tunisia – between 1956, the year these countries gained their independence from French rule, and 2016. The book tracks and explains three manifestations of religious regulation in these states over time: the infusion of Islam into the national curricula of public schools, the balance between autonomous and state-controlled institutions of religious learning, and the training and licensing of religion teachers in schools and in mosques. By analyzing the political processes at work as Morocco and Tunisia regulated religious expression and activity through their education systems, the book sheds new light on the connections between

I

political authoritarianism, government entanglement in religion, and state-religion relations more generally in the Arab world.

I concentrate on religious education – as a locus of state regulation – for several reasons. The first has to do with connections between education and political legitimacy. In the West, the gradual separation of church and state from roughly the sixteenth century onward entailed a process in which the "state gained organizational control over practices and institutions which formerly were placed under 'spiritual' authorities, such as private and civil law, *education*, science, etc."[1] Ambitious secular rulers were eager to wrest education from the control of religious authorities, since education was seen as a pivotal tool for producing a national culture and reinforcing allegiance to the state.[2] In the Islamic world, too, many postcolonial leaders believed that public education offered a means of constructing a national identity and reinforcing their own political legitimacy once the European powers withdrew. Insofar as Arab state leaders in the postcolonial era considered education a crucial tool for bolstering state legitimacy, they had an interest in seizing education from the exclusive control of the learned religious elite, or ulama (sing. *'alim*). The Quranic school was historically the primary institution of the individual's socialization to the values of the Muslim community (*umma*), serving as the intermediary between the family and the Islamic state. As one leading Moroccan sociologist put it, "The school extended the work of the family and anticipated the power of the state. This is very important because all [political] legitimacy, whatever its form, depended on the individual supporting the claim of the leading power to rule."[3] Thus, the education systems of the new states became contested spaces

[1] Matthias Koenig, "Politics and Religion in European Nation-States: Institutional Varieties and Contemporary Transformations," in *Religion and Politics: Cultural Perspectives*, ed. Bernhard Giesen and Daniel Suber (Leiden: Brill, 2005), 295. Italics mine.

[2] The literature on the connections between education and state- and nation-building in the West is vast but a good starting point is Eugen Weber, *Peasants into Frenchmen: The Modernization of Rural France, 1870–1914* (Stanford, CA: Stanford University Press, 1976), 303–38. There is also a rich literature, largely in history and political science, about the manifestation of an emerging political culture in systems and mechanisms of education in the United States. See, for example, David K. Cohen and Susan L. Moffitt, eds., *The Ordeal of Equality: Did Federal Regulation Fix the Schools?* (Cambridge, MA: President and Fellows of Harvard College, 2009); Lawrence Cremin, *American Education, the National Experience: 1783–1876* (New York: Harper & Row, 1980); Carl F. Kaestle, *Pillars of the Republic: Common Schools and American Society, 1780–1860* (New York: Hill and Wang, 1983); and David B. Tyack, *The One Best System: A History of American Urban Education* (Cambridge, MA: Harvard University Press, 1974).

[3] Interview with Mohsine Elahmadi, Rabat, January 7, 2013.

for representatives of state and societal interests debating questions of national identity and political authority. With the possible exception of works by Gregory Starrett and Malika Zeghal on postcolonial reforms of religious education in Egypt and Tunisia, most of the scholarship on the contemporary links between education and nation-building in the Arab world has not focused on religious education *per se*, and where it has, the relevant works remain confined to single country case studies.[4] This book traces the impact of debates over national identity on religious education policy in two Arab countries throughout the decades following independence, with a view to theorizing about the politics of religious regulation more broadly.

A second reason to concentrate on religious education as a target of state regulation in the Arab world derives from the role institutions of religious instruction have played in shaping the interpretation of the religious tradition. In contrast to, say, the Catholic realm, the (Sunni) Muslim world is not overseen by a centralized, hierarchically structured religious institution. In the absence of a central body vested with authority to interpret religious teachings and weigh in on such key matters as the optimal relationship between religion and state, "the control of religious interpretation [and] the devising of state mechanisms of authorization . . . are so crucial to a government that needs to secure its control of state and society."[5] In the postcolonial period, one of the ways in which

---

[4] On the links between education and nation-building in the Islamic world, see, for instance, Betty S. Anderson, "Writing the Nation: Textbooks of the Hashemite Kingdom of Jordan," *Comparative Studies of South Asia, Africa and the Middle East* 21 (2001): 1–14; David Menashri, *Education and the Making of Modern Iran* (Ithaca, NY: Cornell University Press, 1992); and Sam Kaplan, *The Pedagogical State: Education and the Politics of National Culture in Post-1980 Turkey* (Stanford, CA: Stanford University Press, 2006). On the evolving role and tenor of religious education throughout the contemporary Islamic world, see Malika Zeghal, "Public Institutions of Religious Education in Egypt and Tunisia: Contrasting the Post-Colonial Reforms of Al-Azhar and the Zaytuna," in *Trajectories of Education in the Arab World: Legacies and Challenges*, ed. Osama Abi-Mershed (New York: Routledge, 2010), 111–24; Gregory Starrett, *Putting Islam to Work: Education, Politics, and Religious Transformation in Egypt* (Berkeley, CA: University of California Press, 1998); Michel Lelong, "Le Patrimoine Musulman dans l'Enseignement Tunisien Après l'Indépendance" (PhD Dissertation, Université de Provence I, 1971); the excellent collection of essays in Robert W. Hefner and Muhammad Qasim Zaman, eds., *Schooling Islam: The Culture and Politics of Modern Muslim Education* (Princeton, NJ: Princeton University Press, 2007); and Iren Ozgur, *Islamic Schools in Modern Turkey: Faith, Politics, and Education* (Cambridge: Cambridge University Press, 2015).

[5] Malika Zeghal, *Islamism in Morocco: Religion, Authoritarianism, and Electoral Politics* (Princeton: Markus Wiener Publishers, 2008), xvi–xvii.

Arab regimes have sought to control religious interpretation, and thereby assert control over states and societies, is by enacting policies regulating religious education. And in their quest for control, Arab regimes (like all regimes) have faced pressures, constraints, and opportunities that have rendered their efforts to regulate religion more or less effective over the years. Understanding how these pressures, constraints, and opportunities have shaped states' regulation of religion is a central aim of this book.

In pursuing that aim, I build on and contribute to two principal bodies of scholarship. The first is social science literature highlighting the role of political interests, ideology, and social structures in accounting for dynamics of state–religion relations. Consider, for example, the "religious economy" school, which has argued that a state's approach to regulating religious institutions principally reflects the leaders' political and economic interests. Likewise, scholars focused on the role of ideas have shown that ideological debates over religion and secularism – particularly in the period of early state-building – can have long-term ramifications on the nature of religious regulation in that state. And sociologists have demonstrated the role that dominant social groupings, such as tribes, can play in affecting a state's regulation of religious institutions. The arguments advanced in these schools of thought have enriched our understanding of state-religion dynamics, moving us well beyond the simpler, if initially promising, framework of secularization theory.

Still, in certain key respects, these theories leave us with nagging questions. For example, the interest-based assumption of religious economy scholars that leaders prioritize staying in power seems self-evident enough, but it does not tell us much about why and how a leader's desire to stay in power influences policy decisions implicating religion, or why and how that leader's preferences, and by extension the relevant policy decisions, change over time. For their part, ideational theories cannot account for the ostensibly puzzling instances in which policy shifts occur against the backdrop of state elites' unchanging ideological convictions. Sociological explanations have rightly drawn attention to the role of alliances between regimes and dominant social structures, but they have not always considered the reasons those alliances form in the first place. The theoretical propositions coursing through this book seek to fill such lacunas.

The second strand of scholarship I engage addresses the relationship between Arab governance structures and religious actors in society. In the past three decades, much of the scholarship on Middle Eastern politics focused on the durability of authoritarianism and the concomitant emergence of Islamist social movements, conveying the image of an inherently strong, often "secular" Arab autocracy confronting ascendant "religious" opposition movements in society. The presumption of a strong Arab state came under reexamination with the swift downfalls of Zine al-'Abidine Ben 'Ali in Tunisia and Hosni Mubarak in Egypt, but even before the 2011 uprisings, scholars had begun to challenge the notion that states in the postcolonial Arab (and, more generally, Islamic) world had ever been truly "secular."[6] This book extends such challenges to the dominant narratives, highlighting the constraints and pressures facing state institutions and leaders in the formulation of policies regulating religion, and demonstrating that the dichotomy pitting a secular state against a religious society obscures more than it enlightens the complex and shifting relationships between religion and state throughout the region.

REGULATING ISLAM IN MOROCCO AND TUNISIA

The ensuing chapters present a theory of how and why Arab states regulate religion, and demonstrate how that theory has played out through an examination of the politics fueling state regulation of religious education in two Arab countries since their independence in 1956. The comparative exercise follows the logic of John Stuart Mill's *method of difference*, in which selected cases are similar in as many ways as possible except for those to which the observed variation is attributed. Morocco and Tunisia, which have demonstrated both cross-national and within-country variation in regulations affecting religious education over time, share important conditions that enable us to control for certain factors in explaining the observed variation. Both countries emerged from French colonial rule in the mid-twentieth century; both countries enjoyed similar levels of economic development at the outset; and both countries have majority

---

[6] Key works in this vein have included Sayyed Vali Reza Nasr, *Islamic Leviathan: Islam and the Making of State Power* (New York: Oxford University Press, 2001); Zeghal, *Islamism in Morocco: Religion, Authoritarianism, and Electoral Politics*; Colin J. Beck, "State Building as a Source of Islamic Political Organization," *Sociological Forum* 21 (2009): 337–56; Birol Baskan, "The State in the Pulpit: State Incorporation of Religious Institutions in the Middle East," *Politics and Religion* 4 (2011): 136–53; Rachel M. Scott, "Managing Religion and Renegotiating the Secular: The Muslim Brotherhood and Defining the Religious Sphere," *Politics and Religion* 7 (March 2014): 51–78; and Rory McCarthy, "Rethinking Secularism in Post-Independence Tunisia," *The Journal of North African Studies* 19 (2014): 733–50.

Sunni Muslim populations. Yet, Morocco and Tunisia have differed in the configuration of the three factors to which I am attributing much of the observed variation in religious regulation, i.e., in the interplay of each regime's legitimating ideology, political opponents, and institutional endowment. The similarities and differences between these two countries, therefore, lend themselves well to a comparative study.

For each country, I demonstrate the extent to which the interaction of regime ideology, political opposition, and institutional endowment produced shifts in three indicators of religious regulation. The first indicator is the infusion of Islam into the national curricula, i.e., the degree to which Islamic principles and tenets are embedded into the national curricula of public schools. I focus on changes in secondary school Islamic education and philosophy curricula because it is at the middle and high school levels and in these subjects that tensions over religion and secularism have been most acute. Each country underwent several periods of distinct curricular orientation. In Morocco, the curricular stasis of the first decade after independence shifted toward an expansion and reorientation of the curricula beginning in the late 1960s, and in the mid-1990s the regime once again sought a reorientation that continues to this day. In Tunisia, the period between 1956 and 1969 saw a contraction and reorientation of the curricula, followed by an expansion and reorientation in the 1970s and 1980s, and yet another contraction and reorientation from 1989 onward.

The second indicator to be explained is the shifting balance between state-controlled and autonomous institutions of religious instruction. I focus on the evolving administrative status of two institutions: the Quranic school (at the preprimary, primary, and secondary levels) and the mosque-university. Quranic schools and institutes of higher Islamic learning have historically carried tremendous cultural significance as principal sites of religious learning, and thus identity cultivation, throughout the Muslim world. Furthermore, they have retained an importance for substantial numbers of citizens to the present day. By the early 2000s, for example, over 80 percent of Moroccan children enrolled in preschools were attending Quranic schools.[7] On the eve of independence, Morocco and Tunisia possessed numerous institutions of traditional Islamic learning, including Quranic schools for young children and classical institutions of advanced religious learning such as the Qarawiyyin

---

[7] Moroccan Ministry of National Education, *Aperçu sur le Système Educatif Marocain* (International Bureau of Education, 2004).

Mosque-University in Fes and the Zaytuna Mosque-University in Tunis. After 1956, the states diverged in their respective approaches to these institutions. In Morocco, the reigns of Mohammed V and Hassan II (1956–99) saw a blend of autonomy and state control for many institutions of religious learning. Since the early 2000s, Mohammed VI has been asserting tighter state control over Quranic schools and institutions of higher Islamic learning. In Tunisia, the trajectory went from state control in the 1950s and 1960s to a mix of autonomy and state control in the 1970s and 1980s, to a resumption of state control in the 1990s and 2000s. The political tumult of what came to be known as the Arab Spring led to a weakening of state control over religious institutions in Tunisia.

Finally, I examine shifting regulations of training and licensing procedures for teachers of Islam, both in schools and in mosques. Research reveals variation within and between the cases in several ways, including who was enlisted to teach religion classes, which ministries supervised the training and licensing of religion teachers, whether nonreligious subjects and instruction by nonreligious professionals were required as part of religion teachers' training, and the degree to which ulama engaged in teaching received their training and/or salaries from the state. The story of how and why Morocco and Tunisia have regulated religion through their education systems is partly a story of these states' attempts to regulate ideas, but it is also a story of how and why they sought to mold and reform the individuals entrusted to disseminate those ideas.

To tell this story, I rely on evidence drawn from seven years of research. In addition to an extensive review of the secondary literature on modern Moroccan and Tunisian political history, I spent parts of 2011 and 2012, and much of the 2012–13 academic year, conducting field work in Morocco and Tunisia. Living in these countries permitted me to interview nearly seventy officials involved in crafting education, and specifically religious education, policies over the past twenty years – principally, Education Ministry division heads, leading imams, religious seminary professors and deans, and civil society members who consulted on the reforms. In Morocco, I also accessed related texts and documents stored in the National Center for Documentation, the National Library, the King Abdul Aziz Center for the Maghreb in Social Sciences, and the Abderrahim Bouabid Foundation's archives. In Tunisia, I reviewed curricular materials, textbooks, ministry directives, and related documents held in the national archives, the National Museum of Education and its affiliated National Center for Pedagogic Innovation and Education Research, the Institute for Research on the Contemporary Maghreb, the National Documentation Center (particularly for press articles), the Center for Economic and Social Research and Studies, and the Arab Human Rights Institute. To complement the materials located in North Africa, I gathered and analyzed Moroccan and Tunisian school textbooks housed at the Georg Eckert Institute for International Textbook Research in Braunschweig, Germany. Finally, five research trips to the region since 2014 enabled additional interviews with Moroccan and Tunisian ministers of religious affairs, Education Ministry officials, political party leaders, and imam training directors, permitting deeper examination of the states' regulations of religious institutions since the upheavals of 2011.

Stitching these elements together, I begin by presenting my main theoretical argument in Chapter 1. Chapter 2 then dives into the Moroccan case, providing an historical account of how the Alaouite regime's ideology of legitimation, political opposition, and institutional endowment evolved between the country's independence in 1956 and the onset of the Arab Spring in late 2010. In Chapter 3, I describe and analyze the impact of these factors on Morocco's curricular incorporations of Islamic instruction, shifting balances between state control and autonomy for Moroccan institutions of religious learning, and changes in training and licensing procedures for religion instructors between 1956 and 2011. Chapter 3 also introduces the concept of "identity bargaining," my way of characterizing instances in which authoritarian regimes such as the Alaouite monarchy, when faced with limited institutional resources, confront opponents' demands by trading concessions to some aspects of citizens' identities in exchange for lessened pressure to fulfill others. Chapter 4 then turns to the Tunisian case, reviewing how the ideology of legitimation, political opposition, and institutional endowment of the regimes of Habib Bourguiba and Zine al-ʿAbidine Ben ʿAli evolved between independence in 1956 and the departure of Ben ʿAli in 2011. Chapter 5 then demonstrates how these factors interacted to produce curricular reforms, shifting balances between state control and autonomy for religious institutions, and changes to licensing and training procedures for Tunisia's instructors of Islam.

Given the import of recent events in the region, it seemed advisable to devote a separate chapter to the post-Arab Spring landscape. Thus, Chapter 6 examines evolving dynamics of state regulation of religion in both countries since the 2011 uprisings, positioning the whole study in the contemporary context of change and uncertainty in the post-Spring Arab world, and highlighting questions emanating from the study that will hopefully invite further research. For example, while both states' efforts to regulate religious institutions similarly comprised elements of the respective regimes' survival strategies, the divergent paths of Morocco and Tunisia since 2011 – regime survival in one case, regime collapse in the other – raise the possibility that the states' varying approaches to regulating religious institutions throughout their contemporary history may partly explain the differing fates of each regime since 2011. To the extent that the Moroccan regime's skillful management of the religious realm over the years contributed to that regime's relative stability in the aftermath of the Spring, the findings of this book enhance our understanding of why and how the Arab monarchies managed to emerge from the political challenges of the past six years intact. In Chapter 6, I address the possible links between religious regulation and the "monarchical exceptionalism" of the post-Spring Arab world in greater depth.

I

Toward a Theory of Religious Regulation

For much of the late nineteenth and twentieth centuries, the dominant view among Western social scientists studying the relationship between religion and state was that as modernization proceeded, secularization – comprising both a separation of religious and political authority, and a diminishing religiosity in society – would follow. However, world events, including the emergence of Liberation Theology in Latin America in the mid-twentieth century, the 1979 revolution in Iran that resulted in a theocratic regime, and an upsurge in religious revival movements around the world in the 1970s and 1980s, led some scholars to argue that secularization theory should be discarded.[1]

It is true that neither the predicted separation of religion and state, nor the prophesied diminution of public religiosity, came to pass in quite the way secularization theorists had posited. Most governments have continued to exhibit a mix of religious establishment and a separation of religious and state authority, while religion has remained a central part of people's lives around the world. Indeed, this book deals with two modern countries which have not only experienced growing institutional ties between religion and state, but also a persistence (if not growth) in societal levels of religious observance.

---

[1] For compelling critiques of secularization theory, see Jose Casanova, *Public Religions in the Modern World* (Chicago, IL: Chicago University Press, 1994); and Nikki R. Keddie, "Secularism and the State: Towards Clarity and Global Comparison," *New Left Review* 1 (December 1997): 21–40. Classic secularization theory was expounded most forcefully in the works of sociologists such as Emile Durkheim, Auguste Comte, Max Weber and, more recently, Peter Berger.

Still, we should be careful about dismissing secularization theory entirely. For one thing, there are undeniably countries in which secularization – both at the state level and in terms of societal religious observance – *has* accompanied modernization. In places such as Canada, Britain, Australia, and France, to cite a few examples, state and religious authorities *did* separate and levels of church attendance *did* plummet in the last century. In the United States, where religion and state have ostensibly been separated since the founding of the republic, levels of religious observance have remained more or less constant, and relatively high, in the last sixty years.[2] These countries may be exceptions to the rule, but the fact that states have diverged in their degree of secularization only reinforces the need for deeper analysis of the observed variation in state-religion ties around the world.[3] Rather than continue to debate the merits of secularization theory as it was originally conceived, a more fruitful set of questions asks how and why governments regulate religion, how and why such regulations change, and how such regulations reflect ongoing negotiations between states and societies over the contours of national identity. It is to these lines of inquiry that the present book speaks.

In recent years, social scientists and their peers in Middle East studies have begun tackling these questions. Three strands of scholarship on the dynamics of state-religion relations bear mention here. The first is often referred to as the "religious economy" school, as it applies rational choice frameworks borrowed from economics to explain differences in political outcomes, including state regulation of religious institutions. Religious economy proponents have argued that the degree to which a state regulates the "religious market" – that is, the public arena in which religious institutions compete for adherents – is a function of leaders' political and economic interests. Accepting the assumption that political leaders are chiefly concerned with their own survival, their ability to raise revenue, and their success in minimizing social unrest, religious economy scholars have found that where policies restricting religious practice will serve these aims, states are most likely to adopt them. By contrast, where political leaders reason that they would be better served by loosening regulations of religious practice, states are likely to permit greater religious freedom.[4]

4 Self-serving

2 Pippa Norris and Ronald Inglehart, *Sacred and Secular: Religion and Politics Worldwide* (Cambridge: Cambridge University Press, 2004), 2.
3 For a snapshot of this variation, see Jonathan Fox, *A World Survey of Religion and the State* (Cambridge: Cambridge University Press, 2008).
4 For works emblematic of the religious economy approach, see Stathis Kalyvas, *The Rise of Christian Democracy in Europe* (Ithaca, NY: Cornell University Press, 1996); Carolyn

The religious economy school has rightly highlighted the role of political interests in determining policy outcomes, including policies implicating religion. Extending the focus on political interests to the countries under examination here, Moroccan and Tunisian rulers unquestionably sought to lower the costs of ruling, and at times this quest motivated them to adopt certain regulations targeting religious education. But the interest-based argument only takes us so far, for two primary reasons. First, the religious economy literature often assumes that political leaders are distinct from religious leaders (implicitly accepting secularization theory), so it is unclear how a religious economy approach would handle a case such as Morocco, where the head of state is also the chief religious authority and the ruling monarchs have always based their legitimacy, at least in part, on their intrinsic religious identity as descendants of the Prophet Muhammad.

Second, acknowledging the importance that a leader such as Tunisia's Habib Bourguiba (r. 1957–87) or Morocco's Hassan II (r. 1960–99) attached to staying in power does not tell us much about why these leaders reasoned as they did, or how the preoccupation with staying in power translated into specific policies regulating religion. Nor does the assumption of self-interested behavior shed light on why and how these leaders' preferences – and, as a result, their political calculations and ensuing policies – changed over time. There is a tendency in the religious economy literature to chalk up variation in policy outcomes to the rather unsatisfying, and at times borderline tautological, notion that regimes act in their own self-interest. I take it as given that regimes are primarily concerned with their own survival. But a major goal of this book is to identify a logic governing the strategic calculations these regimes make when they resort to the regulation of religion as a means of ensuring their political survival.

In addition to the religious economy school, the arguments at the heart of this book build on an approach that emphasizes the role of ideas in determining the nature and degree of state regulation of religion.[5] Political

they would do anything to stay in power

Warner, *Confessions of an Interest Group: The Catholic Church and Political Parties in Europe* (Princeton, NJ: Princeton University Press, 2000); Anthony Gill, "Rendering Unto Caesar? Religious Competition and Catholic Political Strategy in Latin America, 1962–79," *American Journal of Political Science* 38 (1994): 403–25; Anthony Gill, *Rendering Unto Caesar: The Catholic Church and the State in Latin America* (Chicago: University of Chicago Press, 1998); and Anthony Gill, *The Political Origins of Religious Liberty* (Cambridge: Cambridge University Press, 2008).

[5] For the ideational approach, see Sultan Tepe, *Beyond Sacred and Secular: Politics of Religion in Israel and Turkey* (Palo Alto, CA: Stanford University Press, 2008); Ahmet Kuru, *Secularism and State Policies Toward Religion: The United States, France and Turkey*

include ideology

scientists such as Ahmet Kuru have noted that the rational choice model has trouble explaining why a country such as Turkey pursued aggressively secularist policies for decades, even though such policies raised the cost of ruling considerably. Kuru argues that to understand policies regulating religion, we need to consider the role of ideology. Specifically, in countries where the state-building period was marked by ideological debates concerning secularism and religious accommodation, the ruling elites thereafter adopted an "assertive secularist" stance that left little room for religion in the public sphere and all but eliminated it in the administrations of state power. By contrast, in countries where debates in the state-building period revealed a consensus between secular and religious groups concerning the relationship between state and religious authority, the emerging state tended to adopt policies less restrictive of religion in public, or what Kuru calls "passive secularism."

His focus on democracies notwithstanding, Kuru's emphasis on ideology finds support in authoritarian contexts such as Morocco and Tunisia. To explain the regulation of religious education in Tunisia, for example, without acknowledging President Bourguiba's ideological conviction that religion was an obstacle to modernization would miss a crucial piece of the story. And, in line with Kuru's prediction about the importance of ideological debates concerning religion and secularism in the state-building years, the presence of this cleavage in the Tunisian case and its absence in the Moroccan case did correspond to two different trajectories of religious regulation in the early post-independence years. In Tunisia, where a secularist faction of the nationalist movement managed to exclude its rivals among the traditional religious establishment from the higher echelons of state power at independence, ensuing policies greatly reduced the (already diminishing) role of religion in Tunisian public life. By contrast, in Morocco, where the nationalist movement that had expelled the French was more unified on the question of how religion should inform governance, policies of the post-independence monarchs largely left in place institutions of religious education and public expressions of religious life.

A second relevant finding in the literature on ideology emerges from the works of Joel Fetzer, J. Chris Soper, and Stephen Monsma. These scholars have demonstrated that differences in levels of religious accommodation

---

(Cambridge: Cambridge University Press, 2009); Birol Baskan, "State Secularization and Religious Resurgence: Diverging Fates of Secularism in Turkey and Iran," *Politics and Religion* 27 (March 2014): 28–50.

for Muslim minorities in European democracies have resulted principally from a given country's dominant political ideology, coupled with inherited relations between state and religious institutions (e.g., the foundational relationship between church and state). For example, Fetzer and Soper have found that in Germany the state's longstanding practice of granting corporate status to religious groups and subsidizing religious instruction in public schools has made it easier for Muslim groups to gain religious accommodation. In contrast, France's more rigid ideology of *laïcité*, dictating a removal of religious expression and practice from the public sphere, has made the state less accommodating to Muslim religious practices.[6] In a separate study, Monsma and Soper highlight the impact of cultural assumptions concerning the notion of religious freedom on policies regulating religious institutions.[7] The combined emphasis on ideational and institutional factors in these works finds support in my cases.

Still, the ideological orientations of ruling elites cannot fully explain state regulation of religion. In Morocco and Tunisia, for example, the ideological inclinations of the rulers remained fairly constant over time, yet the states' approaches to regulating religion changed. And because scholarship emphasizing ideology has largely refrained from theorizing about the mechanisms linking ideological debates with different policy outcomes, ideas-based theories have difficulty explaining why the ideological rifts that emerged between Bourguiba's supporters and opponents translated into a win for Bourguiba's secularist camp, how this win informed actual policies, and how ideological divisions among elites continued to affect the nature and degree of a state's regulation of religion well beyond the state-building years. The present book aims to fill these gaps.

A third strand of scholarship upon which this study builds can be found in Mounira Charrad's work on the Maghreb countries' divergent approaches to religious family law. In her seminal book, Charrad asks why Morocco, Algeria, and Tunisia pursued different policies concerning Islamic family law at independence even though all three states emerged from colonial rule under similar circumstances. She argues that North African states' postcolonial regulations of religious law were partly a function of the political coalitions in place once the Europeans left. Since tribal kin networks maintained a keen interest in seeing a greater

---

[6] Joel Fetzer and J. Christopher Soper, *Muslims and the State in Britain, France, and Germany* (Cambridge: Cambridge University Press, 2005).

[7] Stephen V. Monsma and J. Christopher Soper, *The Challenge of Pluralism: Church and State in Five Democracies* (Lanham: Rowman & Littlefield Publishers, Inc, 1997).

incorporation of religious tenets into the emerging family law, the varying degree of Islamization of family law across post-independence Tunisia, Algeria, and Morocco was a function of "the extent to which the newly formed national state built its authority in alliance with kin groupings or, on the contrary, on bases independent of them."[8] In states where the ruling elites allied themselves with tribal and other non-state authorities that had a stake in the maintenance of traditional Islamic family law, reformists had to contend with opposition from traditional sectors of society backed by the regime; in these countries, family reform came late, as in Algeria, or not at all, as in Morocco. In contrast, where reformist elites enjoyed unrivaled political dominance at independence, as in Tunisia, secularizing reforms came early and forcefully.[9] I apply Charrad's argument on the role of political coalitions to a different realm of religious regulation – education – and find support for her argument about the importance of political coalitions beyond the post-independence period.

Finally, the book engages an intensifying debate over the role of Arab governance structures in framing and constraining the spaces in which religious societal actors have flourished. In the past three decades, scholarship on Middle Eastern politics focused on the durability of authoritarianism and the parallel emergence of Islamist social movements, conveying the image of strong, secular states seeking to outbid and defeat rising religious opposition movements. But this narrative failed to consider ways in which the states themselves had appropriated religious language to justify state expansion well before Islamist movements posed a threat, and it overlooked how Arab states had framed the very spaces in which religious actors could emerge in the first place. Much of the scholarship on political Islam also hinged on a problematic framework pitting "secular" states against "religious" societies, ignoring a more complicated and evolving relationship between religion and state in the region. The binary framework of "secular states" versus "religious societies" may have appealed to scholars because it further undercut the assumption of secularization theorists that populations had become less religious over time.[10]

---

[8] Mounira Charrad, *States and Women's Rights: The Making of Postcolonial Tunisia, Algeria, and Morocco* (Berkeley, CA: University of California Press, 2001), 2.

[9] For an earlier exposition of her argument as it played out in the Tunisian case, see Charrad, "Policy Shifts: State, Islam and Gender in Tunisia, 1930s–1990s," *Social Politics* 4 (1997): 284–319.

[10] See, for instance, Mark Juergensmeyer, *The New Cold War? Religious Nationalism Confronts the Secular State* (Berkeley, CA: University of California Press, 1993).

Aware that such portrayals missed important dynamics at play, a growing number of scholars of the Middle East have begun revisiting the dominant story lines. One key thesis to emerge contends that Arab state-building policies of the postcolonial period included processes of Islamization – i.e. processes of increasing the public visibility of religion – that were not aimed at combating Islamist political movements, since the latter had not yet emerged, but rather sought to strengthen the state by making it more reflective of society's cultural mores and delineating the spaces in which religion could serve a public function.[11] Regulating religion, in this new understanding, has been, at least in part, a means of state-building, and the resultant policies belie the notion of "secular" postcolonial states throughout the region. Malika Zeghal, for example, has argued compellingly that the independent Moroccan monarchy initially pursued policies of religious regulation not so much out of fear of religious social forces – many of whom were allied with the regime – as to establish the monarchy's hegemony over both the political and religious realms.[12] More recent works have offered refreshingly nuanced assessments of the relationship between religion and state in countries such as Syria and Saudi Arabia, although these remain confined to single-country studies.[13]

The story of how and why contemporary Moroccan and Tunisian regimes regulated religion in the educational realm builds on and lends credence to these evolving understandings of religion-state dynamics in the Arab world, and the comparative exercise of the book permits more rigorous theoretical propositions than previous works have posited.

BEYOND SECULARIZATION THEORY

The approaches surveyed above have advanced the scholarly debate over secularization theory and uncovered important dynamics fueling state

---

[11] The critique is most compelling in Nasr, *Islamic Leviathan: Islam and the Making of State Power*; Zeghal, *Islamism in Morocco: Religion, Authoritarianism, and Electoral Politics*; Beck, "State Building as a Source of Islamic Political Organization"; and Baskan, "The State in the Pulpit: State Incorporation of Religious Institutions in the Middle East."

[12] Zeghal, *Islamism in Morocco*, xii.

[13] Thomas Pierret, *Religion and State in Syria: The Sunni Ulama from Coup to Revolution* (Cambridge: Cambridge University Press, 2013); Nabil Mouline, *The Clerics of Islam: Religious Authority and Political Power in Saudi Arabia* (New Haven, CT: Yale University Press, 2014); and Bernard Haykel, Thomas Hegghammer, and Stephane Lacroix, eds., *Saudi Arabia in Transition: Insights on Social, Political, Economic and Religious Change* (Cambridge: Cambridge University Press, 2015).

| Legitimating ideology + political opposition + institutional endowment | → | State regulation of religion |

FIGURE 1.1 *The basic argument*

regulation of religion in the Arab world. Still, the admirable drive to develop parsimonious explanations for such a complicated process as religious regulation has yielded theories that tend to come up short in fully accounting for how and why these states regulate religion. Rather than focus on a single explanatory condition, the theoretical proposition at the heart of this book highlights the interactive effect of several factors. My central argument is that the nature and degree of state regulation of religion (or "religious regulation") in the Arab world has been a by-product of authoritarian regimes' strategies of political survival. But more specifically, state regulation of religion in these countries has resulted from the interaction of three factors: (1) the regime's ideology of legitimation, (2) the nature of the regime's primary political opponents in society, and (3) the robustness of the regime's institutional endowment, as reflected in the presence or absence of a hegemonic political party and the relative strength of the state's bureaucratic apparatus. Taken alone, each factor would not adequately account for why and how states regulate religion. Taken together, their interaction explains much of the observed variation. Figure 1.1 depicts this argument, which I flesh out below.

Legitimating Ideology

A regime's *ideology of legitimation* – i.e. the overarching set of justifications a regime offers for its right to rule – influences state regulation of religion. Specifically, the degree to which regimes rely on religious themes, principles, and imagery in their legitimating rhetoric will partially determine the nature and degree of religious regulation. Another way to conceptualize this factor is to ask to what extent religion factors into a regime's justification for its right to rule. Based on the answer, as gleaned from the speeches and writings of ruling elites, foundational documents such as constitutions, and rituals performed by the state, we can imagine regimes falling somewhere along a spectrum of ideological legitimation, ranging from what I call "traditionalist" to "non-traditionalist."

The most traditionalist regimes are those that rely heavily on religious themes and symbolism to justify a leader's right to rule. I prefer the term "traditionalist" to "traditional" because many of the twentieth century's political regimes and social movements grounding their legitimacy in religious notions were thoroughly modern in their interpretations of religious texts and teachings, and in their tactics of political consolidation and social mobilization.[14] That they styled themselves as embodiments of tradition did not reflect a historical reality so much as a self-conscious equating of (a particular reading of) religion with tradition. For the traditionalist regime, religious observances and teachings are presumed to reflect indigenous, and therefore authentic, traditions widely adhered to in the population; for this reason, a traditionalist leader will affiliate himself closely with religious notions in his bid for political legitimacy.

A regime's traditionalism could take several forms. To borrow a term from Clifford Geertz, for some rulers religion could be *intrinsic* to their identity, as in Morocco and Jordan, where the monarchs' legitimating ideologies include frequent reference to their familial descent from the Prophet Muhammad.[15] In other instances, a traditionalist leader could promote his personal piety, guardianship of particular religious norms, or religious knowledge and scholarship as central to his political legitimacy, as the Saudi monarchs and Iranian ayatollahs have done in the modern era. Either way, religion remains a pillar of the traditionalist ruler's strategy of legitimation.

By contrast, non-traditionalist regimes are those for which religion, if present at all, remains peripheral to the ruler's rhetoric of self-legitimation. In some instances, a non-traditionalist regime may even be overtly hostile to religion. Importantly, though, non-traditionalist regimes may instrumentalize religion insofar as they occasionally promote interpretations of religious teachings to justify public policies. (This was certainly the case with Tunisia's presidents, as we shall see.) But non-traditionalist regimes do not ground their right to rule in religious ideas, and the leaders in these countries cannot claim any intrinsic religious identity. Most of the Arab regimes that emerged from colonial rule in the last century fall closer to the non-traditionalist end of the ideological spectrum.

An authoritarian regime's ideology of legitimation influences the nature of religious establishment because the regime's discursive justifications for its right to rule create a framework within which the leadership

[14] Nikki R. Keddie, "The New Religious Politics: Where, When, and Why Do 'Fundamentalisms' Appear?" *Comparative Studies in Society and History* 40 (October 1998): 696–723; Graham Fuller, *The Future of Political Islam* (New York: Palgrave, 2003); Peter Mandaville, *Global Political Islam* (London: Routledge, 2007).

[15] Clifford Geertz, *Islam Observed: Religious Developments in Morocco and Indonesia* (Chicago, IL: University of Chicago Press, 1971): 75–7.

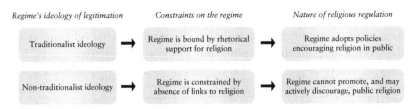

FIGURE 1.2 *Legitimating ideology and religious regulation*

can maneuver, delineating the range of policy options it may adopt without opposing its own stated commitments. In the absence of regularized mechanisms of political turnover familiar to democracies, authoritarian rulers nonetheless know they will be judged by how closely their policies adhere to their expressed ideological preferences. Therefore, the extent to which a regime's self-legitimation includes identification with citizens'/subjects' religious identities will affect the nature and degree of that regime's regulation of religion. In the educational realm, for example, we would expect more traditionalist regimes to insist on a greater incorporation of religious instruction into the national curricula than their non-traditionalist counterparts because such a policy would reinforce the regimes' rhetorical commitments to religion contained in their legitimating ideology. Figure 1.2 depicts the links I am proposing between ideology of legitimation and religious regulation.

The cases examined in this study lend support to what might appear to be an intuitively predictable proposition: Morocco, where the traditionalist Alaouite rulers have always touted their descent from the Prophet, has tended to promote a greater amount of religious instruction in the schools than Tunisia, where the non-traditionalist regimes of Habib Bourguiba and Zine al-'Abidine Ben 'Ali not only lacked intrinsic religious identities but espoused ideologies inimical to religious practices common throughout the country.

However, even if a regime's ideology of legitimation informs state regulation of religion by constraining the regime's policy options, this factor alone cannot fully explain the nature of religious regulation, let alone changes therein. For one thing, even if we can confidently identify a regime as more or less traditionalist, from this classification it is difficult to predict important indicators of religious regulation. In the educational sphere, for example, a regime's incorporation of religious themes into its self-legitimating ideology could dictate greater or less state control of institutions of religious learning: a traditionalist regime such as the

Alaouite monarchy in Morocco could seek greater state control over these institutions on the grounds that the king is also a religious figure (the Commander of the Faithful), but a non-traditionalist ruler such as Tunisia's Bourguiba could similarly find incentive to establish state control over religious institutions in order to prevent them from challenging his religious bona fides. From a regime's ideology of legitimation it is also difficult to predict variation in indicators such as the specific curricular treatment of the established religion.

The stories of how and why Morocco and Tunisia have regulated religious education since independence point to another limitation of ideology as an explanatory factor: were we to rely on governing ideology alone, we would have a hard time accounting for changes in Moroccan and Tunisian regulations of religious education over time, given that both regimes' ideologies of legitimation remained constant throughout the period under review. Explanations relying solely on ideology also have difficulty accounting for instances in which a regime's policies patently contradict its own governing ideology, as when a traditionalist regime like the Moroccan monarchy sought to incorporate a greater number of secular concepts into its religious education curricula despite the regime's continued reliance on a close identification with Islam as a source of political legitimacy. Ideology is a necessary part of the story because it frames the policy choices available to a regime; but once it has done so, it remains inadequate to fully explain the ensuing regulations. To ideology, we need to add an additional factor: the nature of a regime's primary political opponents.

Political Opposition

State regulation of religion in these countries is also shaped by the form and tenor of the group(s) a regime perceives to be its most formidable political opponent(s). Specifically, the degree to which a regime's political opponents frame their demands and base their own legitimacy on religious grounds will color the state's regulation of religion. Whereas Charrad has compellingly demonstrated the role of a regime's political supporters in determining policy outcomes, I emphasize the salience of a regime's political opponents in determining religious regulation, in part because the nature of an aspiring regime's opposition often precedes – and consequently dictates – the very alliances on which this regime will rely in consolidating power. When the post-independence Moroccan monarchs sought out partnerships with certain rural tribes, for example,

POLITICAL OPPOSITION	REGIME'S RESPONSE	RELIGIOUS REGULATION
...demands changes in religious regulation	CO-OPTATION	Regime alters religious regulation in line with opposition's demands
	REPRESSION	Regime does not alter religious regulation, or adopts regulations inimical to opposition
...does not demand changes in religious regulation	CO-OPTATION	Regime does not alter religious regulation
	REPRESSION	Regime alters religious regulation to counteract opponents

FIGURE 1.3 *Political opposition and religious regulation*

it was largely because they hoped such alliances would counter the well-established, urban-based nationalist parties posing the greatest threat to their political hegemony.

The key consideration is the degree to which opposition forces incorporate religious themes into their grievances and issue demands implicating the state's regulation of religion. Faced with these demands, the regime faces two options: it can co-opt the opposition by embarking on "a process of mobilizing and incorporating individuals into state organizations,"[16] and thereby accommodate some of the co-opted opposition's preferences, or it can repress this opposition, thereby rejecting its demands. In the realm of religious education, for example, co-optation of groups demanding less regulation of religious institutions might translate into policies increasing the administrative and pedagogical autonomy of institutions of religious learning. Likewise, repression of opposition groups demanding an increase in public school hours devoted to religious instruction might involve policies that diminish or leave untouched the place of religion in school curricula. Figure 1.3 demonstrates the connections I am proposing between the nature of a regime's political opponents and the regime's approach to regulating religion.

In Morocco and Tunisia, the changing nature of the groups each regime perceived to be its most formidable political opponents unquestionably contributed to the regimes' evolving policies regulating religion. Yet, if

---

[16] Joshua Stacher, *Adaptable Autocrats: Regime Power in Egypt and Syria* (Stanford, CA: Stanford University Press, 2012), 40.

TABLE 1.1 *Primary opponents of the Moroccan and Tunisian regimes,*
1956–2016

Time period (approx.)	Morocco	Tunisia
1950s–1960s	Religious nationalists	Religious nationalists and leftists
1970s–mid-1980s	Religious nationalists and leftists	Leftists and liberals
Late 1980s–2010	Radical Islamists	Islamists
2011–16		Radical Islamists

the nature of the regimes' political opponents helps to explain much of the within-country variation in religious establishment, it cannot fully account for the observed between-country variation. Indeed, Moroccan and Tunisian leaders faced a similarly evolving constellation of political opponents over time (as Table 1.1 recounts), but they did not always pursue similar policies of religious regulation.

Much like a regime's ideology of legitimation, then, political opposition alone cannot always fully explain differing state approaches to regulating religion. This is because, in carrying out its stated ideological preferences and in determining how to minimize opposition and cement alliances, a regime contends with another crucial factor: the strength of the institutional resources at its disposal.

Institutional Endowment

This book focuses on two institutions – the political party structure and the bureaucracy – and argues that the presence or absence of a hegemonic political party representing the regime, coupled with the relative strength of the bureaucracy, can contribute to the nature and degree of a state's religious regulations. I define a hegemonic party as one that dominates the political sphere by enjoying broad popularity and/or a broad presence through local offices, high penetration of associational life, and a high level of membership. The emphasis on bureaucratic strength stems from the literature on state capacity, which has highlighted the crucial role a state's administrative capacities can play in facilitating a regime's policies.[17] I gauge the relative strength of the state's bureaucracy by how

---

[17] Leading works in this vein include Theda Skocpol, Dietrich Rueschemeyer, and Peter Evans, eds. *Bringing the State Back In* (Cambridge: Cambridge University Press, 1985);

you need both hegemonic party & a robust bureaucracy

	BUREAUCRACY	
	ROBUST	THIN
HEGEMONIC PARTY — PRESENT	STRONG Tunisia: 1956–69, 1989–2010	MIXED
HEGEMONIC PARTY — ABSENT	MIXED Morocco: 1990–2016 Tunisia: 1970–88, 2011–16	WEAK Morocco: 1956–89

FIGURE 1.4 *Institutional endowment in Morocco and Tunisia, 1956–2016*

closely it adheres to Max Weber's paradigm of an organization staffed by individuals who are appropriately trained, hired on a merit basis, and possessing professional expertise.[18] As I am principally interested in religious education policy, the focus is on the strength of each state's educational and religious bureaucracies.

A "strong" institutional endowment for the regime would come in the form of a hegemonic political party to which it is allied, and a robust bureaucracy (often headed by regime loyalists) to which it can resort in implementing policies. In contrast, the absence of a hegemonic political party, coupled with a resource-poor (and/or ideologically oppositional) bureaucracy, would translate into a "weak" institutional endowment for the regime. An institutional endowment would qualify as "mixed" if it enjoyed either a hegemonic party without a robust bureaucracy or a strengthened bureaucracy without a hegemonic party. Figure 1.4 is a visualization of what I mean, with designations of each country's institutional endowment for the period under review.

In interaction with a regime's legitimating rhetoric and the nature of a regime's political opponents, institutional endowment can influence

---

Michael Mann, "The Autonomous Power of the State: Its Origins, Mechanisms and Results," *Archives Européennes de Sociologie [European Journal of Sociology]* 25 (1984): 185–213; Joel Migdal, "Studying the State," in *Comparative Politics: Rationality, Culture, and Structure,* eds. Mark Lichbach and Alan Zuckerman (Cambridge: Cambridge University Press, 1997); Joel Migdal, *State in Society: Studying How States and Societies Transform and Constitute One Another* (Cambridge: Cambridge University Press, 2001).

[18] Max Weber, "Politics as a Vocation" in *Max Weber: Essays in Sociology,* eds. H.H. Gerth and C. Wright Mills (New York: Oxford University Press, 1946), 79–82; Max Weber, *Economy and Society: An Interpretive Sociology* (Berkeley, CA: University of California Press, 1978), 956–63.

INSTITUTIONAL ENDOWMENT	REGIME IDEOLOGY	RELIGIOUS REGULATION
STRONG	Traditionalist regime	Regime adopts policies reflecting traditionalist ideology
	Non-traditionalist regime	Regime adopts policies reflecting non-traditionalist ideology
WEAK	Traditionalist ideology	Regime cannot adopt policies in line with traditionalist ideology
	Non-traditionalist ideology	Regime cannot adopt policies in line with non-traditionalist ideology

FIGURE 1.5 *Institutional endowment and religious regulation*

state regulation of religion in two ways. First, institutional resources can condition a regime's success in carrying out policies in line with its ideology of legitimation. To take an example from this study, one reason Bourguiba was able to implement educational policies minimizing the place of religion in the national curricula was because he benefited from a hegemonic political party and a highly centralized bureaucracy in which his allies occupied top positions. These were conditions that his domestic political opponents (and his Moroccan counterpart at the time) lacked. Thus, a strong institutional endowment facilitated the Tunisian regime's success in carrying out policies that reflected and reinforced the marginalization of religion central to its legitimating ideology. The constraints of a weak institutional endowment also help to explain the ostensibly puzzling situations in which traditionalist regimes end up reducing state support for religion. Figure 1.5 spells out what I mean.

Institutional endowment can affect religious regulation in a second way: the presence or absence of a dominant political party and solid bureaucratic apparatus can condition a regime's response to political opposition. Faced with a challenger, the regime's decision to co-opt or repress this challenger will depend in part on the institutional resources available to it. A stronger institutional endowment makes repression easier, while a weak institutional endowment incentivizes co-optation. A feeble institutional endowment may also increase the regime's receptivity to bottom-up demands percolating in society, so if these demands touch on the matter of religious regulation, we can expect institutionally weaker regimes to be more responsive to them.

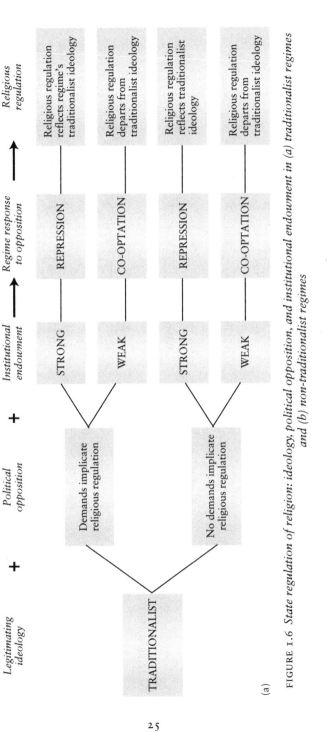

FIGURE 1.6 *State regulation of religion: ideology, political opposition, and institutional endowment in (a) traditionalist regimes and (b) non-traditionalist regimes*

25

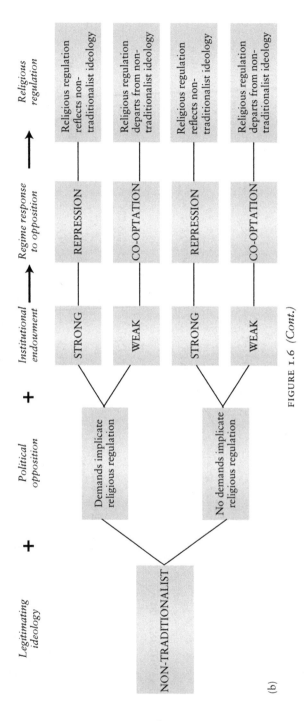

FIGURE 1.6 *(Cont.)*

(b)

26

Two examples from the Moroccan and Tunisian experiences bear out these propositions. In the 1970s, the Alaouite regime faced multiple political challengers, among which were groups calling for greater Arabization and Islamization of the school system. In determining how to respond to these groups, Hassan II could not escape the gnawing reality of an insufficient number of Arabic-speaking teachers to staff the state-run public schools. This limitation led him to co-opt his challengers by splitting the difference: in exchange for a delay in Arabization, he promised (and delivered) greater state support for Islamic education. The regime calculated that by splitting the linguistic and religious dimensions of Moroccan citizens' demands, it could bolster its own legitimacy and undercut the opposition. Or consider the Tunisian case, where the ruling party in the 1970s began losing popular support and succumbing to internal ideological schisms. These chinks in the party's armor facilitated a greater receptivity on the part of the weakened regime to societal demands concerning religion in public life, which in turn fueled changes in the religious education curricula. Shifts in religious regulation were thus partly attributable to institutional liabilities hobbling the regimes.

Having outlined the ways in which ideology, political opposition, and institutional endowment each factor into decisions about regulating religion, it is now possible to incorporate all three in an expanded representation of the basic argument I presented at the outset. For ease of reference, I have divided this expanded form of the basic argument into two part figures. Figure 1.6a depicts the combined effects on religious regulation resulting from the interplay of regime ideology, political opposition, and institutional endowment in cases where the regime's legitimating ideology is traditionalist. Figure 1.6b offers a corresponding representation for instances in which the regime's legitimating ideology is non-traditionalist. The theoretical models reflected in the two flowcharts offer a simplified range of conditions and outcomes facing policymakers. As the ensuing chapters demonstrate, the empirical realities informing a state's regulation of religion, no less than the varied nature of that regulation, are undoubtedly more complex.

2

The Moroccan Ingredients of Religious Regulation

The central argument of this book is that the nature and degree of religious regulation in Morocco and Tunisia have resulted principally from the interaction of three factors: (1) a regime's ideology of legitimation, in particular the degree to which a regime's overarching justification for the right to rule incorporates religious themes; (2) the landscape of political opponents confronting the regime, especially the extent to which these groups make demands concerning state-religion relations; and (3) the regime's institutional endowment, as reflected in the presence or absence of a hegemonic party and a robust bureaucracy through which the regime can implement its political will. In this chapter, I explore these ingredients in the Moroccan context, reviewing the progression over time in the Alaouite regime's ideology of legitimation, political opposition, and institutional endowment from the state's independence in the 1950s to the eve of the Arab Spring in 2010.

THE MOROCCAN MONARCHY'S ENDURING TRADITIONALISM

Throughout the period under review, the Moroccan regime's legitimating ideology was traditionalist insofar as the Alaouite monarchs consistently included overt references to religion in their self-legitimating rhetoric. Two salient aspects of the regime's ideology reflected this traditionalism: (1) emphasis on the monarch's descent from the Prophet Muhammad, or *Sharifism*[1] and (2) the melding of political and religious authority in the designation of the monarch as both the head of state and Commander of the

---

[1] The Arabic term sharif is usually translated as "noble" and, in the Sunni world, has been used to denote one who is descended from the Prophet Muhammad. *Sharifism* or

Faithful (*Amir al-Mu'minin*). Of the two, Sharifism has the deepest roots, while the Commandership of the Faithful is a more recent innovation.

The Alaouite sultans have touted their descent from the Prophet Muhammad since the seventeenth century, when they established dominance over large swaths of Moroccan territory. The Sharifian identity did not immunize the Alaouites from continued challenges to their political and religious authority. On the contrary, for centuries, much of the territory in what later became unified Morocco remained under the control of local tribal confederations, and the Alaouites continued to compete with learned religious elites (ulama) and Sufi brotherhoods for hegemony over the religious realm, especially in areas beyond the control of the central state. In the early twentieth century, a new source of competition came in the form of prospective European penetration, prompting the Alaouites to once again invoke their religious bona fides to justify their leadership. In this vein, a 1908 project for a Moroccan constitution cited the Muslim nature of the state and the eminence accorded to the sultan, who was designated as the defender of religion, the supreme commander of the armed forces, and chief of domestic and international policy. The blending of the sultan's religious and political functions was short-lived, as the French authorities made a clear distinction between the sultan as religious leader and the colonial, elite-led government as the secular, sovereign power of the state.

The Alaouites sought to revive this blend of religious and political leadership after independence, coupling their Sharifian identity with the "historically constructed political fiction" that the sultan, renamed king in 1957, was also the Commander of the Faithful.[2] They presented the monarch as the embodiment of the link between the religious and political identity of Morocco, insofar as the Alaouite descendants of the Prophet's Quraishi tribe had introduced Islam and the institution of the monarchy to Morocco. As Geertz noted in his seminal work on Moroccan Islam, the Alaouite monarchs claimed legitimacy to rule on both *intrinsic* grounds, i.e. that the monarchs possessed a spiritual leadership by virtue of their hereditary link to the Prophet's family, and on *contractual* grounds, i.e. that the monarchs had for centuries been granted the right to rule by the Moroccan public through the investiture ritual of *bay'a*.[3] Both notions conveyed that the monarchy was the only institution capable of unifying an independent Morocco.

Sharifianism is used interchangeably to denote the brand of leadership based on this descent, claimed by the Jordanian and Moroccan monarchies today.

[2] Zeghal, *Islamism in Morocco*, xiv.

[3] Geertz, *Islam Observed*, 75-7.

The traditionalism of the monarchy's legitimacy has been enshrined in Morocco's constitutions since 1962, when the first foundational text adopted after independence declared Islam to be "the religion of the State" and described the king as "the Commander of the Faithful (Amir al-Mu'minin), [who] symbolizes the unity of the nation, guarantees the perennial nature and continuity of the State, and enforces Islam as well as the constitution." The 1962 constitution likewise declared that the king was "sacred and inviolable," and identified the national motto as "God, Homeland, King."[4] Identical language appeared in amended constitutions of 1970, 1972, 1992, and 1996, all of which referred to Morocco as a "sovereign Muslim State" in which the king, as Commander of the Faithful, was "sacred and inviolable."

Royal speeches over the years have similarly reflected the Alaouites' traditionalism. In his Throne Speech of March 3, 1962, Hassan II used language that would become typical of monarchical discourse to situate the construction of the new political order in the context of a broader spiritual revival and to draw links between political reforms and the religious heritage the king purportedly embodied:

Concerned to effectuate a renewal in the Islamic spirit, a revival of thought and of faith and an awakening of the Muslim conscience, and to consolidate the foundation of our religion, we created, after our ascension to the Throne, a state ministry of Islamic Affairs . . . In this same perspective, the Minister of [pious endowments] followed the correct path forged by our beloved father [Mohammed V, r. 1956–1961] to sprinkle the country, especially in the most disadvantaged regions, with mosques designated for prayer and for education, permitting our subjects to fulfill their religious duties . . . It is therefore crucial that the Islamic character of our personality affirm itself in all aspects of this reform. The history of our country demonstrates that the most flourishing periods of our past often coincided with those periods marked by the genius of Islam . . . Every reform we undertake here will be inspired by our tolerant religion, and while it is true that the goods of this world are relative, spiritual riches are absolute.[5]

Such attempts to solidify the king's religious legitimacy remained a staple of Hassan II's addresses throughout the years,[6] and his son continued to promote the Alaouite dynasty's spiritual endowment after assuming

---

[4] For an analysis of Morocco's first modern constitution, see Louis Fougère, "La constitution marocaine du 7 décembre 1962." *Annuaire de l'Afrique du Nord* 1 (1962): 155–65.

[5] "Discours prononcé par sa majesté le Roi Hassan II le 3 Mars 1962," *Annuaire de l'Afrique du Nord* 1 (1962): 755–63.

[6] See, for example, King Hassan's speeches and press conference remarks of May 17, 1963, November 18, 1963, March 3, 1967, March 3, 1968, July 30, 1970, and February 17,

the throne upon his father's death in 1999. Since then, every royal address has opened with praise for God, the Prophet's family, and/or the Prophet's companions – clear references to the Sharifism undergirding the regime – and Mohammed VI has consistently anchored his dynastic legitimacy in religious references. Consider, for example, language from Mohammed VI's first Throne Speech on August 20, 1999:

God wished for us to assume the Throne of our glorious ancestors, in line with the desire of our father [Hassan II], who named me Crown Prince, and in line with our constitution, and in keeping with the practice of bay'a to which the representatives of our nation have adhered . . . Let us work hand in hand toward the realization of our aspirations and the noble actions that await us, in counting on God's help, as He is the greatest master and the greatest protector.[7]

A decade later, the tenor of Mohammed VI's speeches had changed little, offering carefully crafted references to the monarchy's religious bona fides:

Our main advantage, in [achieving our developmental goals] rests in the fundamental national constants that we continually aim to renovate. The first of these constants is the unity of [the] Maliki [legal school of] Sunni Islam, for which we, as Commander of the Faithful, assume responsibility to modernize its institutional structures and cultural spaces.[8]

Such examples point to the enduring traditionalism of the Alaouite regime's legitimating ideology. Yet, while the regime's governing ideology has remained consistent, Morocco's modern monarchs have faced an evolving constellation of political opponents over the years.

THE ALAOUITES' POLITICAL OPPONENTS

Three broad clusters of political opponents have emerged to challenge the Alaouite regime since independence. In the 1950s, the monarchy perceived its main political opponents to be the urban-based religious

---

1972. All are reprinted in the corresponding year's volume of the *Annuaire de l'Afrique du Nord*.

[7] All Throne Speeches of Mohammed VI are accessible on the Moroccan National Center for Documentation's website, at www.abhatoo.net.ma/maalama-textuelle/developpement-economique-et-social/developpement-social/discours-et-interviews-officiels/discours-et-interviews-de-s-m-le-roi-mohammed-vi.

[8] Throne Speech of Mohammed VI, June 30, 2009.

nationalists of the Independence (*Istiqlal*) Party. Then, beginning in the 1960s and extending into the 1970s and early 1980s, the Istiqlalians were joined by a growing number of leftist factions allied with groups such as the National Union of Popular Forces and similarly oriented movements on college campuses. Finally, from the mid-1980s onward, anti-monarchy Islamists (what I will refer to as "radical Islamists," to distinguish them from pro-monarchy groups) emerged as the regime's primary political opponents. Importantly, and in contrast to the Tunisian experience, the Moroccan regime's principal opponents have always included groups challenging the monarchy on religious grounds, a fact that carried important implications for the regulation of religious education. A review of the Alaouites' shifting political opposition will help to demonstrate why.

(1) **1950s: Religious Nationalists.** Founded in 1944, the Istiqlal Party built its popularity on a religiously infused nationalism that blended *Salafi*[9] revivalism with demands for independence, social justice, and universal education.[10] Around the time of its founding, there emerged a split within the Moroccan nationalist movement between, on the one hand, graduates of traditional religious institutions such as 'Allal al-Fassi, the leader of the Istiqlal, who argued that there could be no separation between religion and politics, and the country's first graduates of French universities such as Muhammad Ibn Hassan al-Wazzani on the other, who advocated a political model in which sovereignty resided in the people and Islam did not figure prominently. The sultanate, which had always relied on its religious identity for legitimacy, embraced the Salafism of al-Fassi's Istiqlal, and the alliance enabled the Alaouites and the Istiqlalians to emerge as winners from the struggle against the French. By 1956, nearly 90 percent of Moroccans belonged to the Istiqlal or sympathized with it.[11]

---

[9] The term "Salaf" in Arabic is usually translated as "ancestors" or "predecessors" and refers to the earliest Muslims who lived around the time of the Prophet Muhammad. Salafism is a Sunni legal and theological movement that seeks to redefine Islamic practice according to how adherents believed the faith was practiced by the first three generations of the Prophet's followers. The definitive work on Salafist doctrines remains Roel Meijer's edited volume, *Global Salafism: Islam's New Religious Movement* (Oxford: Oxford University Press, 2013).

[10] Jamil Abun-Naser, "The Salafiyya Movement in Morocco: The Religious Bases of the Moroccan Nationalist Movement," *St. Anthony's Papers* 16 (1963): 90–105; Mohamed El-Mansour, "Salafis and Modernists in the Moroccan Nationalist Movement," in *Islamism and Secularism in North Africa,* John Ruedy ed. (New York: St. Martin's Press, 1994): 53–71; Abdelbaki Hermassi, "The Political and the Religious in the Modern History of the Maghreb," in Reudy, *Islamism and Secularism,* 87–99.

[11] El-Mansour, "Salafis and Modernists in the Moroccan Nationalist Movement," 69.

For the sultanate, fostering an alliance with al-Fassi and other members of what Elbaki Hermassi termed the "nationalitarian-scripturalist elite" put it at odds with the other main locus of religious authority in the country, the Sufi brotherhoods, or *zawiyas*.[12] Salafism had always been hostile to Sufism and other popular forms of Islam, but the divide between the sultanate and the Salafi nationalists on the one hand and the Sufi brotherhoods on the other was also political. Many leading zawaya had lent tacit support to the French colonial administration prior to and during the struggle for independence. The sultanate's alliance with the Istiqlal during the Protectorate allowed it to emerge from the colonial struggle as a leading contender for political power. However, after gaining independence, the Alaouites viewed the movement that had helped bring them to power as a source of political competition, and thus a threat.

The Istiqlal never managed to extend its appeal to rural Morocco, but its presence in the cities challenged the monarchy in two key respects. First, the Istiqlal enjoyed widespread legitimacy for its leadership during the struggle to oust the French, a legitimacy that enabled the party to secure important ministerial posts in the country's first governments. Second, the Istiqlal challenged the king's religious bona fides because leaders such as al-Fassi were widely respected religious scholars in their own right, and much of the party's leadership hailed from venerated institutions of religious learning such as the Qarawiyyin Mosque-University in Fes and the Yussufiyya Mosque in Marrakesh. Though institutions such as the Qarawiyyin had lost much of their vigor during the Protectorate, they retained a deep cultural significance for Moroccans. The Istiqlal's popularity among students and the teachers associated with the country's traditional institutions of religious instruction would carry important implications for the monarchy's regulation of religious education.

(2) 1960s–early 1980s: **Religious Nationalists and** Leftists. The religious nationalists of the Istiqlal remained key rivals of the regime throughout the ensuing decades. In 1963, for example, al-Fassi and other leading figures in the Istiqlal resigned from the coalition government in protest over the growing powers being accorded to Hassan II's Interior Minister, Ahmad Reda Guedira. This prompted the king to form a new cabinet comprised of independents and pro-monarchy parties such as the Berber-dominated *al-Haraka al-Sha'biyya* (Popular Movement, or MP by its French acronym), forcing the Istiqlal into the opposition. A speech

---

[12] Hermassi, *Leadership and National Development in North Africa* (Berkeley, CA: University of California Press, 1972), 101.

al-Fassi made in parliament in 1964 epitomized the challenge he and the Istiqlal's supporters continually posed to the king's religious legitimacy. Discussing the Religious Affairs Ministry's budget, al-Fassi implied that the Commander of the Faithful was failing in his guardianship of the religious realm by neglecting his religious duties:

In our country, we see everywhere that church steeples are surpassing in height our skyscrapers and minarets. This religious propaganda on the part of foreign sects is striking and we are forced to ask ourselves which of the two communities [Christian or Muslim] is better off. There are now in Morocco more churches and temples than mosques and Islamic schools. And all of this foreign religious activity is not being met by action on the part of our government to preserve the Muslim soul.[13]

Similar efforts to challenge the regime's religious bona fides were on display at the Istiqlal's Party Congress in 1965. There, the party issued its political platform, calling for a renewal of "the Islamic conscience and spiritual orientation of the nation," decrying "the sad situation currently facing our country in its religious and social life," and demanding "a religious, moral and social instruction in the schools, the mosques, the social clubs and in the news media, newspapers, radio and television."[14] A year later, al-Fassi published a book entitled *In Defense of Sharia*, in which he criticized the constitutional designation of the king as "sacred and inviolable," writing that "Kings and heads of state do not have power or rights that come to them from heaven . . . This power and these rights belong to the people who – by virtue of the status of its individual members, vice-regents of God on earth – is the source of sovereignty (*siyada*), the source of power."[15] Such statements took aim at the Alaouites' claims to political and religious authority, and the religious nationalists of the Istiqlal remained a central threat to the regime. Still, the party consistently calculated that it would be better off operating within the basic framework of the monarchical political system rather than advocating its overthrow.

Others were less conciliatory, and in the 1960s a growing number of radical leftist groups emerged alongside the religious nationalists to

[13] Al-Fassi's speech is reprinted in André Adam, "Chronique Sociale et Culturelle: Maroc," *Annuaire de l'Afrique Du Nord* 3 (1964): 212.

[14] The party platform is reprinted in Roger Le Tourneau, "Chronique Politique," *Annuaire de l'Afrique du Nord* 4 (1965): 182 and André Adam, "Chronique Sociale et Culturelle: Maroc," *Annuaire de l'Afrique du Nord* 4 (1965): 253.

[15] As cited in Zeghal, *Islamism in Morocco*, 72.

oppose the monarchy. In 1959, a left-wing faction of the Istiqlal broke away to form *al-Itihad al-Watani li-l-Quwat al-Sha'biyya* (the National Union of Popular Forces, or UNFP by its French acronym). Hassan II banned the Communist Party that year and remained unsympathetic to leftist ideologies more generally, but he initially welcomed the creation of the UNFP, most likely because it ensured his opposition would be divided. Along with its student union, the UNFP emerged as the more radical alternative to the Istiqlal, opposing the monarchic regime and denouncing the king's economic policies. When Hassan II invited members of the various parties to sit on a constitutional council in 1961, for example, the UNFP boycotted the initiative. And when a constitutional referendum took place a year later, the UNFP urged its members to vote "no," in contrast to the Istiqlal's (grudging) support for the basic law.

Throughout the 1960s and 1970s the regime's impatience with the UNFP and similarly oriented leftist groups led to violent clashes. In 1963, for example, the regime arrested 130 members of the UNFP and accused them of plotting a coup. One year later, Mehdi Ben Barka (a UNFP leader who was by then in exile), Omar Benjelloun, Abderrahmane Youssoufi, and other prominent members of the party were put on trial and some were sentenced to death. The deterioration in the regime's relations with its leftist opponents inspired Hassan II to suspend the constitution and declare a state of emergency in 1965.

On July 10, 1971, during Hassan II's forty-second birthday celebration at his palace in Skhirat, an army colonel led 1,400 cadets in an attempted coup. The attack, which left one hundred people dead and more than 200 persons injured, ended after one of Hassan II's generals, Muhammad Oufkir, led several army units and the police in putting down the rebels. A year later, on August 16, 1972, the king was flying home from a visit to France when four Moroccan air force jets attacked his plane as it passed over Tetouan, a town on the northern coast. The attempted coup left ten people dead and forty-five injured, but Hassan II survived. It was a measure of the regime's enduring perception that religious nationalists and leftists constituted its greatest political threats that even after the attempted coups, for which no evidence surfaced to implicate the Istiqlal or the UNFP, Hassan II accused them of orchestrating the attacks.[16]

Indeed, the regime's assessment of its enemies endured well into the next decade. In the mid-1970s, as the Palace continued to arrest and

---

[16] J. Gourdon, "Chronique politique: Maroc," *Annuaire de l'Afrique du Nord* 10 (1971): 332–3.

imprison certain student activists and politicians, the UNFP changed its name to *al-Itihad al-Ishtiraqi li-l-Quwat al-Sha'biyya* (the Socialist Union of Popular Forces, or USFP by its French acronym) following a split within the leadership. The USFP fared no better in its relationship with the regime, as occasionally violent confrontations with the government throughout the ensuing decade and a half would demonstrate. As late as 1981, the regime was placing one hundred members of the USFP on trial for allegedly instigating a series of bread riots in which several hundred citizens lost their lives. But shortly thereafter, the regime's perception began to shift and the monarchy increasingly came to view its most formidable opponents in the country's Islamist movements, some of which the regime had initially supported to counteract the Left.

(3) **Mid-1980s–2010: Radical Islamists.** The first signs of Islamism in Morocco appeared in 1969, when Abdelkrim Mouti – a former teacher and member of the UNFP – founded a movement called *al-Shabiba al-Islamiyya* (Islamic Youth). The regime initially considered such groups to be either benign or instrumental in beating back leftist opposition, and in 1972 Hassan II legalized al-Shabiba al-Islamiyya. But three years later, after the group claimed responsibility for the assassination of a prominent leftist politician, Hassan II outlawed the group and it splintered into several offshoots. One branch, led by Abdelilah Benkirane and Saad Eddine al-Othmani, ultimately took a less confrontational route, accepting the monarchy's legitimacy and disavowing violence. The movement would go through several incarnations before emerging in its current form. Throughout the 1980s, Benkirane sought and repeatedly failed to obtain legal recognition for his association, and in 1992 the group changed its name to Reform and Renewal (*al-Islah wa-l-Tajdid*), thereby dropping the reference to Islam. In the mid-1990s, the group once again changed its name to Reform and Unicity (*al-Islah wa-l-Tawhid*) and later merged with another Islamic group to become the Movement of Unicity and Reform (*al-Tawhid wa-l-Islah*). Throughout the 1990s Benkirane's group developed ties to a small political party called the *Mouvement Populaire Democratique et Constitutionnel* (MPDC), and in 1998 the latter renamed itself *Hizb al-'Adala wa-l-Tanmiyya*, or the Party of Justice and Development (PJD).

Alongside groups such as al-Shabiba al-Islamiyya, the 1970s also saw the emergence of 'Abd al-Salam Yassine, a shaykh of Berber origin who would become the most well-known Moroccan Islamist thinker of the twentieth century. At the time of independence, Yassine was working as an inspector at the Ministry of Education, an experience that would inform his later works. In 1973 he published *al-Islam Ghadan* (Islam Tomorrow), in which he argued that the French-imposed educational system had "led to the cultural bifurcation of the society and to the spread of a Western mentality and behavior among the educated elites . . . [that were] alien, backward, and designed in part to disorient and dislocate the future generations of the country."[17]

A year after *Islam Tomorrow* appeared, Yassine sent Hassan II a public epistle, entitled *al-Islam aw al-Tufan* (Islam or the Deluge), in which he accused the monarch of "playing with Islam" and urged him to repent.[18] In Yassine's estimation, hereditary monarchy was not sanctioned in Islam and the Commandership of the Faithful should be chosen by religious scholars (ulama), not bestowed upon someone by virtue of his bloodline. Considering Yassine to be an isolated case, Hassan II locked him up in an asylum for the insane for three years. Upon his release in 1977, Yassine was barred from preaching in mosques, though the regime continued to judge his influence as relatively marginal.

In 1981, this perception began to change as a result of two developments. First, Yassine founded a group called the *Jama'a Islamiyya* (Islamic Movement), which would evolve into the *Jama'at al-'Adl wa-l-Ihsan* (Justice and Charity Movement). Second, following an increase in the price of bread and other basic commodities that year, the country's leading labor unions launched a series of strikes, which turned deadly in Casablanca. The Interior Ministry reported that sixty-six Moroccans had been killed in clashes with security forces, but opposition groups such as the USFP claimed the number of victims was between 600 and 1,000.[19]

The regime's response to the bread riots of 1981 suggested it no longer believed the antimonarchist stance of Islamists such as Yassine to be an isolated affair but rather part of a larger emerging threat to stability. Following the restoration of calm in the capital (and a rescinding of the price hikes), the king issued a decree establishing a High Council of Ulama, over which he would preside and through which the Palace would monitor religious activities taking place throughout the kingdom. In addition to the High Council, the 1981 decree created numerous regional councils charged with managing local mosques, organizing

---

[17] As reprinted in Emad Eldin Shahin, "Secularism and Nationalism: The Political Discourse of 'Abd al-Salam Yassin," in Ruedy, *Islamism and Secularism in North Africa*, 175.

[18] As reprinted in Henry Munson, Jr., *Religion and Power in Morocco* (New Haven: Yale University Press, 1993), 165.

[19] Jean-Claude Santucci, "Chronique Politique: Maroc," *Annuaire de l'Afrique du Nord* 20 (1981): 577.

conferences and other educational initiatives, and implementing directives of the High Council.[20]

The monarchy's shifting perception of its opponents was also apparent three years later, when a second attempt to reduce subsidies on basic goods in 1984 provoked a series of riots in more than fifty locales around the country and the ensuing clashes between protestors and state security forces left nearly one hundred Moroccans dead.[21] Unlike in prior decades, when the regime had confronted such outbursts with harsh repression of implicated leftist groups, this time the regime arrested and put on trial not only leftist activists allegedly involved in the protests but also members of (decidedly anti-leftist) Islamist movements whom the regime accused of participating in the protests. In a harshly worded speech, Hassan II for the first time attributed the social strife to leftist and foreign agitators sympathetic to Ruholla Khomeini's revolution in Iran and the Muslim Brotherhood (among others). From the regime's perspective, Khomeini's ideology and that of the Muslim Brotherhood, while doctrinally at odds with each other, represented threatening deviations from the country's religious traditions – the former because of its Shi'i roots, the latter because of its rejection of the Commandership of the Faithful.[22]

To handle the emerging threat, Hassan II sought to weaken the Islamists by splitting them up. The regime repressed radical Islamists, i.e. those groups espousing violence and/or refusing to operate within the monarchical framework, but tolerated Islamist movements that ostensibly accepted the monarchical system. In this vein, the regime took a harsh approach to Yassine and his followers, imprisoning the shaykh in 1984 for circulating an Islamic newspaper, *al-Subh* (the Dawn), and confining him to house arrest upon his release in 1986. Likewise, in the 1990s the regime disavowed and sought to dismantle violent jihadi groups such as *al-Salafiyya al-Jihadiyya*, a movement claiming to draw inspiration from Sayyid Qutb and other Muslim Brotherhood ideologues.

By contrast, Islamists willing to buy into the monarchical system fared better. By the late 1990s the aging king was ready to integrate, if gradually, Benkirane's group into the government. In 1997, Hassan's Interior Minister invited the MPDC (the PJD's predecessor) to participate in legislative elections in exchange for formal recognition and acceptance of the monarchy,

---

[20] Royal Decree 1-80-270 of April 8, 1981 (Bulletin Officiel du Royaume du Maroc [BORM] 3575 of May 6, 1981, pp. 231–2).

[21] Jean-Claude Santucci, "Chronique Politique: Maroc," *Annuaire de l'Afrique du Nord* 23 (1984): 901.

[22] Ibid., 902.

and one year later the Islamist party joined the coalition government of socialist leader (and former leftist foe) Abderrahmane Youssoufi. The decision to invite the PJD into the political process was motivated in part by a desire to protect Morocco from the fate of neighboring Algeria, where by this point nearly 100,000 people had been killed in a civil war sparked by the regime's response to an Islamist electoral victory. The move enabled the Alaouite regime to balance against the socialists who were on the verge of winning the legislative elections, and to undercut the more radical antimonarchists of al-ʿAdl wa-l-Ihsan and violent jihadi groups that had emerged. Hassan's gradualist approach also found support among PJD leaders, many of whom viewed the devastating fate of their peers in Algeria as a cautionary tale to avoid. If the monarchy hoped that the PJD's entry into politics would chip away at al-ʿAdl wa-l-Ihsan's base of support, the relative weakness of the movement upon Yassine's release from house arrest in 2000 suggested the regime's strategy had worked. Yassine died in 2012 and al-ʿAdl wa-l-Ihsan remains banned.[23]

But the strategy was not foolproof when it came to violent groups. In May 2003, twelve Moroccan citizens blew themselves up in front of five Jewish and European sites in Casablanca, killing thirty-three and injuring more than one hundred. In the year following the bombings, the regime enacted a tough anti-terrorism law, arrested between 2,000 and 5,000 individuals, and announced that 2,112 Islamists had been charged in connection with the May 2003 attack. Of the 903 individuals convicted, seventeen were later sentenced to death. Those who were involved in planning the attacks later claimed to have been inspired by jihadi groups, reinforcing the regime's perception that it faced a home-grown problem of religiously motivated violent opposition.[24]

In the aftermath of the attack, the PJD faced widespread criticism and suspicion in the news media and on behalf of rival factions, some of which alleged the Islamist party had indirectly paved the way for such violence

---

[23] On the PJD's decision to enter the political system, and the regime's attendant acquiescence, see Michael Willis, "Between *Alternance* and the Makhzen: at-Tawhid wa Al-Islah's Entry into Moroccan Politics," *The Journal of North African Studies* 4 (1999): 72–5. For more on the regime's strategy of propping up the PJD in an effort to counteract the Islamists of al-ʿAdl wa-l-Ihsan, see Michael Willis, "Political Parties in the Maghrib: the Illusion of Significance?" *The Journal of North African Studies* 7 (2002): 7; Malika Zeghal, "Religion et Politique au Maroc Aujourd'hui," *Institut Français des Relations Internationales*, Working Paper (November 2003): 16.

[24] Marvine Howe, *Morocco: The Islamist Awakening and Other Challenges* (New York: Oxford University Press, 2005), 324–5; Human Rights Watch, "Morocco: Human Rights at a Crossroads," Vol. 16, No. 6 (2004).

and called on the regime to ban the party outright. That did not come to pass, but the party spent much of 2003 on the defensive and began downplaying its religious ideology in favor of an emphasis on "development" and loyalty to the constitution and the monarchy. Additionally, the leader of the PJD's civil society sister organization, al-Tawhid wa-l-Islah, was forced to resign following what were widely perceived as equivocal comments concerning the religious legitimacy of the monarchy; and the party acquiesced to new regulations issued by the Interior Ministry that effectively ensured the party would not win a mayoral seat in upcoming municipal elections. In the event, the PJD did manage to capture mayoral positions in Meknes, Kenitra, and Temara, though these gains were weaker than expected. The entire episode suggested the PJD had not become a "co-opted" party so much as an opposition faction permitted to "co-habit" alongside its peers in a multiparty system that still reserved the bulk of political power for the ruling monarch.[25]

MAKING THE MOST OF A WEAK INSTITUTIONAL ENDOWMENT

Since independence, the Moroccan monarchy has lacked a hegemonic political party, and until the 1980s the regime's bureaucracy was comparatively weak. Beginning in the mid-1980s, however, several state ministries – including the Ministry of Pious Endowments and Islamic Affairs – underwent reforms that strengthened the regime's administrative apparatus and carried important implications for the regime's regulation of religious education.

From the outset, the Alaouites were careful to avoid appearing to seek absolutist rule. For example, Mohammed V's first national consultative assembly of 1956 included seventy-six representatives of political parties, unions, the agricultural and industrial sectors, religious clergy, the liberal professions, and youth groups. In response, nationalist elites in the Istiqlal – the leading political party at the time – began pushing for the

---

[25] I owe this insight to Matt Buehler, who has argued compellingly that the common designation of the PJD as merely "co-opted" overlooks the nuances of a more contested relationship between the Islamist party and the monarchy. See Buehler, "The Threat to 'Un-moderate': Moroccan Islamists and the Arab Spring," *Middle East Law and Governance* 5 (2013): 231, and Willis, "Between *Alternance* and the Makhzen: at-Tawhid wa Al-Islah's Entry into Moroccan Politics." For more on the PJD's predicament following the 2003 Casablanca attack, see Eva Wegner, *Islamist Opposition in Authoritarian Regimes: The Party of Justice and Development in Morocco* (Syracuse: Syracuse University Press, 2011), 83–6.

establishment of a constitutional monarchy in which the Prime Minister would appoint his cabinet, and the government would be imbued with authority to address all political, economic, and social problems facing the country. The Istiqlal's vision made sense, given that as the strongest political party at the time, its members would likely fill most of the important ministerial posts. Determined to prevent the Istiqlal from cementing its political hegemony, the king quickly asserted control over the main coercive apparatuses of the state – the army and the police force – and appointed a former member of his private cabinet as Interior Minister.[26]

Although Mohammed V lacked a coherent political party that could match the strength of the urban-based nationalists, he managed to turn this institutional liability into a tool of survival by encouraging a multiplicity of parties that could counterbalance the Istiqlal. Such was the motivation behind the 1959 legalization of the Popular Movement (al-Haraka al-Sha'biyya), a party with a strong rural, especially Berber, base of support that could serve as a counterweight to the urban, mostly Arab Istiqlal. His son pursued a similar course. For example, Hassan II saw to it that the 1962 Constitution outlawed a one-party system, the model then emerging in Tunisia and Algeria and one that the Istiqlal, perhaps for obvious reasons, would have preferred.[27] Hassan's allies consistently argued that "the complexity of the Moroccan society necessitated competition among multiple groups for governmental power, and that one-party rule would endanger the fundamental stability of the government,"[28] even as the king repeatedly noted that his responsibilities as monarch did not permit him to interfere with the people's choice of representatives in the parliament.[29] The Palace's role in the creation of parties such as the National Rally of Independents (Rassemblement National des Independents, or RNI) in 1978 and the Constitutional Union (Union Constitutionnel, or UC) in 1983 reflected a similar rationale of wishing to preclude the emergence of a single dominant party.

There were at least three advantages to inviting so many voices into the political sphere. First, the tactic increased the chances of these voices coming into conflict with one another. Indeed, faced with the monarchy's evident intention to both reign and govern, the Istiqlal became divided

[26] Hermassi, *Leadership and National Development in North Africa*, 173.

[27] James Sater, "The dynamics of state and civil society in Morocco," *The Journal of North African Studies* 7 (2002): 104.

[28] Hermassi, *Leadership and National Development in North Africa*, 175.

[29] See, for example, Hassan's speeches to parliament on May 17, 1963 and November 18, 1963.

over how to respond. The 1959 break-up of the party – which gave birth to the leftist UNFP – largely reflected disagreements over whether to participate in an emerging government that was increasingly comprised of the king's direct appointees. Second, encouraging multiple political parties reinforced the notion of a king in direct relationship with his people by creating the impression of a monarch hovering above a cacophony of competing, but presumably equal, voices clamoring for influence in the Moroccan political system. John Waterbury, a leading historian of Morocco, put it this way: "A sort of circular strategy is thereby put into effect: by encouraging intergroup rivalry, the necessary conditions for discontinuous political leadership are maintained, and the need for a symbol of political continuity is accentuated."[30] Third, promoting a multiplicity of parties permitted pro-monarchy ones such as the MP, the RNI, and the UC to emerge as counterweights to Istiqlalians and others advocating limits on the king's power or the abolition of the monarchy altogether.[31]

As early as 1963 the monarchy began reaping the rewards of this strategy: in that year's election for the Chamber of Representatives (one of the two houses of parliament), out of 144 seats the largest bloc – sixty-nine seats (48 percent) – went to a coalition of pro-monarchy parties called the National Front for the Defense of Constitutional Institutions. The remaining seats were split between the two main opposition parties, the Istiqlal with forty-one seats and the UNFP with twenty-eight seats, and a smattering of independent candidates.[32] The multiparty system has continued to yield dividends for the monarchy: as recently as 2009, the Palace-backed Party of Authenticity and Modernity (PAM) swept local elections and replaced the Istiqlal as the leading party in parliament. Founded in 2009 by a close friend and advisor to Mohammed VI and former interior minister, PAM embodies the most recent example of the regime's longstanding strategy of transforming what was ostensibly an institutional weakness – the lack of a hegemonic party – into an asset.

By contrast, the Alaouites took much longer to strengthen their weak bureaucracy. Unlike Tunisia, which had undergone a degree of bureaucratic centralization even before the French Protectorate, Morocco in the precolonial and colonial periods possessed an inchoate bureaucracy,

[30] John Waterbury, *The Commander of the Faithful: The Moroccan Political Elite – A Study in Segmented Politics* (New York: Columbia University Press, 1970), 146.
[31] Michael Willis, "Political parties in the Maghrib: ideology and identification. A suggested typology," *The Journal of North African Studies* 7 (2002): 3.
[32] Octave Marais, "L'élection de la chambre de représentants du Maroc," *Annuaire de l'Afrique du Nord* 2 (1963): 85.

staffed by officials with varying ties to the sultan and existing alongside tribal leaders who frustrated the central state's efforts to extend control over rural areas. For centuries, the country had been divided into a *bilad al-makhzan*,[33] or land of the government, and territories escaping the sultanate's control – the *bilad al-siba,* or land of dissidence. At independence, the bilad al-siba constituted as much as half of Moroccan territory.[34]

Before the Protectorate, the sultan's central administrative structures consisted of a few ministers with poorly delineated functions, positions that often became hereditary, and salaries that were not fixed – a far cry from Max Weber's archetype of a modern bureaucracy. In his management of the bilad al-makhzan, the sultan relied on governors (*qayids*) to collect taxes and perform other administrative functions but his sway over these regional governors was limited since most of them "were not direct representatives of central authority . . . but local notables whose influence in the tribe the sultan had ratified."[35]

The sultanate's administrative hold on the country only further deteriorated after 1912, when French authorities took advantage of the decentralized administrative apparatus they found and began pitting regional power brokers against one another – and against the sultan – in a bid for political control. Thus, when the Alaouites finally did regain political authority in the late 1950s, they inherited a poorly equipped and decentralized bureaucratic structure. As one scholar noted, "[t]his not quite centralized but no longer wholly tribal society provided the framework around which some of the fundamental Moroccan social and political institutions were to develop."[36] The lack of a robust bureaucracy, in turn, made it difficult for the state to extract resources from society and perform other key functions in the early post-independence years. In this vein, Morocco in the 1970s stood out among its neighbors for its "poor performance in collecting taxes . . . while the Tunisian state increased its tax revenue to 28% of GNP . . . Morocco has lagged behind at barely 15.3% in the 1960s."[37]

Or consider the educational realm, where Morocco's administrative weaknesses since independence have been evident in the chronic shortage

---

[33] The term "makhzan," from the Arabic word for "warehouse," is used in Morocco to denote the administrative, religious, military, and economic state structures on which the monarchy relies to rule. It can be more loosely translated as "political elite."

[34] Charrad, *States and Women's Rights,* 104.

[35] Ibid., 106.

[36] Edmund Burke, III, *Prelude to Protectorate in Morocco: Precolonial Protest and Resistance, 1860–1912* (Chicago: University of Chicago Press, 1976), 150–1.

[37] Hermassi, *Leadership and National Development in North Africa,* 183.

of qualified school teachers. In the early decades after independence, annual reports issued by the Ministry of Education repeatedly noted that the state's teacher training objectives were not being met. At the primary school level, for example, the state in 1961 needed to fill 3,536 posts but only had 1,100 graduates of elementary school teacher training institutes on hand. In 1963, the percentage of primary school teachers with formal training stood at only 24 percent. By the 1980s the state was doing better, reporting that 86 percent of primary school teachers had received formal training. Still, as recently as 2008, primary schools in Morocco faced a deficit of 1,390 instructors.[38]

At the secondary school level, the percentages of fully trained teachers available to staff the schools started out even lower than their primary school counterparts, reaching only 67 percent by 1980. In the 1990s the Ministry of Education reported that the departure of middle school teachers for high school teaching posts had left too many unfilled vacancies, and as recently as 2008, the ministry reported a dearth of middle school classrooms and an alarming rise in the ratio of students to teachers, with the percentage of classrooms holding forty or more students per teacher at 20 percent nationwide, and as high as 40 percent in some regions. High schools also continued buckling under the weight of too many students and not enough teachers: in 2008, the Education Ministry reported that the percentage of high school classrooms with over forty-one students per teacher was 15 percent nationwide, and as high as 79 percent in some areas.[39] These bureaucratic limitations provided an important context to the country's regulation of religious education over the years, a point I flesh out in the next chapter.

Much like its underequipped educational bureaucracy, Morocco in the first three decades after independence also lacked a robust administrative apparatus that could manage the religious realm. In contrast to Tunisia,

[38] Georges Granai and André Adam, "Chronique Sociale et Culturelle: Algérie-Maroc-Tunisie," *Annuaire de l'Afrique du Nord* 1 (1962): 565; Moroccan Ministries of Education and Culture, *Le Mouvement Educatif au Maroc, 1973–4 et 1974–5* (Rabat: September 1975), 22; Moroccan Ministry of Education, *Le Mouvement Educatif au Maroc durant la Période 1980–1 et 1983–4* (Rabat: 1985), 40; Moroccan Ministry of Higher Education, *Rapport National sur le Développement de l'Education, Préparé pour la Conférence Internationale de l'Education de 2008* (Rabat: 2008), 21.

[39] Moroccan Ministry of Education, *Harakat al-Ta'lim fi-l-Maghreb khilal al-Fatra ma bayna 1980–1, 1983–4* [The Progression of Education in Morocco during 1980–1 and 1983–4] (Rabat, 1985), 40; Moroccan Ministry of Education, *Le Mouvement Educatif au Maroc durant la Période 1990–1 et 1991–2* (Rabat: 1994), 60; Moroccan Ministry of Higher Education, *Rapport National sur le Développement de l'Education, Préparé pour la Conférence Internationale de l'Education de 2008*, (Rabat: 2008) 24–5 and 28.

which created a civil service of religious functionaries early on, Morocco refrained from organizing a state-sponsored corps of ulama, primarily out of concern to keep the religious realm fragmented and thus less of a political threat. A 1957 law outlining the responsibilities of the Ministry of Pious Endowments and Islamic Affairs (henceforth, Ministry of Islamic Affairs) did make reference to religious judges and other functionaries, but the wording of the law was vague and in practice the ministry's work over the next three decades remained largely confined to managing the pious endowments.[40] Similarly ineffectual attempts at bureaucratization occurred in the 1970s, when a new law decreed that the Ministry of Islamic Affairs' Directorate of Islamic Affairs was henceforth responsible for assisting in the training of preachers. The law never specified what this training should entail, and the training remained optional.[41]

However, beginning in the 1980s the regime took steps toward developing a more robust religious bureaucracy, a development that partly reflected the regime's shifting perception of its political opponents. Recall that following the bread riots of 1981, the king established a High Council of Ulama, over which he presided, and a host of regional and local affiliated councils reporting back to the central body. The High Council, whose members were appointed by the king, began advising the king on matters relating to Moroccan religious practices. The local councils, which initially numbered fourteen, were chaired by royal appointees, and charged with overseeing instruction taking place in mosques and consulting with communities on questions pertaining to religious ritual.

Three years later, the king issued a decree regulating mosque construction, the permit for which would now have to be issued by local governors. The 1984 decree stipulated that the management of mosques would fall under the Ministry of Islamic Affairs' purview; all imams would need to be approved by local governors, in consultation with the central ministry; and the text of the imams' sermons would have to be similarly approved.[42] In the 1990s the expansion of the religious bureaucracy continued with the reorganization of the Ministry of Islamic Affairs to include

---

[40] The endowments, or *habous* in Moroccan Arabic, have been a key source of revenue for the Palace and likely explain why the monarchy early on took control of this ministry, which has remained one of four "sovereign" ministries under the Palace's purview to this day. The other sovereign agencies are the ministries of defense, foreign affairs, and the interior.

[41] Dahir (Royal Decree) 1-57-214 of December 16, 1957 (BORM 2359 of January 10, 1958, pp. 63–4); Dahir 1-75-300 of April 12, 1976 (BORM 3313 of April 28, 1976, pp. 529–30).

[42] Mohamed Tozy, "Islam et Etat au Maghreb," *Maghreb Machrek* 126 (1989): 42–3.

TABLE 2.1 *Legitimating ideology, political opposition, and regime endowment in Morocco, 1956–2010*

Time period (approximate)	Legitimating ideology	Primary political opponents	Institutional endowment
1956–1960s		Religious nationalists	
1970s–mid-1980s	Traditionalist	Religious nationalists and leftists	Weak
Late 1980s–2010		Radical Islamists	Mixed

a Directorate of Studies and General Affairs responsible for "the training of mid- and upper-level religious functionaries, as well as preachers."[43]

A more dramatic expansion of the state's administrative apparatus in the religious realm began in the early 2000s, when the regime under Mohammed VI reorganized the Ministry of Islamic Affairs and overhauled the system of clerical councils, enlarging the High Council of Ulama's functions and increasing the number of local councils to thirty. The regime created a Directorate of Traditional Education within the ministry, and the new office began granting official permits to the schools and overseeing all matters related to traditional religious schooling in consultation with regional councils of state-appointed ulama responsible for inspecting schools and carrying out policies at the local level.[44] This period also saw the transformation of mosque-based educators into state employees on the government payroll, and between 2004 and 2012 the budget for the Ministry of Islamic Affairs increased from $15 million to $203 million.[45] Such bureaucratic investments, in turn, facilitated shifts in the state's regulation of religious education, as we will see in the next chapter.

Before turning to those shifts, I summarize in Table 2.1 the progression in ideological, political, and institutional trends covered in this chapter.

---

[43] Decree 1-80-270 of April 8, 1981 (BORM 3575 of May 6, 1981, p. 231), Decree 1-84-150 of October 2, 1984 (BORM 3753 of October 3, 1984, p. 386); Decree 1-93-164 of November 8, 1993 (BORM 4279 of November 2, 1994, p. 530).

[44] Dahir 1-03-193 of December 4, 2003 (BORM 5174 of January 1, 2004, p. 105); Dahir 1-03-300 of April 22, 2004 (BORM 5210 of May 6, 2004, p. 698).

[45] The 2004 figure is cited in "Mashru' Wizarat al-Awqaf wa-l-Shu'un al-Islamiyya hawl al-Waqf . . . Tamuh Kabir Yahtaj ila Irada Siyasiyya li-l-Taf'il" [The Ministry of Pious Endowments and Islamic Affairs' project for the endowments: a big ambition that will need the political will to implement] *al-Tajdid*, January 20, 2004. The 2012 operating budget was obtained from the Ministry's website on January 13, 2014.

3

Striking an Identity Bargain in Morocco

I first met Amine Gwafa[1] in January 2013 while I was living in Rabat as a graduate student. At the time, he was pursuing his master's degree at *Dar al-Hadith al-Hassaniyya*, a university specializing in religious studies. I wanted to understand how and why he had chosen that course of study, and to get his assessment of the instruction he was receiving. Gwafa is of Berber origin and grew up in Sefrou, a town roughly twenty miles southeast of Fes that had once been a thriving center of Jewish life in Morocco. He attended public schools but around the time he turned fifteen he decided to also attend classes at a local *msid*, the Moroccan term for a traditional religious school, outside his regular school hours. I asked him why.

"I was a pretty rambunctious child," he recalled. His home life had been difficult, his father had physically and verbally abused him, and he ultimately found some solace in the religion classes at the msid. "My mother prayed," he added. "But she never encouraged me to."

Gwafa did not get good enough grades in middle school to enter the science track in high school, so he chose a track known as *al-taʿlim al-ʾasil* (roughly, "original education"), which devoted more time to religion courses and Arabic study. "The ʾasil students were typically the weakest," Gwafa said candidly, "and the state neglected the track for a long time. But I guess I was always interested in combining scientific and religious studies." It spoke for his drive and self-discipline that Gwafa was ultimately

---

[1] I have changed the name to protect my interlocutor's privacy. This account is based on interviews I conducted in Rabat on January 6, 2013, October 7, 2015, and December 1, 2016.

admitted into Dar al-Hadith al-Hassaniyya, a prestigious and selective institution that for decades had been training scholars of religion who could staff the state's religious bureaucracy and teach university-level religion courses. In 2005 the school had undergone its first major curricular reform in sixty years, requiring instruction in foreign languages and lessening the school's traditional emphasis on prophetic sayings and behaviors (the *hadith* in the institution's name) in favor of bolstering training in Islamic jurisprudence and the social sciences. Gwafa's education at Dar al-Hadith was an experiment of the state.

At Dar al-Hadith al-Hassaniyya, first as a bachelor's student and then in his master's degree program, Gwafa chose to concentrate in *'usul al-fiqh* (foundations of Islamic jurisprudence) because, in his estimation, "as a science grounded in some amount of reasoned analysis, it would let me speak to foreigners and open up possibilities of communicating with other cultures." Over coffee at that first meeting, he spoke enthusiastically of his plans to finish the master's program and matriculate into Dar al-Hadith al-Hassaniyya's PhD program. He would focus on Islamic finance, what he deemed "a nice blend of science and religious studies."

Two years later, on a return visit to Morocco, I reconnected with Gwafa and inquired as to how his studies were advancing. This time he was decidedly less enthusiastic. He had completed his master's degree but then encountered opposition when he had proposed to write his dissertation on Islamic finance. "At Dar al-Hadith today," he explained, "there are two subjects that are off-limits: political Islam and Islamic finance." The dean of the university, an academic and former jurist named Ahmed al-Khamlishi, had written a tract debunking the foundations of Islamic finance, and students were discouraged from pursuing it as a research topic. Gwafa thought Khamlishi's allergy to the subject stemmed from a desire to push back against ultra-conservative interpretations of Islamic law that had made their way into Morocco, allegedly with the help of Saudi and other Gulf patrons. Gwafa was sympathetic to Khamlishi's broader goal, but he took issue with his method of achieving it. "There *is* a jurisprudential foundation for Islamic finance," Gwafa told me, "but we don't need to adopt the Wahhabi variant of it, as Islamists in Morocco seem so intent on doing!" Feeling dejected, he had decided to transfer to the Faculty of Arts and Letters of Mohammed V University, the country's main public university, and continue his doctoral work there.

I caught up with Gwafa once again in late 2016 over dinner at a Japanese restaurant in Rabat. By this time, he was wrapping up his thesis and he had secured a job as a compliance officer in a private bank, where he was advising the management team on how to ensure that its Islamic finance instruments were in keeping with jurisprudential norms. According to Gwafa, his predecessor had been deeply influenced by Wahhabi interpretations of these norms, so he was spending much of his time trying to re-educate his colleagues. Pausing from his meal, he looked up and mused, "You know what? In retrospect, Khamlishi was right. I understand why he didn't want students writing about Islamic finance!" If the state was to succeed in counteracting unwanted religious dogma, then setting limits on the intellectual pursuits of university students seemed to Gwafa a reasonable trade-off.

* * * * * *

This chapter examines Morocco's evolving approach to regulating religious education between the country's independence from French rule in 1956 and what turned out to be the eve of the Arab Spring in 2010. I first delve into the Alaouite regime's curricular policies, demonstrating how and why the state left unchanged the incorporation of Islamic principles into the national secondary school curricula throughout the first decade after independence, expanded and reoriented the religious content of curricula between 1965 and 1999, and once again reoriented the curricular content in the first decade of this century. I then turn to the shifting balance between state control and autonomy for institutions of religious instruction, namely the Quranic schools and institutions of higher Islamic learning. On this indicator of religious regulation, the Moroccan regime pursued a mixed strategy of control and autonomy throughout the reigns of Mohammed V and his son, Hassan II, and then shifted toward greater state control following the ascension of Mohammed VI in 1999. Finally, I trace and analyze evolving training and licensing procedures for religion instructors in schools and mosques. These procedures remained largely unchanged throughout the 1950s and 1960s, underwent an expansion in the 1970s and 1980s, and were increasingly standardized throughout the 1990s and 2000s. The chapter demonstrates how the observed shifts in state regulation of religion resulted from the interplay of the regime's ideological self-legitimation, political opposition, and institutional endowment.

Along the way, the chapter also introduces the concept of "identity bargaining," denoting instances in which authoritarian regimes with limited institutional resources confront opponents' demands by trading concessions to some aspects of their constituents' identities in exchange for lessened pressure to fulfill others. The Moroccan regime engaged in identity

bargaining when Hassan II responded to calls for a fully Arabized education system that would include extensive Islamic instruction by offering
to increase the amount of religious instruction in exchange for postpon-
ing full-scale Arabization. The regime calculated that by splitting the linguistic and religious dimensions of Moroccan citizens' demands, it could
bolster its own legitimacy and weaken the opposition. Identity bargaining in Morocco constituted a tool of regime survival that carried important implications for the nature of religious regulation. More generally,
identity bargaining represents an under-explored tactic that regimes can
employ in co-opting their opponents, and enhances our understanding of
how authoritarian regimes in the Arab world and beyond have survived.

CRAFTING CURRICULA

Before the French Protectorate (1912–56), the typical educational trajectory for Moroccan Muslim children began with attendance at a traditional Quranic school, or msid, between the ages of four and ten, and,
if desired, continued studies in a larger establishment – either a *madrasa*
(when located in a mosque) or a zawiya (when attached to a Sufi lodge) –
where the focus shifted from Arabic language and Quranic memorization
to deeper examination of religious texts. Whereas the teacher (*fqih*) of the
lower level msid usually lacked a formal education beyond having memorized the holy book, lessons in a madrasa/zawiya most often involved
students learning from respected scholars, or *shuyukh*. Students in the
madrasa/zawiya ranged in age from ten to thirty-five, and those who
wished to pursue advanced studies would continue on to the Qarawiyyin
Mosque-University in Fes or its smaller sister school in Marrakesh, the
Yussufiyya.[2]

During the Protectorate, the majority of Moroccan Muslim children
attending school continued to learn in the traditional msids that had
existed in the country since the arrival of Islam in the eighth century,
where the curriculum focused on Quranic memorization and the rudi-
ments of Arabic grammar. In some cases older students in the msids also
took lessons in Islamic law, in preparation for advanced studies at the
Qarawiyyin in the Fes or the Yussufiyya in Marrakesh.

---

[2] Daniel A. Wagner and Abdelhamid Lotfi, "Traditional Islamic Education in Morocco:
Sociohistorical and Psychological Perspectives," *Comparative Education Review* 21
(June 1980): 241–3.

Although the French largely left in place the msids, they introduced a competitor in the form of modern public elementary schools. In addition to opening nonelite primary schools to teach children an upgraded (but rudimentary) curriculum in Arabic, the French opened several *écoles des fils de notables* for the children of aristocratic Moroccan families. There, classes were taught in French and Arabic, and the curricula were modeled on the French system. By the 1920s the French-run elementary schools had attracted several thousand Muslim Moroccan children, mostly in urban centers. Still, at the end of the Protectorate only 13 percent of Muslim primary school-aged children were enrolled in school.[3]

At the secondary school level, the French opened vocational schools for the children of farmers and lower-class workers. For the sons of Morocco's governing elites, the makhzan, the colonial administration created tuition-based *collèges musulmans*, in hopes of producing a new and compliant generation of state functionaries and religious leaders. Though the French initially intended for these elite schools to include a heavy dose of Arabic and Islamic instruction, and only 1 hour per day of French, pressure from Moroccan families wanting their sons to access the highest levels of the colonial (i.e., Francophone) bureaucracy led the administrators to abandon most of the Arabic and Islamic instruction in favor of Western-style, French-based schooling. Between 1912 and 1955, an estimated 1,000 Moroccan Muslim youth completed secondary school and obtained the baccalaureate diploma. By the end of the Protectorate, only 2 percent of Moroccan Muslim children were attending secondary schools.[4]

Between the traditional msids and the Protectorate schools, there emerged a hybrid alternative in the form of "Free Schools," so named because they were free of government control. Dismayed by the poor quality of instruction in the traditional Quranic schools, and concerned that the French schools were alienating Muslim children from their own culture, the founders of the Free Schools aimed to offer an education that

---

[3] Data on school enrollment throughout the Protectorate is thin, but secondary sources have placed the total number of Moroccan Muslim children enrolled in primary and secondary schools at around 6,000 in the 1920s and around 650,000 in 1956. See Granai and Adam, "Chronique Sociale et Culturelle, Algerie-Maroc-Tunisie," 563; John Damis, "The Origins and Significance of the Free School Movement in Morocco, 1919–1931," *Revue de l'Occident Musulman et de la Méditerranée* 19 (1975): 76; Spencer Segalla, *The Moroccan Soul: French Education, Colonial Ethnology, and Muslim Resistance, 1912–1956* (Lincoln: University of Nebraska Press, 2009), 248.

[4] Segalla, *The Moroccan Soul*, 87–9; Hermassi, *Leadership and National Development in North Africa*, 102.

would promote the Arabic language, revive the religious instruction the French schools were neglecting, and teach both religious and secular subjects, including a smattering of foreign languages. The first Free Schools opened in 1919, and by 1930 there were over thirty free schools educating 1,500–2,000 Muslim students (roughly one-quarter of the Muslim students enrolled in school at the time). By the late 1940s, over 120 Free Schools were educating nearly 25,000 Moroccan children – around 50 percent of all Muslim children enrolled in school.[5]

Such were the contours of the Moroccan education system that the newly independent regime inherited in 1956. Over the next half century, the place of Islamic instruction in this education system would evolve through three distinct phases.

1956–1965: Stasis. In the first decade after independence, the Moroccan regime largely left in place the minimal curricular focus on Islamic education that had characterized most secondary schools during the French Protectorate (1912–56). In 1957 the government did introduce religious education in public middle and high schools, through the 'asil (original) or *taqlidi* (traditional) track, as it was alternatively referred to. This track, which absorbed many of the students who had been studying in traditional institutions of religious education during the Protectorate, taught entirely in Arabic and devoted a greater proportion of the curriculum to religious instruction than the standard public school curriculum. However, secondary school students in the 'asil/taqlidi tracks represented only 10 percent of the total number of students in public secondary schools, so for the vast majority of Moroccan secondary school students, religious education featured minimally in their course of study and most students continued to study in French.[6]

The low priority given to religious education for most secondary school students was apparent in exam requirements for the middle school completion certificate, and in the baccalaureate exam requirements for the high school diploma. These exams typically consisted of written and oral sections, some of which were required and some of which were optional. The coefficients assigned to each section corresponded to the relative weight accorded each section. Written sections were weighted

[5] Damis, "The Origins and Significance of the Free School Movement in Morocco, 1919–1931," 76 and 81; Moha Ennaji, *Multilingualism, Cultural Identity, and Education in Morocco* (New York: Springer, 2005), 204–5.
[6] Adam, "Chronique Sociale et Culturelle: Maroc" (1964), 195; Zeghal, *Islamism in Morocco*, 41.

more heavily than oral sections, while required sections generally counted for more than oral sections in the final scoring. The distribution of exam subjects and coefficients, therefore, offers an indication of how the state was prioritizing students' knowledge of these subjects. In middle and high schools, Islamic instruction ranked low among the subjects being tested during this period. At the middle school level, for example, a 1957 decree listed Islamic education among the optional subjects on which students could choose to be tested. In 1960 the state dropped the Islamic studies section from the exam, thereby removing the option of demonstrating any knowledge of religious subjects to receive the middle school certificate. Three years later, the state added a section on "Islamic disciplines" to the oral portion of the exam, but the requirement remained meager, representing a mere 6 percent of the total exam score. The 1963 ordinance did require that students in the 'asil tracks pass a written exam in "Islamic sciences" that would count for 26 percent of the final score, but for the vast majority of middle school students, the requirements to demonstrate knowledge in religious subjects remained low.[7]

High school requirements in this period similarly carved out minimal space for religious instruction. In 1962, the state instituted a baccalaureate exam for prospective high school graduates, modeled on the French system. That year, students could register for one of five baccalaureate tracks: classical letters, modern literature, mathematics, experimental sciences, and economics. Only one of these tracks – classical letters – required students to demonstrate knowledge of Islam, and the relevant section made up 20 percent of the exam questions. A 1964 ordinance reorganizing the baccalaureate system left these requirements unchanged.[8]

The relatively minimal emphasis on Islamic instruction after independence was surprising, given the nationalist movement's demands for an Arabized education system that would place greater emphasis on Islamic instruction. As early as 1934, the *Comité d'Action Marocain* (the main body of the nascent nationalist movement) had pressed for a unified education system for Moroccan Muslim students in which Islamic instruction would be a top priority. And in the final years of the Protectorate the sultan himself had encouraged the spread of Free Schools as an expression

7   Decree 2-57-0084 of March 14, 1957 (BORM 2318 of March 29, 1957, p. 417); Decree
    2-60-374 of July 2, 1960 (BORM 2491 of July 22, 1960, p. 1425); Ordinance 219–63 of
    May 7, 1963 (BORM 2639 of May 24, 1963, p. 750).
8   Ordinance 039-63 of December 26, 1962 (BORM 2623 of February 1, 1963, p. 178);
    Ordinance 315–64 of May 29, 1964 (BORM 2697 of July 8, 1964, p. 841).

of nationalist objection to the French system.[9] Given the Alaouites' heavy reliance on religious symbolism in their legitimating ideology, it stood to reason that the independent regime would heed the nationalists' demands and expand on the Free School model to reinforce its religious bona fides. Instead, the independent regime retained the bilingual curricula of the vast majority of French Protectorate public schools that paid relatively marginal attention to religious instruction.

Only by taking into account the regime's institutional resources and the emerging landscape of political opponents confronting it can we explain the stasis of the post-independence years. As we saw in the last chapter, the Moroccan monarchs who inherited the independent state from French rule lacked a hegemonic political party through which the regime could easily implement its rule. At the same time, the regime during this period was chiefly concerned with undermining its main political challenger, the religious nationalist Istiqlal Party. In the regime's ensuing efforts to consolidate its rule, the weak institutional endowment and the nature of its primary political foes produced a stasis in religious education curricula.

In contending with the lack of a hegemonic political party, the sultanate/monarchy sought to turn this liability into an asset by presenting itself as the only institution capable of unifying the diverse threads of Moroccan society and fostering a pluralistic political environment in which multiple parties would compete with one another for influence. Simultaneously, to blunt the challenge posed by its rivals in the Istiqlal, the Palace cultivated alliances with rural notables, tribal leaders, and wealthier Francophone elements of the bourgeoisie that had remained outside the nationalist party's base of support. Since many of these groups had been discredited by their cooperation with the French during the colonial period, it made sense for the monarchy to reach out to them in an attempt to weaken the regime's main rival.[10]

Significantly, the groups upon which the regime came to rely for political survival in this early post-independence period had varying stakes in the degree to which religion should be incorporated into the curricula. Thus, the regime's reliance on them for political survival decreased the chances that it would pursue a radical reform in either direction – i.e., toward more or less incorporation of religion into the curricula – since

---

[9] Spencer Segalla, "French Colonial Education and Elite Moroccan Muslim Resistance, from the Treaty of Fes to the Berber Dahir," *The Journal of North African Studies* 11 (2006): 96; Ennaji, 204.

[10] Charrad, *States and Women's Rights*, 147.

such a move would have risked antagonizing a necessary base of supp(
This predicament reflects Charrad's argument that policy outcom(
postcolonial states often depended on the strength of the political coalitions that included groups with the greatest interest in these outcomes.
In postcolonial Morocco, individuals with the greatest interest in expanding religious education – for instance, the learned religious elite (ulama)
who could work as religion teachers, or adherents of Salafi movements
committed to increasing public access to religious education – were
spread out among the regime's supporters and opponents. The net effect
was to dilute their impact.

Indeed, despite a consensus among the nationalist leaders that
Moroccan schools should reserve a prominent place for religious instruction, the Alaouites' encouragement of a pluralistic political realm created
spaces for divergent preferences to emerge among those who had fought to
remove the French and were now in a position to staff the nascent bureaucracies of the state. The government's 1960–64 Five Year Development
Plan called for the unification of the various educational tracks to "give
to all Moroccans a proper Islamic education that would immerse them
once again in Muslim civilization." However, translating this goal into
policy was more complicated, since proponents of the Free School model
now had to contend with fellow nationalists who had graduated from
the French system and were congregating around rival political parties.[12]
The regime's encouragement of a pluralistic political realm – an encouragement fueled by the monarchy's institutional weaknesses – brought to
the fore divisions that precluded major policy shifts.

These divisions were on display at a 1964 colloquium convened by the
king to address problems surrounding the unification and Arabization
of the educational system. In a demonstration of his self-assigned role as
supreme arbiter, and in what was to become a pattern of his reign, Hassan
II invited to the conference a diverse array of interests and encouraged

[11] Waterbury's assessment of Moroccan politics in the early post-independence period
points to another possible explanation for the stasis: "To activate a program, to strike
out energetically, and to do so meaningfully, would require nation-wide support, mobilized into some sort of organizational form. But it is precisely the creation of such a force
that the monarchy wished to avoid." See Waterbury, *The Commander of the Faithful: The
Moroccan Political Elite – A Study in Segmented Politics*, 148.

[12] Damis, "The Origins and Significance of the Free School Movement in Morocco, 1919–
1931," 89. The 1960–64 Development Plan is reprinted in Mohamed Souali and Mekki
Merrouni, "Question de l'Enseignement au Maroc," *Bulletin Economique et Social du
Maroc* 143–144 (1981): 147–55.

them to reach a consensus on how to proceed. In attendance were civil servants from the Ministry of Education, professors from the Qarawiyyin Mosque-University and affiliated institutions of traditional Islamic learning, representatives of parents, elected members of provincial assemblies, members of the committees of cultural affairs from both houses of parliament, and representatives from student unions and youth associations.

Throughout the conference, union representatives, Qarawiyyin students, and some (but not all) members of the Istiqlal Party urged a more aggressive Arabization and Islamization of the schools. However, there were also voices calling for gradualism. Ministry officials, including some Istiqlalians, endorsed the goals of Arabization and Islamization in principle but cautioned that rapid reforms would undermine the system more generally because there was not a sufficient number of teachers available to teach religion courses in Arabic – a hint of emerging bureaucratic constraints. The Education Minister, a French-trained lawyer, acknowledged the need to train native Moroccans as teachers but also praised the virtues of bilingual education, demonstrating the regime's delicate balancing act.[13]

The split between the gradualists on the one hand, and advocates of immediate Arabization and the expansion of religious instruction on the other, reflected a rift between the Francophone elites who had been running the Ministry of Education since independence – many of whom considered the Qarawiyyin and other traditional religious instructions sclerotic – and the Arabic-speaking elite representing rural populations, segments of the ulama, and the urban petit bourgeoisie for whom an Arabized bureaucracy would open access to the upper echelons of state power. But the divisions did not stop there. Even within parties such as the Istiqlal, whose leadership had always been urban-based and mostly French-educated, there was a disagreement between those advocating quicker Arabization and increased attention to religious education, and those self-proclaimed "modernists" who in their positions at the Education Ministry had overseen the continuation of a bilingual system marginalizing religion.[14]

Such divisions precluded any major policy initiative. The conference participants cobbled together a series of motions, which called for: a unified public education system that would eliminate the distinction between what attendees termed "original" (i.e., Arabic/Islamic) and "modern"

---

[13] Adam, "Chronique Sociale et Culturelle: Maroc," (1964), 201–2.
[14] Ibid., 203. See also Mohamed Chekroun, "Système d'Enseignement et Education Religieuse au Maroc," Série Colloques et Séminaires 22 (Rabat: Publications de la Faculté des Lettres et des Sciences Humaines, 1992), 420.

(i.e., French/secular) education by incorporating the former into the latter; an immediate Arabization of the elementary and secondary education system, to be achieved within ten years; and the elimination of all non-Moroccan teaching faculty and staff. But no consensus emerged on the matter of religious education curricula. The lack of a loyal hegemonic party had inspired Hassan II to pursue a fragmented political sphere and to seek alliances with diverse factions in an effort to undermine his opponents in the Istiqlal. These conditions ultimately precluded a more robust incorporation of Islamic instruction into the curricula.

1966–1993: Expansion and Reorientation. Beginning in the late 1960s there was a steady expansion and reorientation in the incorporation of Islamic education into the Moroccan curricula, reflected in two trends. First, the amount of Islamic instruction increased. Second, the content shifted to include teachings that framed the religion as a moralizing force to protect students against dangerous, usually secular, ideologies. These trends were evident in royal speeches, decrees regulating weekly curricular hours, ordinances determining the weight of Islamic studies on the baccalaureate exam, and Ministry of Education reports detailing substantive changes in the Islamic education curricula of secondary schools.

The first sign of a change came in December 1966, when Hassan II announced that prayer would henceforth be obligatory in all government-run primary and secondary schools, and in all public institutions of higher education. Then, beginning in the mid-1970s, the Ministry of Education implemented a series of reforms increasing the amount of religious education in the public secondary schools, not only for students in the ʾasil track but also for the majority of Moroccan students making their way through the general track.[15] Ensuing regulations made the following changes: they doubled the hours devoted to Islamic studies classes at the middle school level, from 1 hour per week in the late 1970s to 2 hours per week by the mid-1980s; they made Islamic education a required class in every grade of primary and secondary school; they added religious topics to history, Arabic literature, and philosophy curricula; they increased the coefficient of Islamic studies on the baccalaureate exam; and they increased the number of baccalaureate tracks requiring students to be tested in Islamic studies.[16] The increasing presence of Islamic studies

[15] Mohamed El Ayadi, "Entre Islam et Islamisme: la religion dans l'école publique marocaine," *Revue Internationale d'Education de Sèvres* 36 (2004): 115–17.
[16] Moroccan Ministry of Education, *Le Mouvement Educatif au Maroc, 1978–1979 et 1979–1980* (Rabat: Moroccan High Council of Education, 1981), 29; Hassan Rahmouni, ed.,

on the baccalaureate exam was striking: whereas in 1962, only one out of five baccalaureate tracks (20 percent) was testing students' religious knowledge, in 1971 four out of six baccalaureate tracks (67 percent) were requiring knowledge of Islam. In 1974 the proportion climbed to 71 percent. With the exception of a dip in 1979 (due to the addition of accounting, mechanics, and electrical engineering tracks), the trend toward greater Islamization continued, and by 1987 the state had made Islamic education a required subject on every baccalaureate exam.[17]

There were also substantive changes to the curricula, previewed in numerous royal speeches in 1972, 1974, and 1975 addressing religious education. On April 6, 1974, for example, Hassan II announced his intention to review all Islamic studies curricula and textbooks. A year later, in a speech before the League of Moroccan Ulama, he announced that a committee of experts would "review all [religious education] textbooks being used in our schools and remove any false theories or excessive terms that should not be inculcated to the youth of a people proud of its Muslim faith and its holy book, the Quran."[18] The committee would then issue recommendations for revisions to the textbooks.

There was a sense in these speeches that religious education ought to serve as a moralizing force for Moroccan youth, and this intimation infused the new Islamic education curricula and textbooks. For example, the 1979 Arabic Language and Islamic Studies curriculum for secondary schools noted that "for the Muslim student, Islamic instruction should be considered of primary importance, since the value of all education depends on the influence it exerts on the student's psychology and on the formation of his personality." Whereas textbooks of the 1960s and early 1970s had defined the goal of Islamic education as "forming a Moroccan citizen who is proud of his Arab and Muslim identity, and open to the world," the later textbooks reframed Islamic education as part of a broader effort to moralize Moroccan youth, and emphasis shifted from

---

La Grande Encyclopédie du Maroc (Rabat: 1988), 177; Mohamed El Ayadi, "De l'Enseignement Religieux," *Prologues: Revue Maghrébine du Livre* 21 (2001): 39; Abdellatif Felk, "Idéal Ethique et Discours d'Orthodoxie dans l'Enseignement Marocain," *Bulletin Economique et Social du Maroc* 157 (1986): 173.

[17] Ordinance 039-63 of December 26, 1962 (BORM 2623 of February 1, 1963, p. 178); Ordinance 500-71 of June 23, 1971 (BORM 3061 of June 30, 1971, p. 732); Ordinance 26-74 of February 1, 1974 (BORM 3203 of March 20, 1974, p. 376); Ordinance 182-79 of February 1, 1979 (BORM 3464 of March 21, 1979, p. 160); Ordinance 1446 of November 17, 1987 (BORM 3916 of November 18, 1987, p. 370).

[18] El Ayadi, "De l'Enseignement Religieux," 37.

lessons on religious rituals and dogma to teachings on Islamic ethics and morals. Curricula and textbooks in the late 1970s began referring to students as "the children" of teachers, reframing the teacher–student relationship in terms akin to a father–child relationship, likening the teacher's role to that of a father responsible for inculcating his children with religious morals.[19]

If Islamic instruction was to serve as a moralizing force, it also became an inherently defensive enterprise. For instance, the preface to the 1979 secondary school curriculum for Arabic Language and Islamic Studies stated that instruction in Islam would "grant our youth an immunity from all danger, arming them with a powerful weapon to defend their religion, their authenticity and their values against the invasion of destructive ideational currents, ideologies inciting doubt, and temptations that threaten their faith." The curriculum also stressed that teachers of Islamic studies should possess proper convictions, reflected in the instructor's "enthusiasm" for the discipline and "eagerness to defend Islam [as] an example of morality."[20]

The state's evolving approach to religious education curricula in the 1970s and 1980s could not have stemmed solely from the regime's ideology, since the Alaouites' traditionalism had evidently not produced a robust incorporation of Islamic instruction into the curricula during earlier periods. But ideology mattered insofar as it increased the burden on the regime to justify policies ostensibly limiting the incorporation of Islamic instruction into the curricula. These policies had partly reflected bureaucratic constraints (especially the teacher shortages) confronting the regime after independence, and they ultimately became targets of the regime's two leading opponents in this period, the religious nationalists of 'Allal al-Fassi's Istiqlal Party and the pro-republican leftists of Mehdi Ben Barka's UNFP. In interaction with the regime's ideology of legitimation, then, institutional limitations and political opposition produced the curricular innovations of this period. Two specific examples are instructive.

In 1957 the government had outlined a four-point education policy of "unification, generalization, Arabization, and Moroccanization." But thereafter, the shortage of qualified teachers who could speak in Arabic limited the regime's ability to follow through on its stated promise to Arabize the education system. In 1962 the state had sought to remedy the situation by launching a three-year training program for 14,000

19 Felk, "Idéal Ethique et Discours d'Orthodoxie dans l'Enseignement Marocain," 172–4.
20 Ibid.

secondary school teachers aimed at improving their Arabic skills so they might eventually teach math and science courses in Arabic. The state had also begun recruiting Arabic-speaking teachers from Egypt and Iraq to help compensate for the shortage.[21]

By 1965 the problem of insufficient secondary school teachers remained acute. With the departure of 700 foreign-born (principally French) teachers that year, the state needed to fill 2,347 positions, of which 650 were for disciplines taught in Arabic. But the main teacher training academy had only graduated 180 students the previous year, leaving a considerable gap.[22] As the school system began showing signs of distress from too many students, too few classrooms and too few qualified teachers, the government began limiting access to the schools. In February 1965, the Education Minister, Youssef Ben Abbes, issued a directive establishing an age limit for students wishing to enter the second cycle of high school, hoping to alleviate some of the pressure stemming from these trends. Ben Abbes's decree prevented a sizeable portion of students who were set to enter this cycle from doing so, and it provoked a swift response.

On March 22, high school students went on strike in Casablanca. Soon thereafter, students at the universities in Rabat and Fes joined in the protests. Riots broke out and the regime responded with force, sending in the army to quell the demonstration. After nearly a week of protests, at least seven people had been killed, sixty-nine injured, and 168 arrested in Casablanca.[23] Many of those arrested were later pardoned, a development welcomed by the UNFP and the leftist student unions, and on March 29 the students returned to school. But tensions remained and in June, Hassan II declared a state of emergency, dissolved parliament, and replaced Ben Abbes with Mohamed Benhima. At the same time, demonstrating his role as supreme arbiter, the king convened a diverse group of ulama, educators, and others to review problems with the education system and to try to find a way out of the impasse.

At the 1965 conference, conflicting discourses emerged on the role of the school in Moroccan society. Some attendees, particularly those from the unions and leftist political parties, argued that the school should be a democratic institution open to the masses. Others noted that the impulse to open schooling to every child was already having disastrous consequences on the quality of instruction, arguing that the schools should

[21] Granai and Adam, "Chronique Sociale et Culturelle, Algerie-Maroc-Tunisie," 566.
[22] Adam, "Chronique Sociale et Culturelle: Maroc" (1965), 242.
[23] Le Tourneau, "Chronique Politique" (1965), 183.

concentrate on producing elites who could more effectively manage the country. The conference may have provided an opportunity for many to express grievances – what the director of the Ministry of Education's Office of Curricula later referred to as "the genius of Hassan II" – but the compromises struck at the meeting made for relatively minor policy changes.[24] For example, some attendees argued that the state should shut down the Mission Française schools since they were forming a small cadre of elites who were purportedly detached from their Arab-Muslim heritage. In the resulting compromise, the Mission schools were allowed to remain open, but they would now be required to teach a course in Arabic.[25]

The lack of a radical change fueled continuing protests over the next year. In response, the regime went after its opponents, arresting students and members of the left-leaning student unions deemed subversive. In January 1966, for example, the vice-president of the UNFP's student union was sentenced to six months' imprisonment, prompting a new round of strikes and arrests of students, including a number at the Islamic Institute in Meknes. In March of that year, police arrested eleven students protesting in Fes and Meknes, and Omar Benjelloun, a prominent UNFP leader, was arrested and charged with distributing incendiary material. When on March 24, students in Fes, Meknes, Casablanca, and Rabat renewed their strikes, the Minister of Education declared the closure of various educational institutions in these cities.[26]

Against this contentious backdrop, Benhima gave a press conference in April 1966 outlining a new educational doctrine intended to replace the government's previous four-point policy of "unification, generalization, Arabization, and Moroccanization."[27] The revised plan, which called for a selection process to limit access to secondary school and halted the Arabization of secondary school instruction, implicitly acknowledged that the country's effort to "unify, generalize, Arabize, and Moroccanize" the schools all at once had failed. This failure was probably inevitable, since the policies required to meet each of these four goals often worked at cross-purposes. For example, to generalize the system while also

---

[24] Interview with Fouad Shafiki, Rabat, January 3, 2013.

[25] For more on the conflicting education policy preferences of the various political parties at the time, see Souali and Merrouni, "Question de l'Enseignement au Maroc," 260–325.

[26] André Adam, "Chronique Sociale et Culturelle: Maroc," *Annuaire de l'Afrique du Nord* 5 (1966): 326–7; Roger Le Tourneau, "Chronique Politique," *Annuaire de l'Afrique du Nord* 5 (1966): 240.

[27] This policy had been first outlined in 1957. See Adam, "Chronique Sociale et Culturelle: Maroc" (1966), 324.

"Moroccanizing" its teaching corps forced the state to accommodate a rapidly growing number of students (from 220,000 in 1955 to over a million by 1962) while drastically reducing the number of available teachers. Benhima's new doctrine was an attempt to mitigate the impact of these conflicting imperatives.

Six days after Benhima's press conference, the Istiqlal formally rejected the new plan and accused the Minister of "undermining the foundations of our personality and the unity of our country in destroying the mother tongue [and] its cultural unity that is based on the national language, the language of the Quran."[28] Such statements drew a direct link between Moroccans' linguistic and religious identities. Neglecting instruction in Arabic, "the national language," was akin to abandoning Islam, "the language of the Quran." The regime itself had drawn similar links between language and religion. The 1960–4 Development Plan, for example, portrayed instruction in Arabic as the necessary medium of Islamic education: "[Cultural instruction] in the Arabic language will be indispensable to Moroccans for the acquisition of Islamic civilization."[29] But now, by supporting bilingual education, the king had opened himself up to the charge that he was rejecting, or at least insufficiently promoting, Islam – a difficult predicament for a Commander of the Faithful.

The Istiqlal kept up the pressure in a detailed memorandum to the king outlining its own preferences for reform. An official statement in August 1966 urged: "It is absolutely necessary that civic, moral, religious and physical education take their proper place in the primary and secondary school curricula. These aspects of education are indispensable for the formation of a good citizen and the consecration of the values of the Moroccan nation."[30] Later that year, al-Fassi published *In Defense of Sharia,* in which he castigated the regime – and the Ministry of Education in particular – for failing to improve religious education in the country.

The religious nationalists of the Istiqlal were among the more vocal critics of the Benhima doctrine, but they were not alone. Joining the chorus of criticism were numerous groups, including the Istiqlal's student union, the General Union of Moroccan Workers, various parents' associations, and the League of Moroccan Ulama, a group created out of a

[28] Adam, "Chronique Sociale et Culturelle: Maroc" (1966), 325.
[29] The Development Plan is reprinted in Souali and Merrouni, "Question de l'Enseignement au Maroc," 151.
[30] Istiqlal's statement is reprinted (in French) in Souali and Merrouni, "Question de l'Enseignement au Maroc," 283.

meeting of 300 religious scholars in Rabat in 1960. The Istiqlal's alliance with the League was particularly problematic for the regime, since
it further called into question the monarchy's traditionalist ideology of
legitimation. Seeking to appease his critics, while not antagonizing his
supporters in the Ministry of Education who remained partial to a bilingual curriculum that minimized religion, Hassan II dismissed Benhima
from his post as Minister but maintained the halt on Arabization. And in
December of that year, he announced that prayer would be obligatory in
all state-run schools.

Hassan II's move to make prayer obligatory was an example of what
I am calling *identity bargaining*, whereby a regime confronts identity-
related demands by trading concessions to certain aspects of their constituents' identities in exchange for lessened pressure to fulfill others. In this
instance, Hassan II calculated that he could blunt his opponents' demand
for more Arabic and Islamic instruction by decoupling the religious and
linguistic components of this demand, effectively trading a concession to
the former for reduced pressure to fulfill the latter. And it was significant
that increasing prayer in the schools did not require hiring additional
teachers. On the contrary, the identity bargain offered the regime a low-
cost option in the face of severe resource constraints. A year later, in his
1967 Throne Speech, Hassan II tried to shore up support for a planned
constitutional referendum by emphasizing the government's increased
attention to religious education in the public schools.[31] At the very least,
his speech implied, those angered by the king's inability or unwillingness
to fully Arabize the system would now have a harder time arguing that
the stalled Arabization was undermining Islamic education.

A second example of ideology, political opposition, and institutional
constraints jointly contributing to curricular shifts occurred in the aftermath of the two attempted coups d'état in 1971 and 1972. Those attacks
had reinforced the vulnerabilities of an increasingly isolated king and
prompted the monarchy to seek ways to bolster its legitimacy. To that
end, Hassan II began building support among constituencies that could
counteract opposition groups rallying around the Istiqlal and UNFP, and
leaning more heavily on his identity as a religious leader for legitimacy.
The decision to carve out greater space for religion in the schools was
part of this broader strategy.

---

[31] The speech is reprinted in Roger Le Tourneau, "Chronique Politique," *Annuaire de l'Afrique du Nord* 6 (1967): 305.

In its efforts to reach out to elements in Moroccan society that could undercut the major opposition parties, the regime turned to the urban-based ulama represented by organizations such as the League of Moroccan Ulama. Peeling the League away from its alliance with Istiqlal and other regime opponents would weaken the traditional parties by strengthening the king's religious credentials. The imperative to isolate the Istiqlalians was especially strong because pressure from the ulama had been building for some time. In 1968, the League had published its charter, defining its goals as "the renewal of Islamic values, the revitalization of the Prophetic Sunna [sayings and practices of the Prophet Muhammad] and the combat against *bid'a* [unwanted innovation], namely secularism, atheism, and licentiousness," and stipulating that education in Morocco should be "submitted to religion."[32] In 1970, 500 ulama, political figures, union leaders, and academics signed a manifesto demanding an end to bilingualism and a renewed attention to Islamic education.

The 1970 manifesto was significant, both for the breadth of its signatories and for the nature of its demands. Linking the religious and linguistic dimensions of Moroccan identity, the manifesto declared that "the policy of bilingualism . . . has only reinforced the foreign language [French] within the Moroccan bureaucracy, to the detriment of the national language – the language of the Quran" and blamed bilingual secondary education for "weakening the moral and spiritual values of [the young] generations, insofar as it discriminates against Islamic education."[33] The accusation that the king was neglecting religious education provoked a series of protests in 1971, when a group of secondary school teachers in the 'asil tracks went on strike to demand the same pay and benefits as teachers in the regular public school system. Shortly thereafter, students in the Faculty of Sharia in Fes went on strike to protest the lack of jobs available to graduates of traditional educational institutions.[34]

In the aftermath of the two coup attempts, and still lacking the bureaucratic resources needed to Arabize the secondary schools and universities at the pace many were demanding, the regime could no longer ignore such pressure. To break the alliance between the national opposition parties on the one hand, and the teachers, students, and graduates of

[32] Mohsine Elahmadi, *La Monarchie et l'Islam* (Casablanca: Ittissalat Salon, 2006), 108.

[33] The manifesto is reprinted in Moroccan Ministry of Education, *al-Madrassa al-Maghrebiyya: As'ila wa Ruhanat.* [The Moroccan School: Questions and Stakes] (Rabat: Moroccan High Council of Education, 2009), 193–200.

[34] Chekroun, "Système d'Enseignement et Education Religieuse au Maroc," 423.

religious institutions angered by the lack of Arabization on the other, the king once again identity bargained. Decoupling the religious and linguistic demands of his constituents, Hassan II delivered the series of speeches outlining his plans to revise and strengthen religious education curricula and textbooks in the country.[35] Most of these speeches occurred on religious occasions in front of gatherings of ulama, many of whom had been among the king's most vocal critics. For example, just three months after the second failed coup, Hassan II told a group of ulama commemorating the holiday of *laylat al-qadr* that the responsibility to instill in children the gifts of Islam fell equally on fathers, teachers, and schools. That same year, the king changed the label of the traditional educational tracks from *'asli* to *'asil* ("authentic"), reflecting the regime's efforts to fortify its religious legitimacy after the attempted coups.[36] At the same time, the state began recruiting teachers, students, and graduates of traditional education – notably, representatives of the constituents who had gone on strike in 1971 – to write new textbooks and curricula for Islamic education classes that would appear later in the decade.[37] In this way, the regime's efforts to appease frustrated opponents in the context of severe bureaucratic limitations (most glaringly, the lack of Arabic-speaking teachers) ultimately led to an expansion and reorientation of Islamic education in the national curriculum.

The increasingly defensive tone injected into the Islamic education curricula also made sense in light of the two attempted coups. In part, the tone reflected the regime's co-optation of the morality-laden rhetoric used by its critics in traditional circles. And in part, the tone spoke to the regime's perception that it *was* under attack – from leftists, from students frustrated at the lack of educational and employment opportunities, from factions within the army, from the ulama, and so on. By portraying the

[35] See, for example, the king's speeches of November 4, 1972, January 24, 1974, April 16, 1974, and April 15, 1975.

[36] The Ministry of Education's annual reports to UNESCO between 1973 and 1984 indicated that throughout this period there was a steady growth in the number of secondary 'asil students (from roughly 8,300 in 1975 to 18,000 in 1984), though the overall percentage of 'asil students never exceeded 2.5 percent of secondary school students. See the Moroccan Ministry of Education's *Le Mouvement Educatif au Maroc, 1973–1974 et 1974–1975*; *Le Mouvement Educatif au Maroc, 1975–1976 et 1976–1977* (Rabat: Moroccan High Council of Education, 1977); *Le Mouvement Educatif au Maroc, 1978–1979 et 1979–1980*; *Harakat al-Ta'lim fi-l-Maghreb Khilal al-Fatra ma bayna 1980–1981, 1983–1984* (Rabat: Moroccan High Council of Education, 1985).

[37] Chekroun, "Système d'Enseignement et Education Religieuse au Maroc," 423.

religion of most Moroccans as a defense against foreign, unwanted ideologies (principally Marxism and other leftist movements then in vogue),
the king could rally Moroccans around the flag.[38] The growing incorporation of Islamic education into the national curricula became a potent
tool at the regime's disposal as it sought to counter the threats to its grip
on power. This pattern of crisis-and-response would repeat itself in the
early- and mid-1980s. In 1984 riots broke out in reaction to a series of
structural adjustment policies and an increase in the high school tuition
fees; and in 1985 and 1987, the state resumed its Arabization of the secondary schools and made Islamic education a required subject on the
baccalaureate, echoing the regime's earlier use of religious education as a
tool of crisis management.

1994–2010: Reorientation. Beginning in the mid-1990s, Moroccan
religious education curricula underwent another reorientation. The
amount of Islamic instruction in the secondary schools remained fairly
constant throughout the 1990s and 2000s, as reflected in weekly hours
devoted to the subject and the ongoing presence of the subject on the baccalaureate exam. In 1987, ninth graders were spending 2 hours per week
(6 percent) on Islamic education; twenty years later, the 2007 Islamic
studies curriculum indicated that tenth graders in all tracks were spending 2 hours per week (7 percent) on religious instruction. In 1995 all
baccalaureate tracks were requiring examination in Islamic studies, continuing the trend that had begun in the 1970s. Between 1996 and 2000,
the exam was dropped from one track, but by 2001 it had returned. Two
years later the coefficient attached to Islamic instruction increased in two
of the nine tracks. And as of 2004, all baccalaureate tracks were still
requiring examination in Islamic studies.[39]

---

[38] Promoting a defensive Islam in the curricula was not the only tactic the regime employed
in this enterprise. There were other, more overt examples, as when Hassan II mobilized
350,000 Moroccans and 20,000 troops to march into the Western Saharan territory
in 1975 and recover it from Spanish control. For more on the Green March, see Susan
Gilson Miller, *A History of Modern Morocco* (New York: Cambridge University Press,
2013), chapter 7.

[39] Rahmouni, *La Grande Encyclopédie du Maroc*, 177; Moroccan Ministry of Education,
*al-Tawjihat al-Tarbawiyya wa-l-Baramij al-Khassa bi-Tadris Mada al-Tarbiyya al-
Islamiyya bi-Suluk al-Ta'lim al-Thanawi al-Ta'hili* [*Educational Orientations and
Curricula for Islamic Education at the Secondary School Level*] (Rabat: Moroccan High
Council of Education, 2007); Ordinance 55–95 of June 20, 1995 (BORM 4318 of August 2,
1995, p. 559); Ordinance 18–96 of January 12, 1996 (BORM 4352 of February 15,
1996, p. 55); Ordinance 1082 of June 20, 1997 (BORM 4506 of August 7, 1997, p. 755);
Ordinance 2070 of November 23, 2001 (BORM 4992 of April 4, 2002, p. 259); Ordinance
950–3 of May 8, 2003 (BORM 5148 of October 2, 2003, p. 1213); Ordinance 1051 of

During this period, the regime similarly retained the curricular emphasis on religious morals and ethics. What changed were the ethics being stressed, as curricula began promoting Islamic principles compatible with concepts such as democracy, human rights, and tolerance. The conceptualization of Islam as a moralizing, defensive force in Moroccan society remained, but there was a shift in the identified threats against which the religion was being marshaled to defend.

The curricular reorientation traced back to a development that actually had little to do with religious education *per se*. In 1994, the Education Ministry and a newly established Ministry of Human Rights signed a statement of cooperation pledging to add lessons on human rights to the public school curricula.[40] Many of the principles outlined in the 1994 agreement made their way into the National Charter on Education and Training (henceforth, "Charter"), a document the Education Ministry adopted in 1999 outlining a comprehensive reform of the education system. The Charter, in turn, served as the blueprint for a series of reforms in the 2000s, and it addressed the matter of religion at the outset. The opening section on "Fundamental Principles" stated:

The education system of the Kingdom of Morocco is based on the principles and values of Islam. It seeks to create citizens of virtue, models of rectitude, of moderation and of toleration, who are open to science and knowledge, and imbued with a spirit of initiative, creativity and enterprise. The education system . . . respects and reflects the ancestral identity of the Nation. It reflects the Nation's sacred and intangible values: belief in God, love of the homeland, and attachment to the Constitutional Monarchy.[41]

On the basis of these and other principles laid out in the Charter, a Permanent Committee on Curricula issued a broad set of guidelines for all curricula, textbooks, and pedagogical materials in 2002. The guidelines called for "the values of Islam, the values of a modern identity and its ethical and cultural principles, the values of citizenship, and values of

---

March 3, 2004 (BORM 5210 of May 6, 2004, p. 704); Ordinance 763–4 of April 13, 2004 (BORM 5222 of June 17, 2004, p. 916).

40 Bashir Tamer, "*al-Nizam al-Ta'limi al-Maghrebi Khilal al-Qarn al-'Ashrin: Ishkaliyyat al-Islah wa-l-Tatawur al-Kronologi* [The Moroccan Educational System Throughout the Twentieth Century: Reforms and Chronology]," *Al-Madrassa Al-Maghribiya* 1 (Rabat: Moroccan High Council of Education, 2009), 188.

41 Moroccan Special Commission on Education and Training, *Charte Nationale d'Éducation et de Formation* [National Charter on Education and Training] (Rabat: Special Commission on Education and Training, 2000), Articles 1 and 2.

human rights and associated principles" to inform all future curricula; it also stipulated that the school system had to attend to the personal, religious, spiritual, and developmental needs of students; and it urged the schools to contribute to the formation of balanced, independent, and open students who were knowledgeable of their religion, their language, and the history of their nation.[42]

Curricular innovations soon followed. In 2004 the Ministry of Education issued new directives for middle school Islamic studies textbooks requiring that they promote sustainable development (for instance, through lessons on respect for the environment), reflect principles of equality, reject violence, conform to the Maliki legal school of Islam, endorse the recently revised personal status law (*al-mudawanna*), comply with all international treatises to which Morocco was a signatory, and reinforce respect for individual and social rights. Two years later a series of Education Ministry directives required that high school Islamic studies textbooks respect the reformed mudawanna, encourage individual and social rights, comply with all international treatises to which Morocco was a signatory, and promote openness, coexistence, respect for differences, and "the value of tolerance contained in true Islam."[43] By the mid-2000s, sectorial committees had revised nearly 120 textbooks, including those being used in Islamic studies courses.[44]

These changes stemmed largely from shifts in two of our three key ingredients of religious regulation. The ascension of a new king in 1999 had not altered the regime's prevailing ideology of legitimation. Royal speeches, for example, continued to justify Alaouite rule by touting the monarch's descent from the Prophet and by portraying the Commandership of the Faithful as the ideal unifying institution for the country. But two conditions had changed: the landscape of political opponents facing the regime,

---

[42] Moroccan Ministry of Education, *al-Wathiqa al-'Itar al-Ikhtiyarat wa-l-Tawjihat al-Tarbawiyya [Document on the Framework of Educational Choices and Orientations]* (Rabat: Moroccan High Council of Education, 2002), 3–4.

[43] For the text of the 2004 and 2006 directives, see Moroccan Ministry of Education, *Daftir al-Tahamulat al-Khassa al-Muta'alaq bi-Ta'lif wa Intaj al-Kutub al-Madrassiyya: Kitab al-Talmidh wa Dalil al-Ustadh [Specifications for the Writing and Production of School Textbooks: Student's Workbook and Teacher's Manual]* (Rabat: Moroccan High Council of Education, 2004), 2; Moroccan Ministry of Education, *Daftir al-Tahamulat al-Khassa al-Muta'alaq bi-Ta'lif wa Intaj al-Kutub al-Madrassiyya [Specifications for the Writing and Production of School Textbooks]* (Rabat: Moroccan High Council of Education, 2006), 9.

[44] Moroccan High Council on Education, *L'évaluation de l'impact des programmes de l'éducation aux droits humains et à la citoyenneté du Ministère de l'Education Nationale* (Rabat: Moroccan High Council of Education, 2011), 27.

and the relative strength of the regime's religious bureaucracy. Recall that by the 1990s, the Alaouites' perception of their principal opponents had shifted from a combined concern with the Istiqlalians and leftists to a growing threat from Islamists. The emergence of Islamism as the leading (perceived) threat to the regime ultimately inspired Hassan II's son, Mohammed VI, to embark on an overhaul of the religious bureaucracy by, for example, increasing the number of regional and local councils of ulama. Such developments enabled the king to spearhead reforms in the religious realm, including reforms affecting religious education curricula, and in so doing he repeatedly invoked his identity as Commander of the Faithful. The interaction of a traditionalist ideology, a religiously oriented political opposition, and a mildly improved institutional endowment produced a reorientation in religious education curricula.

We saw in Chapter 2 that Hassan II had sought to counter the emerging threat of Islamist opposition groups by incorporating nonviolent and regime-friendly Islamists into the political system as part of a broader strategy of controlled political liberalization. One by-product of this political opening was the emergence of civil society organizations (CSOs). Throughout the first three decades of independence, Moroccan labor unions, human rights organizations, youth associations, and women's rights groups had most often been tied to political parties. The close relationship between the parties and CSOs had been a liability for the latter, especially for groups tied to the opposition parties because the parties' marginalization meant civil society groups also enjoyed limited effectiveness. But in the early 1990s, CSOs – some new and some formerly linked to the Istiqlal and USFP – began demanding independence from both the monarchy *and* the traditional parties.

An important result of the financial and institutional decoupling of the political parties from CSOs was the emergence of elites who were autonomous from the traditional institutions of political power. The regime seized on the opportunity to begin co-opting civil society activists who had been urging change in areas like human rights, women's empowerment, and liberalization of the media. This co-optation had the dual effect of undercutting the traditional parties, as when the regime tapped the head of an independent human rights association for Minister of Justice in 1997, and enabling the regime to present itself as a leading participant in Morocco's march toward social and economic progress.[45] In this way, the emergence of nominally independent CSOs – which by

[45] Sater, "The Dynamics of State and Civil Society in Morocco," 116.

the late 1990s numbered around 30,000 – presented a new potential ally for the regime.[46]

Significantly, the political opening in Morocco coincided with the United Nations' (UN) "Decade for Human Rights Education" (1995–2004), which called on member states to include human rights, democracy, rule of law, and tolerance in the school curricula. The growing public space for civil society activism in the 1990s enabled the UN's program to gain traction among Moroccan CSOs. Faced with mounting pressure to teach human rights in the schools, Education Ministry officials in 1994 signed the accord with the Ministry of Human Rights for this to happen. And in 1998, the state created a Directorate of Curricula within the Ministry of Education to oversee the integration of human rights education into the curricula and to coordinate all future curricular development.[47]

The state's response to growing calls for human rights education spoke to its broader strategy of co-opting certain elements of opposition within civil society in an effort to manage them. From the regime's standpoint, adopting the cause of human rights education was risky because many of the CSOs calling for this education were also eager to draw attention to the regime's human rights violations. Teaming up with these groups to promote human rights education would presumably contribute to citizens' awareness of their basic rights, but this could undermine the regime's legitimacy by highlighting its own abuses of these rights. On the other hand, partnering with these groups offered the regime a chance to form alliances with elites who were unaffiliated with the traditional opposition parties. Also, the regime could now point to the curricular reforms as evidence of its commitment to human rights more generally, thereby bolstering its legitimacy. Crafting the 1994 inter-ministerial agreement on human rights education and creating a Directorate of Curricula mitigated the risks associated with permitting public debate on human rights by bringing its participants under a degree of state control.

A similar strategy of co-optation was apparent in the process that produced the National Charter on Education. In typical fashion, Hassan II convened a broadly representative commission to devise the broad contours of the education reform. The *Commission Spéciale de l'Education et de la Formation* included representatives from the national parties,

---

[46] Driss Maghraoui, "The Dynamics of Civil Society in Morocco," in *Political Participation in the Middle East*, eds. Ellen Lust-Okar and Saloua Zerhouni (Boulder: Lynne Rienner Publishers, 2008), 198.

[47] Interview with Mohammed Melouk, Rabat, December 18, 2012.

unions, Education Ministry officials, teachers, university presidents, leadership from various organizations of ulama, roughly 80 members of parliament, and CSOs unaffiliated with the parties.[48] The impact of the latter was apparent in the Charter's numerous references to citizenship, rights, and responsibilities – notions that had become familiar to those engaged in the debate over human rights. The human rights discourse also made its way into a *Document des Choix et des Orientations,* the main road map for all future curricular revisions that was conceived two years after parliament adopted the Charter. That document, written by a group of forty-eight intellectuals appointed by the Education Ministry, listed "universal human rights" as one of the four key principles to be included in all future curricula.

Ultimately, Islamic education could not remain immune from this human rights discourse. In 2002, following the release of the *Document des Choix et des Orientations,* the Education Ministry convened subcommittees to revise curricula and textbooks for each subject (e.g., history, physics, philosophy, language instruction, and Islamic studies). These subcommittees comprised no more than eight members who were appointed by Ministry inspectors based on their expertise in a given subject. The experiences of Mohammed Melouk and Mohammed Boutarboush are instructive. Melouk is a linguist who teaches in the Faculty of Education Sciences at Mohammed V University in Rabat. In the early 2000s, an inspector at the Ministry of Education asked Melouk to serve on a committee reviewing the foreign language curricula and textbooks. Boutarboush is a professor of Islamic studies at Ibn Tufayl University in Quneitra, and he chairs the king's regional council of ulama in Salé, a town bordering Rabat. Around the time Melouk began evaluating the foreign language curricula, Boutarboush was appointed to chair the subcommittee on Islamic studies.

The profiles of these men reflected the state's successful co-optation of non-party elites in civil society, and the growing role for an expanded religious bureaucracy. Melouk had become active in civil society in the 1990s, when he began meeting (initially in secret) with representatives of Amnesty International. He later joined a working group, funded by the Council of Europe, tasked with evaluating the incorporation of human rights – especially notions of religious pluralism and tolerance – into school curricula. Boutarboush divided his time between his teaching responsibilities at the local university and his position as head of the

---

[48] Ibid.

local council of ulama.[49] Created in the 1980s, these councils had undergone a significant expansion in the early years of Mohammed VI's tenure and by the time Boutarboush was appointed, the number of regional
councils had increased from the original fourteen to thirty. The councils
reported directly to the country's High Council of Ulama, a body presided by the king and tasked with coordinating relations between the
local councils, the Royal Cabinet, and the Ministry of Islamic Affairs.
Boutarboush's work on the Salé council reflected the expansion of the
religious bureaucracy and the attendant extension of state control over
the religious realm.

The Ministry of Education's supervision of the education reform
brought together people such as Melouk and Boutarboush. Upon passing review in the subcommittees, the curricula and textbooks were subjected to a final round of evaluation by an ethics committee charged with
ensuring that the values being transmitted in the lessons complied with
the *Document des Choix et d'Orientations* and derivative regulations.
Melouk and Boutarboush served on the ethics committee together, and it
was here that the Islamic studies textbooks – some of which had already
been approved by Boutarboush's committee – were reviewed once more
to check that the lessons endorsed notions associated with human rights,
such as individual liberties, gender equality, and tolerance. For example,
when the group arrived at a passage discussing the need to cut off the
hand of a thief (in accordance with some interpretations of Islamic law),
a debate broke out among the members of the committee. But since the
majority of members on the ethics committee were secularists and relatively progressive ulama like Boutarboush, who opposed such interpretations, the passage was removed from the text. The inclusive nature of
the process – e.g., the fact that ulama were even invited to serve on the
ethics committee – minimized public opposition to the reforms once they
were adopted.[50]

The elimination of passages like the one concerning the thief was not
only a matter of majority rule, however. The growing concern with religious extremism more generally made it increasingly unlikely that such
passages would make it through the final review. Between the parliament's
adoption of the Charter in 2000 and the publication of the *Document des
Choix et des Orientations* in 2002, the attacks of September 11, 2001 had
brought international attention to the question of Islamic education, and

---

[49] Interview with Mohammed Boutarboush, Salé, January 3, 2013.
[50] Interview with Mohammed Melouk, Rabat, December 18, 2012.

especially to the instruction being offered in Quranic schools throughout the Muslim world. The terrorist attack in Casablanca two years later, in which thirty-three individuals were killed and more than one hundred civilians injured, confirmed for the regime that its efforts to stamp out violent Islamist groups had failed.

In his first public address after the Casablanca attacks, Mohammed VI decried the "terrorist aggression" as "contrary to our tolerant and generous faith [Islam]" and argued that "the perpetrators of this aggression . . . cannot in any way claim to represent Morocco or the true Islam, so long as they ignore the tolerance that characterizes our religion." The king then declared that the state would adopt a "global, integrated, and multidimensional strategy" to "combat . . . the under-development, the ignorance, the decline and the ostracism" embodied in the terrorists. Education would be a pillar of this strategy: "In its religious, educational, cultural, and media dimensions, this strategy will educate and form the citizen by instilling in him the values of openness, modernity, rationalism, seriousness of purpose, righteousness, moderation and tolerance."[51]

Two months later, in his annual Throne Speech, the king drew a direct link between the "ostracism and other aspects of moral impoverishment" behind the Casablanca attacks and the revision of curricula: the fight against "ignorance" and "intellectual illiteracy . . . is only possible with a qualitative reform of our education system, and in particular its curricula and courses. We must implement what the Permanent Committee [on Curricula] called for in the National Education Charter so as to . . . revise the curricula in time for the 2003–04 school year."[52] The Throne Speech of the following year similarly highlighted the education reforms in connection with broader efforts to restructure and reform the religious realm. One of the seven goals informing policy over the next five years would be "the anchoring of values of an engaged citizenry, notably through the implementation of the Charter of Education and Training, and through the reform of the religious and cultural realms." In this way, the reforms of the education system were considered "complementary to" the reforms in the religious realm which were aimed at "consolidating the values of our generous and tolerant religion."[53]

Echoes of these speeches made their way into the curricular reforms of that period. Since independence, Education Ministry reports had

[51] Speech of King Mohamed VI, May 29, 2003.
[52] Speech of King Mohamed VI, July 30, 2003.
[53] Throne speech of King Mohamed VI, July 30, 2004.

consistently noted that Moroccan education was based on the "principles of Islam," but in the early 2000s the Ministry began referring to an
education system based on "a tolerant Islam" that would help to combat
extremism.[54] Mohammed Boutarboush, the religious scholar who had
chaired the Education Ministry's Islamic studies subcommittee, later captured the defensive enterprise motivating the curricular reforms:

> Because Morocco is a Muslim country, the state has the right to manage the reli-
> gious sphere and especially now. Why? Because these days there are many ideas
> being touted in the name of Islam and calling for things like killing people and
> bombing. So it's the responsibility of the state to remain steadfast in managing the
> religious realm because in so doing, it will maintain the sanctities of the country
> and protect the country from extremist ideas.[55]

As in the past, the Moroccan regime turned to the schools, and to religious education curricula specifically, in the context of broader efforts to
contend with threats to its survival. What had changed was the nature of
these threats and the relative strength of the institutional resources upon
which the regime could rely in managing them.

BALANCING AUTONOMY AND STATE CONTROL

To appreciate the evolving balance between autonomy and state control
for Morocco's Quranic schools and mosque-universities after independence, it is useful to review key characteristics of these institutions prior
to 1956.

Three features of Morocco's traditional lower schools are worth
noting. First, although the msids and the medrasas/zawiyas traditionally played a central cultural role in both rural and urban communities
throughout Morocco, these Quranic schools cannot be said to have carried a political significance, beyond garnering rhetorical and occasional
material support from the ruling sultan at any given time. By contrast,
as we shall see, institutions of higher Islamic learning traditionally *did*
carry political significance insofar as the sultanate often relied on graduates of the mosque-universities to staff his (admittedly thin) bureaucracy.
Furthermore, these institutions of advanced religious instruction retained

---

[54] The reference to Islam appears in every Ministry of Education report submitted to
UNESCO's annual International Conference on Education since 1956. Copies of these
reports are available at www.ibe.unesco.org/en.html.

[55] Interview with Mohammed Boutarboush, Salé, January 3, 2013.

their political salience during the colonial period, with important implications for the independent state's management of them after 1956.

Second, there was always a close affiliation between Quranic schooling and Sufism in Morocco, as elsewhere in the Muslim world. This connection was especially pronounced in rural areas, where until the mid-twentieth century most of the country's inhabitants resided. Not only were Quranic schools often attached to zawiyas, but between the sixteenth and nineteenth centuries many Sufi lodges were also centers of advanced religious learning.[56] The Sufi affiliation would have important ramifications on the regime's treatment of these schools post-independence, when the Alaouites began reaching out to Sufis in an effort to counteract the religious nationalists of the Istiqlal Party.

Third, traditional Quranic schools in Morocco (as throughout the Muslim world) had never been state-financed. Rather, they relied on revenues from private pious endowments. Additionally, local communities often offered teachers donations of food and other goods in exchange for their instruction, as well as their performance of rituals related to marriage, birth, and death. Beginning in the 1930s, the Protectorate government took administrative control of the larger endowments, but this did not amount to government funding for schools so much as government management and distribution of the private funds already destined for these schools.[57]

Indeed, of the three main schooling options available to Moroccan Muslim children throughout the Protectorate (msids, French schools, and Free Schools), only the French-run system of primary and secondary schools was under complete state control. By contrast, the Free Schools for primary and secondary students (founded by nationalists in protest against the French system) remained unaffiliated with the state and continued to be privately funded through pious endowments, individual donations and tuition payments from families that could afford to pay them. Likewise, the traditional msids continued to be self-sustaining and largely free of state sponsorship during this period.

As for institutions of higher Islamic learning, although the percentage of Moroccans studying at mosque-universities prior to independence was

---

[56] Dale F. Eickelman, "The Art of Memory: Islamic Education and Its Social Reproduction," *Comparative Studies in Society and History* 20 (October 1978): 496.

[57] Dale F. Eickelman, "Madrassas in Morocco: Their Vanishing Public Role," in *Schooling Islam*, eds. Robert W. Hefner and Muhammad Qasim Zaman (Princeton, NJ: Princeton University Press, 2007), 131; Eickelman, "The Art of Memory," 492.

always small,[58] the import of institutions such as the Qarawiyyin lay not so much in the numbers of affiliated students and professors but in their cultural prestige and political significance as leading centers of advanced Islamic learning. Since at least the seventeenth century, the ulama of the Qarawiyyin had lent legitimacy to the ruling dynasty by declaring allegiance to a given sultan through the ritual investiture (bay'a) ceremony. The Qarawiyyin and Yussufiyya Mosque-Universities also produced a high percentage of the individuals working in local government administration, both before and during the early years of the Protectorate. In the late nineteenth century, for example, Sultan Moulay Hassan I (r. 1873–94) encouraged higher Islamic learning – particularly on the part of reformist-oriented scholars returning from the Arab East – by filling many of the positions in his administration with graduates of the Qarawiyyin and Yussufiyya. As Dale Eickelman notes, the sultan's "concern for higher religious studies was integrally linked to his efforts to strengthen and expand the makhzan [and] these efforts necessarily involved recruiting madrasa graduates for administrative posts."[59]

The close link between the makhzan and institutions of higher Islamic learning persisted until the 1940s, when graduates of the colonial schools began replacing their traditionally educated counterparts in the ranks of the colonial administration. Competition between traditional institutions of Islamic learning and the emerging colonial schools led the Qarawiyyin to become a hotbed of political resistance to European domination during the Protectorate. The institution's identification with anti-imperialism, in turn, prompted the French to "reorganize" the school in 1931, bringing it under state control and transforming the faculty who retained their teaching posts into civil servants.[60] A crucial task facing the independent Alaouite regime was to determine how, or even if, the state would manage institutions of religious learning such as the Qarawiyyin now that the colonial power was ostensibly gone.

---

[58] A 1931 census recorded approximately 1,200 students in the Qarawiyyin and Yussufiyya Mosque-Universities, corresponding to a mere 0.02 percent of the total population of 5.8 million at the time. See Eickelman, "The Art of Memory," 497.

[59] Eickelman, "The Art of Memory," 497. For more on the cultural and political significance of the Qarawiyyin and Yussufiyya mosques, see Pierre Vermeren, "Une Si Difficile Réforme: La Réforme de l'Université Qarawiyyin de Fès Sous Le Protectorat Français Au Maroc, 1912–1956," *Cahiers de La Méditerranée* 75 (2007): 121; and Eickelman, "Madrassas in Morocco: Their Vanishing Public Role," 133.

[60] A similar reform of the Yussufiyya followed in 1939. Eickelman, "The Art of Memory," 507.

1956–1990s: Mix of Autonomy and State Control. Throughout the reigns of Mohammed V (1955–61) and Hassan II (1961–99), the Alaouites pursued a mixed approach toward Quranic schools and higher Islamic seminaries such as the Qarawiyyin, allowing some institutions to retain their autonomy while bringing others under a degree of state control.

Consider first the regime's handling of the lower Quranic schools. The vast majority of the traditional msids dotting the Moroccan landscape continued to function with minimal interference from the state after independence. In some cases, the state began offering financial assistance to these schools, but such assistance came with no strings attached and thus did not represent a dramatic increase in state control so much as an informal state affiliation with them. In 1964, for example, Hassan II issued a decree allocating a portion of the state budget to traditional msids, particularly in rural areas. This was followed by a 1965 decree granting financial stipends to Quranic schoolteachers, though the gifts remained minimal and unsystematic.[61]

In 1968 the Quranic schools received a symbolic boost from the state in the form of "Operation Msid," an initiative encouraging Moroccan families to send their children to traditional schools prior to entering the modern public school system. In a speech on October 10, 1968, the king explained that the goals of Operation Msid would be to teach children aged five to seven to read and write, and to introduce them to the Quran. The teacher of each school would be entrusted to bring the children to the mosque every Friday to hear the imam's sermon. And children attending a msid for at least two years would be given preferential treatment when applying for entrance into a public primary school.

Operation Msid theoretically signaled greater state sponsorship of these institutions, as all new msids were henceforth required to obtain a permit from the state in order to open; also, the syllabi and textbooks would need to be approved by the Ministry of Education; and a cadre of state-trained inspectors would supervise instruction in the schools. However, the king's speech did not translate into a financial commitment to these schools on the part of the state, and the bureaucratic commitments

---

[61] Interview with Abdelwahab Bendaoud, Rabat, January 16, 2013. For more on the state's support for msids, see Ministry of Islamic Affairs, *'Ashar Sanawat min al-'Ahad al-Muhammadi al-Zahir: I'adah Haykalat al-Haql al-Dini wa Tatwir al-Waqf [Ten Years of the Glorious Reign, 1999–2009: Reorganization of the Religious Realm and the Development of Pious Endowments]* (Rabat: Moroccan Ministry of Pious Endowments and Islamic Affairs, 2012), 121.

implied by the new initiative never came to pass. For example, even as the number of Quranic schools (not limited to preschools) swelled from 30,000 in the late 1960s to 70,000 by 1980, the number of state-trained inspectors remained around 200 throughout this entire period and thus never came close to matching the need. As a result, the vast majority of Quranic schools remained functionally autonomous and bereft of state funding until the 2000s.[62]

Beginning in the 1970s and continuing well into the 1980s, the regime encouraged a proliferation of autonomous Quranic schools. There emerged a growing number of independent private schools and associations dedicated to Islamic learning. These schools often had names such as *Dar al-Quran* (House of Quran) and *Dar al-Hadith* (House of Hadith), and they were prevalent in the southern area around Marrakesh and the northern region around Tetouan. The schools, which were often financed by wealthy patrons from Saudi Arabia and other Gulf states, did not receive material support from the state but the regime initially lent them rhetorical support and viewed them favorably. Though regulated by a 1959 law on private schools, which required that all such schools be directed by Moroccan citizens and adopt curricula in line with the national curricula of the public schools, in practice most of these schools were not closely monitored by the state.[63] Beyond verifying that the schools were nominally run by Moroccan citizens, the regime did not establish formal links with them and largely refrained from regulating the lessons and activities taking place within their walls.[64]

Yet, even as it granted autonomy to some lower religious schools, the regime sought to control others. Most of the Free Schools, for example, were converted into public schools or integrated into the public schools as separate tracks devoting greater attention to religious instruction than the dominant public school curriculum. These special tracks were

---

[62] Precise data on Quranic schools for this period is not widely available. The figures I cite here are from Dale F. Eickelman's work on Moroccan schools. A leading scholar of Moroccan education, Eickelman estimates that the number of Quranic schools (not limited to pre-schools) increased from 30,000 in 1968 to 70,000 in 1980. See Eickelman, "Madrassas in Morocco: Their Vanishing Public Role," 144. In 1991 the Moroccan Ministry of Education reported that over 750,000 children across the country were being educated in nearly 37,000 Quranic pre-schools. See Moroccan Ministry of Education, *Le Mouvement Éducatif au Maroc durant la Période 1990–1991, 1991–1992* (Rabat: Moroccan High Council of Education, 1994), 57.

[63] Dahir 1-59-049 of June 1, 1959 (BORM 2433 of June 12, 1959, p. 987).

[64] Interview with Lahcen Haddad, Rabat, June 10, 2011; Interview with Abdelwahab Bendaoud, Rabat, January 16, 2013; El Ayadi, "Entre Islam et Islamisme," 112.

designated *al-ṭaʻlim al-ʼasli* ("original education") and brought under the
administrative purview of an "Office of Original Education" within the
Ministry of Education. At the primary school level, most ʼasli tracks were
eventually phased out, while at the secondary school level, separate ʼasli
tracks continued to exist within and alongside the dominant public school
system well after independence. The state took pedagogical, administrative, and fiscal responsibility for these tracks, and in the early 1970s the
state budget for "original education" increased to 65 million Moroccan
dirham, most of which went to creating new ʼasli secondary schools and
tracks. Similar efforts to establish state sponsorship of some religious
schools occurred in the early 1980s, when the Ministry of Islamic Affairs
asserted government control over some schools connected to Sufi lodges,
organizing roughly sixty schools in mosques and zawiyas at the primary
and secondary levels for graduates of traditional msids.[65]

In the realm of higher Islamic education, too, the regime deliberately
left some key institutions alone while seeking to control others. Consider
the regime's treatment of the Qarawiyyin after independence. In 1956,
some 15,000 Moroccans were studying in the Grand Mosque and its
annexes.[66] Malika Zeghal has demonstrated that after independence,
Mohammed V was loath to involve the state in the management of the
institution, in contrast to Bourguiba's handling of the Zaytuna Grand
Mosque at that time. Instead, the Alaouites met continuing demands for
reforms to the Qarawiyyin with largely symbolic gestures, as in 1956
when the monarchy oversaw the opening of a new secondary school at the
Qarawiyyin that introduced modern classrooms with tables and chairs.
Between 1957 and 1959, Mohammed V concentrated instead on devoting the state's scarce resources to the country's first modern university,
the University of Rabat, which itself included a Faculty of Islamic Law.[67]

But in 1963, what had been a largely hands-off approach to the
Qarawiyyin gave way to a law transforming the lower schools affiliated with the Qarawiyyin system into state-run ʼasli secondary schools
and reorganizing what remained into a public university with three
faculties: a Faculty of Sharia in Fes, a Faculty of Theology in Tetouan,
and a Faculty of Arabic Language in Marrakesh (where the Yussufiyya

---

[65] For the budgetary allocation to ʼasli tracks in the 1970s, see Zeghal, *Islamism in Morocco*,
56. For data on the schools affiliated with zawiyas, see Wagner and Lotfi, "Traditional
Islamic Education in Morocco: Sociohistorical and Psychological Perspectives," 245.

[66] Vermeren, "Une Si Difficile Réforme," 125.

[67] Zeghal, *Islamism in Morocco*, 37–8. The decree establishing the University of Rabat was
Dahir 1-58-390 of July 21, 1959 (BORM 2441 of August 7, 1959, pp. 1326–7).

Mosque-University had stood). The 1963 decree stipulated that each faculty would offer advanced degrees with the same status as those granted at Mohammed V University, and the Qarawiyyin University was to be administered through the Ministry of Education in the same manner as the country's largest public university in Rabat.[68]

Another prominent example of the state's effort to control institutions of advanced religious learning was Dar al-Hadith al-Hassaniyya, created in 1964. In a royal address before a group of ulama gathered for the *Durus Hassaniyya*, an annual series of lectures by leading religious scholars from Morocco and elsewhere delivered in the king's presence during the holy month of Ramadan, Hassan II explained that Dar al-Hadith al-Hassaniyya would fill a growing need for younger generations of religious scholars who could replace those passing on. The institution would focus on scholarship in hadith (the sayings and behaviors attributed to the Prophet Muhammad), and the hope was that graduates of Dar al-Hadith al-Hassaniyya might go on to staff the Ministry of Islamic Affairs and fulfill other religious functions throughout the country.[69] The law formalizing its establishment in 1968 stipulated that Dar al-Hadith al-Hassaniyya would only be open to graduates of the Qarawiyyin or other universities who already possessed a bachelor's degree in Islamic studies, so while it would not compete with state-run public universities then offering bachelor's degrees, it would present an alternative to the advanced degree programs at the Qarawiyyin. Fiscal control over the institution resided in the Palace, while the Ministry of Education handled pedagogical matters.

Rational choice theories emphasizing the regime's imperatives to lower the cost of ruling would have difficulty explaining the blend of autonomy and state control for institutions of religious learning throughout the reigns of Mohammed V and his son, Hassan II. For example, the king's decision to create new institutions like Dar al-Hadith al-Hassaniyya entailed significant start-up costs that the regime could have avoided by devoting its limited resources to existing institutions such as the Qarawiyyin.

[68] Dahir 1-62-249 of February 6, 1963 (BORM 2626 of February 22,1963, pp. 260–1). In practice the doctoral program was not formalized at the Qarawiyyin until 1988, and the first doctoral degrees were only conferred in 1991. Interview with Muhammad Ramh, Fes, December 31, 2012.

[69] Interviews with Khalid Saqi and Hssein Khtou, Rabat, December 9, 2013. See also Hssein Khtou, "Reforms in the Religious Sphere and Their Educational Repercussions Vis-à-Vis Islamic Schools: The Case of Dar El Hadith El Hassania Institution in Morocco," Unpublished report (Rabat: Dar al-Hadith al-Hassaniyya, 2012).

Ideological explanations similarly do not tell the full story. the central state in Morocco, such as it existed, had never e trol over institutions of religious learning, so the Alaouites' tra could reasonably have been expected to dictate a continuati hands-off approach. On the other hand, Hassan II unquestional on, and sought to promote, his religious legitimacy in creating institutions such as Dar al-Hadith al-Hassaniyya, with its emphasis on the traditions of a prophet from whom the Alaouites claimed familial descent. Ideology was an important factor but on its own it could not have accounted for the blend of autonomy and control for institutions of religious learning after independence. That blend only makes sense if we consider the nature of the regime's opposition and the institutional resources – especially the bureaucratic capacities – available to the regime. These two factors, in combination with the Alaouites' traditionalist ideology of legitimation, conditioned the regime's policies over time.

Consider first the regime's preoccupation with its chief political opponents. To blunt the momentum of the Istiqlal after independence, the monarchy began fostering alliances with two other groups who, though discredited by their affiliations with the French during the Protectorate, could now assist the Palace in checking the power of the Istiqlal: the Sufi brotherhoods and some of the leading tribes. The decision to seek political support from Sufi orders after independence had direct bearing on the fate of the Quranic schools because many of these schools, especially in rural areas, were being run by members of zawiyas. As there had historically been a close association between Sufi practitioners and Quranic schools, allowing these Sufi-run schools to continue functioning with minimal state interference and (beginning in 1964) minimal financial support for the teachers in these schools frustrated the Istiqlalians' efforts to eliminate the Sufi imprint on the country. To the extent that many of the schools had traditionally been financially self-sustaining, leaving them alone offered the regime a low-cost way to undermine its chief political opponents while also reinforcing the notion of a king directly connected to the people, over and above political parties and elites.

A similar preoccupation with undercutting their political opponents fueled the Alaouites' decision to take control of the Free Schools and incorporate them into the emerging system of public education. In the late 1950s Mohammed V gave the Education Ministry to members of the Istiqlal, though not to its leader, 'Allal al-Fassi, who likely remained too much of a threat. Integrating the Free Schools into the education system represented a concession to Istiqlalians who had been clamoring for a generalization of the Free School model, a demand the regime was reluctant to carry out. The policy had the additional advantage of bringing Mohammed V's chief political rivals into the government where they might be managed, rather than allowing them to challenge the king's political power from the outside.[70]

Efforts to undermine their political rivals also explained the regime's decision to leave the Qarawiyyin alone after independence, while directing resources to a new institution that would compete with the ancient university. The regime's early treatment of the Qarawiyyin exemplified the Alaouites' strategy of pluralizing centers of power so as to keep potential opposition fragmented. Allowing the Qarawiyyin to remain open, while also refraining from establishing formal state control, enabled Mohammed V to bring on board an old guard of ulama who could serve as a check against the Istiqlal and the younger nationalists, many of whom had been advocating reforms to the institution which this old guard rejected. Establishing formal state sponsorship and embarking on a major reform of this institution would have invited certain ulama – and the students allied with them – to join in national debates about education, thereby granting them a platform for political mobilization that the regime could ill-afford. Instead, by leaving the institution alone and starving the Qarawiyyin of state support, the regime could devote its limited resources to new institutions that would attract students who might have otherwise entered the traditional mosque-university. This enabled the infant regime to keep potential centers of political opposition divided and to avoid antagonizing a class of ulama the regime felt it needed to keep at bay in establishing its political hegemony.[71]

But if the monarchy's perceived weakness vis-à-vis the Istiqlalians precluded a more confrontational approach to the Qarawiyyin immediately after independence, by the early 1960s the regime felt it was in a stronger position to act. In this context, the evolving approach to the Qarawiyyin becomes clearer. The 1963 law followed several years of growing demands for reform on the part of Qarawiyyin students frustrated by the lack of equivalency between their degrees and those being granted at Mohammed V University, a situation that was preventing many of them from entering the labor market. In the years following independence, the relatively weak regime deftly managed such demands, at times granting rhetorical support to reform initiatives while also siding with factions at

---

[70] Zeghal, *Islamism in Morocco*, 27–8.
[71] Ibid., 35.

the Ministry of Education who wished to see the institution marginalized, if not eliminated.[72]

The ascension of Hassan II in 1961 and the Alaouites' increasingly solid grip on power thereafter enabled the regime to act more decisively, bringing the Qarawiyyin under state control while refraining from imposing pedagogical reforms for which many ulama still had little appetite. Asserting state control over the Qarawiyyin also undercut the argument of regime opponents that it was neglecting religious education. At the same time, reducing the institution to a faculty within an ascendant, modern university represented a victory in the regime's quest to undermine the ulama more generally.

The decision to create new, state-affiliated institutions such as Dar al-Hadith al-Hassaniyya similarly stemmed from Hassan II's perception of his rivals. A plethora of institutions of religious learning would keep the Istiqlal's sympathizers among the ulama in a weakened position vis-à-vis the regime, and it would produce religiously oriented college graduates who could undermine the strength of leftist student movements then dominating college campuses. Dar al-Hadith al-Hassaniyya would create competition for the students at the Qarawiyyin by building a new cadre of religious scholars who could staff the Ministry of Islamic Affairs and other offices in the state's emerging bureaucracy. At the same time, as Zeghal notes, the new institution's emphasis on the sayings and traditions of the Prophet Muhammad allowed Hassan II to reinforce the Alaouites' prophetic lineage and "launch into a sanctification of his territory [to] more effectively weaken the Left, which was still very powerful in the university sphere."[73]

In addition to concerns to counteract their main political opponents, resource limitations contributed to the mix of state control and autonomy for institutions of religious learning during this period. The rapid unification and generalization of public education after independence had produced a situation in which too many school-aged children were seeking access to an under-equipped and understaffed school system, and throughout this period the regime faced persistently insufficient numbers of classrooms and teachers. Such constraints limited the degree to which the regime could extend state control over institutions of religious learning.

Consider the decision to leave the msids alone after independence. Since most Muslim children enrolled in school throughout the Protectorate were learning in msids, establishing formal state sponsorship would have

---

[72] Ibid., 36.
[73] Ibid., 51.

demanded a greater expenditure of the nascent state's fiscal resources, placing considerable strain on an already underfunded educational bureaucracy. By contrast, the relatively negligible number of students in the Free Schools prior to independence (only about half of the roughly 50,000 Muslim Moroccans enrolled in school) meant that incorporating the Free Schools into the emerging public school system offered a low-cost way to throw a bone to Istiqlalians and other religious nationalists calling on the regime to demonstrate its commitment to the country's indigenous ("original") system of education.

Bureaucratic constraints likewise fueled Operation Msid in 1968. By imposing a new requirement on students wishing to enter primary school (two years' attendance at a msid), the initiative would ease the pressures arising from too many students wishing to enter too few available elementary schools. Operation Msid thus offered the regime a way to reinforce its rhetorical commitment to religious learning while also mitigating the impact of glaring bureaucratic limitations.[74]

The state's encouragement of an increasing number of autonomous *dour al-Quran* in the ensuing decades similarly made sense in light of the regime's scarce bureaucratic resources. Encouraging the growth of independent Quranic schools that, while nominally run by Moroccans, relied on funding and teachers coming from the Arab Gulf states, enabled the regime to follow through on its stated commitment to religious learning without depending on Moroccan teachers who had not yet been trained. In this way, promoting Quranic education in this period was as much about alleviating the pressures of a weak bureaucracy as it was about promoting the monarchy's religious bona fides and undercutting the regime's opponents.

2000–2010: State Control. Beginning in the early 2000s, what had been a mixture of state control and autonomy for institutions of religious learning throughout most of Hassan II's reign gave way to a concerted effort on the part of his son, Mohammed VI, to extend state control over the entire system of religious education.

The first indication of greater state control came in the form of a definition. For decades the Moroccan state had lent rhetorical and occasional material support to traditional religious education, but until the first decade of this century, the state had never felt compelled to actually

---

[74] Eickelman, "Madrassas in Morocco: Their Vanishing Public Role," 143; Khadija Bouzoubaa, "Renover le préscolaire coranique au maroc," in *Tradition et Innovation dans l'Éducation Préscolaire* (Paris: INRP-CRESAS, 2000), 5.

define this education. That changed in 2002 with the promulgation of Law 13.01, which outlined the goals of traditional religious education as "aiming to enable students . . . to know the Quran by heart, to study the sciences of *Sharia*, to acquire the principles of modern science, to develop their knowledge in the domain of Islamic culture, and to open themselves to other sciences and cultures, respecting the principles and values of tolerance contained in Islam."[75] This phrasing was significant: the state was for the first time establishing a standard definition of traditional religious education, and that education was meant to incorporate ostensibly secular subjects.

The blending of religious and secular subjects pointed to another aspect of increased state control: a growing equivalency between the system of traditional religious education and the system of public education. Law 13.01 stipulated that traditional religious education would be dispensed in traditional preschools, traditional primary and secondary schools, and the Qarawiyyin – that is, in schools that paralleled the public education system. The new regulations also required all traditional religious schools, such as Quranic preschools and the Qarawiyyin University, to teach foreign languages and devote two-thirds of their curricular hours to subjects drawn from the national curricula of the public schools. The matching curricula would permit bridges between the two systems so that students could transfer from one to the other if they desired. Similarly, the regulations introduced undergraduate education at Dar al-Hadith al-Hassaniyya in an effort to make its degrees equivalent to those conferred in the Islamic Studies departments of the public universities.[76]

By 2010, the growing state control over various institutions of traditional religious learning was undeniable. Between 2003 and 2008 the number of new Quranic preschools requesting an official permit to open had jumped from 16 to 711, bringing the total number of Quranic preschools registered with the state to 1,626 out of an estimated 12,811 throughout the country. In parallel, the number of traditional religious schools (at all levels) using textbooks revised at the Ministry of Islamic

---

[75] Law 13.01 of January 29, 2002 (BORM 4980 of February 21, 2002, pp. 108–12), Article 1.
[76] The relevant regulations here are: Law 13.01 (2002), Articles 2, 4 and 17; Moroccan Special Commission on Education and Training, *Charte Nationale d'Éducation et de Formation [National Charter on Education and Training]*, Article 88; Dahir 1-05-159 of August 24, 2005 (BORM 5352 of September 15, 2005, pp. 643–7), Article 20. For the reforms to Dar al-Hadith al-Hassaniyya, see Khtou, "Reforms in the Religious Sphere and Their Educational Repercussions Vis-à-Vis Islamic Schools: The Case of Dar El Hadith El Hassania Institution in Morocco."

Affairs to reflect the requirements of Law 13.01 increased from 46 in 2006/2007 to 136 in 2007/2008.[77]

Greater state control over religious learning during this period could not have stemmed principally from the regime's traditionalist ideology, even if the Palace could justify such control by invoking the ruling monarch's religious bona fides as Commander of the Faithful. In earlier periods, that same ideology had evidently allowed for a mix of state control and autonomy for institutions of religious learning. Rather, the increasing degree of state control over these institutions stemmed principally from shifts in the regime's perception of its greatest political threats, combined with improvements in the state's bureaucratic capacity, particularly in the religious realm.

The regime's encouragement of independent religious schools throughout the 1970s and 1980s succeeded in diminishing the influence of leftist movements, but this policy eventually came back to haunt the Alaouites because the lack of government oversight of Quranic schools created fertile ground for religiously inspired opposition movements that ultimately posed a threat to the monarchy. Many of the dour al-Quran that cropped up in the 1970s and 1980s, for example, were financed by Saudi patrons seeking, or at least tacitly allowing, the spread of ultra-conservative Salafi doctrines undergirding the Gulf kingdom. Lessons at these schools often challenged the unity and hegemony of the Maliki rite that had persisted in Morocco for centuries (despite the diversity of cultural practices among Muslims), rejecting the Commandership of the Faithful, and urging that the Amir al-Mu'minin be replaced by an Islamic Caliphate (*khalifa islamiyya*).[78] Whereas Hassan II may have found it beneficial to tacitly sanction these schools in an effort to counter leftist groups, the regime ultimately had to acknowledge that Wahhabi teachings were also inimical to the Commandership of the Faithful, a core tenet of the Alouites' traditionalism.

Even Dar al-Hadith al-Hassaniyya, the king's prized creation, was not immune from antimonarchist discourses. Since its inception, the institution had recruited teachers from Syria and Egypt, mostly out of concern to ameliorate conditions resulting from the state's bureaucratic

---

[77] See Moroccan Ministry of Pious Endowments and Islamic Affairs, *'Ashar Sanawat min al-'Ahad al-Muhammadi al-Zahir: I'adah Haykalat al-Haql al-Dini wa Tatwir al-Waqf*, 125–32.

[78] Interview with Abdelwahab Bendaoud, Rabat, January 16, 2013; Interview with Jaafar Kansoussi, Rabat, January 17, 2013.

limitations. But many of these instructors sympathized with the Muslim Brotherhood, and as a result the Brotherhood's ideology and derivative strains of Islamism began trickling into the classrooms.[79] By the 1990s groups with names such as *al-Salafiyya al-Jihadiyya* were cropping up, labeling Moroccans who supported the king as apostates, and urging the restoration of the Caliphate.

In the wake of the September 11, 2001 terrorist attacks, and again after the 2003 bombings in Casablanca, Mohammed VI evidently felt compelled to launch a reform of the entire system of religious education. A year after the 2001 attacks, the king appointed Ahmed Toufiq as the new Minister of Islamic Affairs. Toufiq, who has advanced degrees in history and archaeology (but not theology), is a member of the Boutchichia, a prominent Sufi order with deep roots in the country. Much as Hassan II had tacitly encouraged Sufi institutions after independence in hopes of countering the Istiqlal, his son's appointment of Toufiq was a deliberate attempt to more actively promote Sufi practices as a counterweight to Islamist discourses. Toufiq was a leading architect of the 2002 law and the affiliated decrees that later established greater state sponsorship of institutions of religious learning.

Interviews with education officials and others involved in these reforms confirmed that the terrorist attack of 2003 in Casablanca had reinforced the regime's suspicion that it would have to establish greater state control over the schools and Quranic institutes to which it had previously turned a blind eye.[80] Whereas the regime had previously calculated that permitting a degree of institutional autonomy to religious schools worked to its advantage, by the early 2000s the regime considered this blend of state control and autonomy a liability. To save itself, the monarchy determined it would need to assert greater control over institutions in which its political opponents had thrived. And in so doing, the regime benefited from an increase in the state's administrative capacities, especially in the religious realm.

With the 2003 reorganization of the Ministry of Islamic Affairs, particularly the creation of a Directorate of Traditional Education, the regime began investing more heavily in its religious administration.

---

[79] Zeghal, *Islamism in Morocco*, 50.

[80] Interviews with Abdelwahab Bendaoud, Rabat, January 16, 2013; Jaafar Kansoussi, Rabat, January 17, 2013; Mohsine Elahmadi, Rabat, January 7, 2013. For more on the state's reforms to the religious realm during this period, see Driss Maghraoui, "The Strengths and Limits of Religious Reforms in Morocco," *Mediterranean Politics* 14 (July 2009): 202.

I noted at the end of Chapter 2 that the budget for the Ministry of Islamic Affairs increased from $15 million in 2004 to roughly $200 million a decade later. During the same period, the Ministry's expenditures on the *atiq* system increased from $300,000 to $30 million, facilitating the state's growing sponsorship of traditional institutions of religious learning.[81] For example, between 2004 and 2007 the state spent 8.5 million dirham (roughly 1 million US dollars) on projects modernizing nearly 150 traditional schools, and by 2009 this figure had nearly doubled. The state could also open its coffers to increasing numbers of students in traditional schools, though the percentage of schools relying on state subsidies to function remained low. Of the nearly 25,000 students enrolled in all levels of traditional schooling in 2008/9, the Ministry of Islamic Affairs offered financial support to just under 10,000. And between 2004 and 2009 the state's expenditures on grants and bonuses for students, teachers, and school directors of traditional education increased almost threefold, from 16.9 million to 50 million Moroccan dirham (roughly 2–6 million US dollars at the time).[82] The state's growing administrative apparatus enabled a greater degree of control over these institutions.

The expanded administrative apparatus also facilitated the regime's efforts to bring a greater number of religious institutions under the supervision of the Ministry of Islamic Affairs. For example, the reforms transferred management of institutions such as Dar al-Hadith al-Hassaniyya from the Ministry of Education to the Ministry of Islamic Affairs, which would now handle both the institution's budget and its pedagogy; and the Minister of Islamic Affairs would henceforth preside over Dar al-Hadith al-Hassaniyya's scientific council, the body responsible for carrying out the curricular orientations contained in the 2005 reform.[83] Bringing

---

[81] The increase in budgetary expenditures on the *atiq* system was cited in a speech before parliament by Minister Toufiq in December 2015. See *Wizarat al-Awqaf: Tarfa' Mayzaniat al-Ta'lim al-'Atiq min Thalathat Milayeen ila 300 Milayun Dirham* [Ministry of Endowments: Increase in the Budget for Traditional Education from 3 million to 300 Million Dirhams] *PJD.ma* (December 15, 2015).

[82] See Moroccan Ministry of Pious Endowments and Islamic Affairs, *'Ashar Sanawat min al-'Ahad al-Muhammadi al-Zahir: I'adah Haykalat al-Haql al-Dini wa Tatwir al-Waqf*, 139–40. The Director of Traditional Education at the Ministry of Islamic Affairs estimated that a mere 4 percent of traditional religious schools depend wholly on state subsidies to survive; the rest are fiscally self-sustaining, even if pedagogically they must abide by the latest reforms. Interview with Abdelwahab Bendaoud, Rabat, January 16, 2013.

[83] Dahir 1-05-159 of August 24, 2005, Articles 1, 8, 9, 12, and 25.

these institutions of religious learning under the management of the Islamic Affairs Ministry was significant because this Ministry has always been one of the monarchy's "sovereign" agencies, funded by and even physically housed within the Palace in Rabat. Removing traditional education from the Ministry of Education's purview, therefore, brought it under the monarchy's direct control and out of the government's hands. With the Ministry of Islamic Affairs' capacities enhanced in the wake of the 2003 reorganization and accompanying financial investments, the regime could now formally sponsor – and thus control – a greater number of traditional schools.

REGULATING TEACHERS OF ISLAM

Finally, I turn to Morocco's evolving approach to regulating the individuals entrusted to teach religion. At independence, the regime's traditionalist ideology of legitimation and its preoccupation with undermining its political opponents incentivized a stasis in regulations concerning religion instructors. Then, in the 1970s and 1980s, the regime's efforts to fragment and weaken the religious nationalists of the Istiqlal and leftist groups such as the UNFP and USFP – against a backdrop of persistent bureaucratic constraints plaguing the higher education system – resulted in an expansion in the pool of Islam instructors, and in the array of teaching programs available to them. Finally, with the emergence of Islamist groups as the regime's primary opposition in the 1990s, and a strengthened religious bureaucracy in place, the Palace pursued a reorientation and standardization of training and licensing procedures for the country's religion instructors.

1956–1970: Stasis. In the decade and a half following independence, the monarchy refrained from imposing regulations (training or otherwise) on imams and other mosque- and zawiya-based educators, and it left the training of instructors in the traditional msids alone. As I noted in Chapter 2, a 1957 law did imbue the Ministry of Islamic Affairs with authority over religious functionaries such as judges, but this did not translate into discernible standards for mosque-based educators.[84] Instead, the Ministry's work in the ensuing decades focused on managing the pious endowments, a key source of revenue for the monarchy.

Whereas the regime was content to leave imams and teachers in traditional schools alone during this period, it did begin standardizing the

---

[84] Dahir 1-57-214 of December 16, 1957 (BORM 2359 of January 10, 1958, pp. 63–4).

training of teachers destined for the public school system, where religious instruction would figure into the national curricula, albeit minimally. In 1958, the state established the Pedagogic Institute of Secondary Education to train future secondary school teachers. The Institute was open to high school graduates who had passed the baccalaureate exam, and a limited number of spots were reserved for those who could demonstrate that they had completed their high school coursework even if they had not passed the baccalaureate. The Institute offered a three-year training program for students wishing to teach scientific subjects, and a two-year program for future humanities teachers. From 1958 to 1961, students who had received or were working toward their *alimiyya* (secondary school) diplomas at the Qarawiyyin and other classical institutions of religious learning could enroll in the new teacher training institute for one year, after which they would be hired to teach Arabic in a secondary school for a minimum commitment of five years. Regardless of their provenance, none of the Institute's students was required to study religion as part of his or her training.[85]

In 1963 the Pedagogic Institute of Secondary Education became the École Normale Supérieure (ENS) and was divided into two cycles: an initial one for those wishing to teach at the middle school level, and a second cycle for future high school teachers. Candidates applying for admission to the ENS had to have completed the baccalaureate exam, and at the ENS they could work toward a three-year bachelor's (*license*) degree or a two-year diploma known as the Certificat d'Aptitude Pédagogique à l'Enseignement Secondaire (CAPES). A certain number of spots were reserved for high school graduates who did not pass the baccalaureate exam, but these students would only be eligible for the two-year CAPES diploma. In 1970, the state created Regional Pedagogic Centers to train future middle school teachers, and the ENS was reduced to a one-year program reserved for aspiring high school teachers. None of the degrees being granted at these institutions required training in religious subjects, and this would remain the case until later in the decade.[86]

---

[85] Decree 2-57-1947 of January 15, 1958 (BORM 2368 of March 14, 1958, pp. 475–6).

[86] The relevant regulations here are Decree 2-62-621 of June 7, 1963 and Ministerial Orders of June 8, 1963 (BORM 2642 of June 14, 1963, pp. 949–53); Ministerial Orders 326-64 and 327-64 of June 22, 1964 (BORM 2700 of July 29, 1964, pp. 908–10); Decree 2-70-454 of October 7, 1970 (BORM 3027 of November 4, 1970, pp. 1507–9); Decree 2-70-455 of October 7, 1970 (BORM 3027 of November 4, 1970, pp. 1509–11); Ministerial Order 332-72 of March 7, 1972 (BORM 3102 of April 12, 1972, pp. 604–5);

It was perhaps not surprising that the new teacher training institutes did not include courses in religion, given the minimal amount of Islamic instruction being taught in the regular public secondary school curriculum during this period. As noted earlier, while religion featured prominently in the curriculum of the ʾasli/taqlidi tracks and schools, the latter were only educating 10 percent of the secondary school students in the post-independence years. During the 1950s and 1960s most of the individuals hired to teach religion courses in these "original" tracks came from the Qarawiyyin and other traditional schools, particularly in the south. This meant that most religion teachers in the early post-independence years had studied a curriculum largely unchanged since the Middle Ages, emerging from their classical training with expertise in theology and Islamic law.[87]

The 1963 nationalization of the Qarawiyyin reorganized the courses of study there, granting degrees a long-sought equivalency to the degrees being conferred at the modern universities. But the contents of what future educators were learning remained largely unaltered. The 1963 law created two bachelor's degree (*ijaza*) programs, one in Islamic law (*sharia*) and one in theology (*ʾusul al-din*), but the traditional pedagogy and curricula remained in place. Likewise, Dar al-Hadith al-Hassaniyya, the other leading institution of higher Islamic learning during this period, focused on training future teachers in religious sciences, and in hadith (the sayings and behaviors attributed to the Prophet Muhammad) specifically.[88] Thus, traditional institutions of higher Islamic learning remained focused on imparting almost exclusively religious knowledge to those who would be teaching religion in the emerging public school system.

As was the case with the school curricula and the degree of state control over institutions of religious learning, the regime's regulation of religion instructors during the decade and a half post-independence reflected a mix of ideological, political, and institutional considerations. To begin with, the regime's ideology of self-legitimation contributed to the stasis of this period. Recall that the monarchy's traditionalist ideology emphasized the sultan/king's role as chief guardian of Morocco's religious heritage. For centuries the Alaouite dynasty (consistent with most political rulers throughout the Arab-Muslim world) had refrained from regulating the activities of the country's religion teachers – whether in mosques,

---

Ministerial Order 633-75 of May 7, 1975 (BORM 3269 of June 25, 1975, pp. 824–5); Decree 2-76-313 of June 11, 1976 (BORM 3320 of June 16, 1976, pp. 718–20).

[87] Vermeren, "Une Si Difficile Réforme," 125.

[88] For more on the 1963 Qarawiyyin nationalization law, see Zeghal, *Islamism in Morocco*, 47.

zawiyas, or schools – so it made sense for the independent regime to refrain from intervening in the traditional trajectories of its religion instructors. After independence, the Alaouites could point to the regime's treatment of these traditional educators as evidence of the monarchy's direct connection to the Moroccan people and their religious heritage.

However, ideology only takes us so far in understanding the regime's treatment of religion instructors after independence. For example, we might have expected a traditionalist regime to dedicate resources to training religion instructors, in an effort to demonstrate the extent of its commitment to religious knowledge. Yet, in response to demands for investments in the Qarawiyyin, Mohammed V and Hassan II were largely silent. Insofar as these investments might have reinvigorated the ancient institution, it stood to reason that a traditionalist regime would jump at the chance to implement its stated commitment to religious education. Furthermore, during the Protectorate, Mohammed V and the nationalists had championed religious education and those who were entrusted to teach it, so one would have reasonably expected the post-independence regime to honor the nationalists' demands for reforms to the Qarawiyyin.

In Morocco, unlike in Tunisia, the introduction of modern schooling and the concomitant diminution in the ulama's role as educators had been by-products of colonialism. As a result, the changing profile of the nation's educators became closely associated with the Western incursion. This presented the Alaouite sultan with a different point of departure from the one facing the nationalists in Tunisia, where bilingual and Western-style schooling had predated the French takeover, and where the ulama's diminishing sphere of influence had not been so much a direct result of European imperialism as a homegrown affair, albeit one not free of controversy. In Morocco, by contrast, it made sense for the Alaouites to forge alliances with ulama of the Qarawiyyin during the struggle to oust the French; antagonizing members of the learned religious class, many of whom blamed the Western power for their diminished role in society, would have conveyed a close association between the sultanate and the colonial administration, undermining the sultan's legitimacy as a champion of the nationalist cause. So what changed after independence?

A clearer picture emerges when we recall the political significance of the Qarawiyyin. By the mid-twentieth century, three competing groups of scholars at the institution vied for influence. The first was an old guard of classically trained ulama, many of whom had resisted earlier efforts to upgrade the institution's pedagogy and curricula. The second was a small coterie of students loyal to the Democratic Party of Independence, a rival of the Istiqlal's. And a third group – the largest of the three – comprised the *Young Tolbas*, who were closely affiliated with the Istiqlal, and who had been demanding many of the modernizing reforms to which the older guard objected.[89] During the Protectorate, the reformist/Istiqlalian camp had allied with the sultanate in the struggle for independence. But with independence achieved, the Alaouites came to view the Istiqlal's base of support at the Qarawiyyin as a political threat.

Indeed, the institution had played a key role in the nationalist struggle against the French, producing many of the elites who were now in a position to compete with the monarchy for political power and religious prestige in the vacuum left by the French withdrawal. Investing in the Qarawiyyin's programs for future religion instructors, therefore, amounted to heeding the demands of Istiqlalians and strengthening a key base of the party's support. With his political hegemony far from secured, Mohammed V could not afford to reform an institution such as the Qarawiyyin and risk empowering factions loyal to his primary political opponents. As a result, the demands for reforms to the institution's curricula went largely ignored throughout the late 1950s and early 1960s.[90]

Even after the promulgation of the 1962 constitution, which enshrined the king's status as Commander of the Faithful, Hassan II continued to face pressure from the Istiqlal to reform the country's system of traditional religious education, including the Qarawiyyin. Most of the Istiqlal's supporters echoed the demands of reformists at the Qarawiyyin who had sought curricular reforms and degree equivalency, so granting both would have empowered the king's primary challenger. At the same time, imposing far-reaching curricular reforms – along the lines of those being introduced at al-Azhar in Egypt at around the same time – risked antagonizing those supporters of the king who were urging the elimination of the entire system of traditional education, and the old guard of conservative ulama at the Qarawiyyin who remained loath to upgrade the institution's curricula[91]

Granting degree equivalency between the Qarawiyyin faculty and the modern faculties at the University of Rabat, while refraining from radically altering the curriculum of the traditional institution, offered a middle way for the monarchy. The king could point to the degree equivalency as a concession to the Istiqlalians who had been demanding it, but by reducing

[89] Vermeren, "Une Si Difficile Réforme," 123.
[90] Zeghal, *Islamism in Morocco*, 35.
[91] Ibid., 35–6.

the institution to a mere undergraduate faculty of theology, the monarchy effectively ensured its neglect in the ensuing years. Bringing the institution under the tutelage of the Ministry of Education would appeal to the Istiqlalians still dominating that Ministry, but eliminating the Qarawiyyin's 'alimiyya (highest level) degree program also ensured that its students would never achieve the coveted status of 'alim, or an advanced scholar. Instead, this title would be reserved for those coming out of Dar al-Hadith al-Hassaniyya, an institution under the direct control of the monarchy.[92]

1970s–1980s: Expansion. In the 1970s, the state continued to leave the training of imams and teachers in the traditional schools unregulated, but three changes occurred in the training of public school religion instructors. First, the profile of the secondary school religion teacher expanded to include not only graduates of the modern teacher training institutes but also graduates of the Qarawiyyin faculties who had been previously restricted to teaching in the ʾasli/ʾasil tracks and, after 1980, graduates of the newly established faculties of Islamic Studies in the modern universities. Second, there was an expansion in the country's programs of higher Islamic learning from which most future religion instructors were expected to emerge. Third, the opening of university departments of Islamic Studies, coupled with curricular reforms at the main institutions responsible for training future religion teachers, increased the amount of religious knowledge required of future teachers.

The first sign of a change came in 1973, when the king announced that henceforth, graduates of the Qarawiyyin and other traditional institutions could apply for teaching jobs in the public schools – including in the non-ʾasil tracks, where religious instruction was increasing and Arabization was underway. Ensuing reforms continued to diversify the profile of secondary school religion teachers. In 1979, for example, the state widened the pool of potential middle school teachers to include not only graduates of the Regional Pedagogic Centers (where religious instruction had featured minimally) but also those with diplomas in classical Arabic, i.e., those more likely to have graduated from traditional schools and the Qarawiyyin Faculty of Arabic Language. High school teaching positions were also opened to middle school instructors who had been teaching for at least two years, meaning the pool of applicants wishing to teach high school would eventually include more graduates of the classical institutions.[93]

---

[92] Ibid., 46.
[93] Decree 2-78-608 of January 25, 1979 (BORM 3457 of January 31, 1979, pp. 68–70), Articles 16 and 19.

The broadening pool of prospective secondary school religion teachers coincided with an expansion in programs of higher Islamic learning. For instance, in 1980 the state opened Islamic Studies departments within the modern university faculties of letters and established a new (non-Qarawiyyin) bachelor's degree in Islamic Studies (*ijaza fi-l-dirasat al-islamiyya*). The ijaza in Islamic Studies was a four-year program that combined courses in Quranic interpretation, hadith, and other religious subjects with courses in Arabic literature, contemporary Islamic thought, and foreign language instruction. Importantly, the new degree program was less focused on Islamic law than either of the ijaza programs at the Qarawiyyin, and this difference would become more pronounced in the ensuing years.[94] Below, I will return to the significance of this widening gap.

A second example of the expansion in higher Islamic learning came in 1988, when the regime reinstated religious studies at the Qarawiyyin Mosque for the first time in thirty years. The reforms to the Qarawiyyin in the late 1950s and early 1960s had situated the university on physical premises separate from the centuries-old Grand Mosque. The 1988 program, though largely informal, invited students (especially from rural areas) who had demonstrated knowledge of the Quran and wished to pursue a career in religious instruction to attend classes in the ancient mosque for the first time in thirty years. At the same time, Hassan II encouraged these students to pursue studies in ostensibly secular subjects, such as foreign languages, alongside their classical religious studies.[95]

Finally, this period saw an increase in the amount of religious knowledge required of future public school religion teachers, as reflected in changes to the training programs at the modern teacher training institutes and at the Qarawiyyin, the main incubators of future religion instructors. In 1978, a decree reorganizing studies at the ENS extended the course of study from one to four years and stipulated that all students would now receive "a complementary training in . . . Islamic culture." The subject remained a required component of ENS training through the ensuing decades. Similarly, in the mid-1980s the state added "Islamic Studies" to the list of subspecialties students could pursue at the ENS and in all CAPES programs, where it would remain for the next three decades.[96]

---

94 Ministerial Order 1180-79 of January 11, 1980 (BORM 3522 of April 30, 1980, p. 285); Decree 2-79-637 of May 12, 1980 (BORM 3527 of June 4, 1980, pp. 380-2).
95 Interview with Abdelwahab Bendaoud, Rabat, January 16, 2013.
96 Decree 2-78-455 of September 28, 1978 (BORM 3440 of October 4, 1978, pp. 1099–101), Article 21; Decree 2-84-142 of February 15, 1985 (BORM 3777 of March 20, 1985, p. 161); Decree 2-88-293 of August 3, 1989 (BORM 4020 of November 15,

The Qarawiyyin also increased the amount of religious instruction required of future teachers. In 1983, the state reorganized the ijaza (bachelor's) programs in sharia and theology, extending the time to completion from three to four years and adding curricular requirements. For example, the new curriculum for the ijaza in sharia replaced the earlier period's courses on general philosophy, logic, and sociology with new courses on comparative schools of Islamic jurisprudence, personal status jurisprudence, and Islamic jurisprudence regarding philanthropy. For theology students, the differences between the earlier and later periods were more pronounced. Whereas in the 1960s, graduates of the ijaza program in theology would have spent roughly 67 percent of their time on strictly religious subjects, this percentage increased to 77 percent in the later period, as new courses were added in Islamic theological doctrines, Prophetic jurisprudence, personal status jurisprudence, Sufism, and modern Islamic thought. And in another sign of shifting priorities, a previously required course on "History of Islam and the Arab World" gave way to a required course entitled "History of Islam and Islamic Organizations," dropping the reference to the Arab identity in favor of emphasis on the religion.[97]

These policies reflected the combined effect of a weak bureaucratic endowment and the growing threat of religious nationalist and leftist opposition facing the traditionalist regime. Consider first the matter of institutional resources, particularly the ongoing pressures acting on the country's educational bureaucracy. The decision to invite graduates of the Qarawiyyin and other centers of religious learning to apply for teaching jobs in the public schools was necessary in light of the Islamization and Arabization of school curricula Hassan II was pursuing at the time. If the state was going to find teachers who could instruct primary and secondary school students in a growing number of religious subjects – and in Arabic, no less – it made sense to lean more heavily on institutions of traditional religious learning to staff the schools.

Resource limitations were also behind the opening of Islamic Studies departments in the early 1980s. The Arabization of the nation's secondary school curricula had produced increasing numbers of high school graduates who were ill-suited to the vast majority of university studies which, up to that point, had remained in French. The growing number

---

1989, pp. 1448–53); Ministerial Order 1643-92 of November 5, 1992 (BORM 4184 of January 6, 1993, p. 8).

[97] Decrees 2-82-319 and 2-82-320 of January 31, 1983 (BORM 3666 of February 2, 1983, pp. 158–64).

of Arabic-speaking high school graduates placed greater demands on the higher education system, rendering the philosophy and other Francophone departments in the universities less relevant. The closing of many philosophy departments and the redirection of resources to the new Islamic Studies departments at the modern universities were "the result both of poor top-down planning designed to satisfy student 'needs' and a low-cost way to accommodate political demands . . . for greater access to higher education."[98] In this sense, the opening of the Islamic Studies departments was a response to continuing bureaucratic pressures.

But such pressures were only part of the story. The state's policies toward future ulama during this period also reflected the Alaouite regime's drive to weaken its opponents. Recall that in the 1960s and 1970s, vociferous opposition to Hassan II was coming from religious nationalists in the Istiqlal and leftist groups loyal to the UNFP and USFP. The latter were especially prominent on college campuses, where protests against the king's consolidation of power only increased after the 1965 state of emergency and the suspension of the constitution. Faced with mounting opposition from the Left, which at times produced violent clashes between leftist youth and state security forces, the king began leaning more heavily on conservative religious circles for support. As the latter were often allied with the religious nationalists of the Istiqlal, courting them also offered an opportunity to peel the ulama away from the monarchy's rivals in the party and, in so doing, keep his religious opponents fragmented.

Many of the ulama active in associations such as the League of Moroccan Ulama had expressed hostility to the leftist movements then in vogue, since the latter struck them as inherently hostile to religion. Hassan II capitalized on this shared opposition to leftist ideologies and "beginning in the 1970s . . . used the anti-socialist sentiments of the ulama in responding positively to their calls for the . . . Islamization of education."[99] In much the same way that Hassan II's growing alliance with conservatives to check the Left fueled his promotion of religious education in the primary and secondary school curricula, this consideration fed the expansion and promotion of the nation's religion instructors.

The desire to weaken the Left was evident in the series of meetings that culminated in the regime's decision to open up teaching positions in the public schools to graduates of traditional religious institutions.

---

[98] Eickelman, "Madrassas in Morocco," 144.
[99] Zeghal, *Islamism in Morocco*, 56.

In June 1971, the king hosted a gathering of representatives from the League of Moroccan Ulama, the deans of the three Qarawiyyin departments, the dean of Dar al-Hadith al-Hassaniyya, the Prime Minister, the Minister of State for Religious Education, and the Minister of Religious Affairs. Hassan II indicated to the attendees that he sought to promote religious education and pull back on the regime's support for those who had sought to marginalize the products of this education since independence.

A year later, in late 1972 (and following the second attempted coup d'état), Hassan II made good on his promise and convened his cabinet to examine the matter of religious education. It was here that the king replaced the term 'asli (original) with 'asil, emphasizing the *authentic* nature of this traditional education. Also at this cabinet meeting, Hassan II appointed a special committee to oversee the expansion of the 'asil tracks to include courses in science, so that beginning in 1973 graduates of 'asil high schools could continue their studies in the modern faculties, and would no longer be limited to attending the Qarawiyyin. The special committee saw to it that the budget for traditional education was increased substantially for the 1973–7 period, and shortly thereafter the government began offering graduates of the traditional schools teaching jobs in the public schools.[100]

But if promoting more traditionally oriented individuals to counteract the Left fulfilled a core demand of those who had attended the June 1971 meeting and those who served on the king's special committee a year later, the policies that ostensibly conceded the ulama's demands for an Islamization of the education system simultaneously furthered the king's goal of keeping these religious elites divided. In this vein, the opening of the Islamic Studies departments at the modern faculties in the late 1970s and early 1980s was key, as it reflected the regime's desire to encourage anti-leftist student movements on college campuses. But a proliferation of training programs for future religion instructors also meant that becoming a member of the learned religious elite – becoming an 'alim – would never mean just one thing. By making it impossible for a standard profile of an 'alim to emerge, the regime precluded the consolidation of the ulama into a force that might escape its control and mobilize politically. Similarly, reinstating classical studies at the Qarawiyyin mosque – supervised by the Ministry of Religious Affairs – furthered the regime's goal of

[100] Ibid.

"fragment[ing] the networks of religious training," while maintaining a modicum of control over the proliferating religious institutions.[101]

Keeping the ulama divided made sense because in addition to opposition from leftist groups, religious scholars such as 'Allal al-Fassi, and, from the mid-1970s onward, opponents such as 'Abd al-Salam Yassine, were challenging the king's assertion of spiritual authority. The curricular variation throughout the institutions responsible for educating future religion instructors reflected the regime's concern with these opponents. I noted above that the new Islamic Studies departments and Dar al-Hadith al-Hassaniyya were teaching courses that decreased emphasis on Islamic law relative to the Qarawiyyin, which was becoming increasingly specialized in Islamic law (sharia) and jurisprudence (fiqh). The import of these curricular differences was not lost on an 'alim such as al-Fassi, whose objections to the king's assumption of religious and political authority rested on the argument that only by adhering to Islamic law could a leader claim legitimacy to rule. But future ulama were not receiving a strong training in this law. Instead, those entering an institution such as Dar al-Hadith al-Hassaniyya would take courses focusing on the Prophetic traditions – i.e., traditions that emphasized the Alaouites' Sharifian identity. Curricular innovations at the institutions training future religion instructors thus partly reflected the political considerations of a traditionalist regime keen on maintaining its religious bona fides while weakening its religiously oriented opponents.

2000s: Reorientation and Standardization. In the 2000s, the state embarked on a series of comprehensive reforms affecting the training of future religion instructors. These reforms included initiatives upgrading and standardizing the training and licensing of teachers in the traditional school system (al-ta'lim al-'atiq), altering curricula at Dar al-Hadith al-Hassaniyya (where many future religion professors were studying) to emphasize the social sciences, and developing new training programs for mosque-based educators such as imams and imam supervisors.

The reforms began with an effort to provide continuing education for teachers in the traditional ('atiq) schools. The state began organizing educational workshops for instructors who had not advanced far in their own formal schooling. These workshops aimed to impart religious knowledge but also knowledge of modern pedagogy and child psychology. Between 2004 and 2008 the number of teachers and school directors

---

[101] Ibid., 171.

participating annually in these workshops increased threefold, from 244 to 731.[102]

Likewise, in 2006 the Ministry of Islamic Affairs issued a slew of regulations concerning the training and licensing of those managing the traditional schools. Individuals wishing to open and direct traditional primary schools, for instance, would have to complete at least six years of secondary schooling and teach in a public, private, or ʿatiq school for at least three years to qualify. Those wishing to direct traditional middle schools would have to pass the baccalaureate exam or a recognized equivalent and teach in a public, private, or ʿatiq school for at least five years. Future directors of ʿatiq secondary schools had to have an ijaza (bachelor's degree) from a Moroccan university and teach in a school for at least five years.[103]

The 2006 regulations affected teachers in the ʿatiq system as well. Individuals wishing to teach in traditional preschools (msids) – with the exception of those who were already working as imams in mosques, and therefore fell under a different set of regulations – had to have a certificate in Quranic memorization issued by a local council of ulama. Those wishing to teach in primary ʿatiq schools had to obtain the high school baccalaureate or already be teaching in the schools. Future teachers in the ʿatiq middle schools had to complete a bachelor's degree at the Qarawiyyin or an Islamic Studies Department within a Faculty of Letters of any Moroccan university, or already be teaching at the time of the decision. And those wishing to teach in the ʿatiq secondary schools had to obtain an ijaza at the Qarawiyyin or an Islamic Studies Department of another Moroccan university, or already be teaching at the time of the decision. Finally, those who wished to teach in higher institutions of Islamic learning had to first obtain a doctorate from the Qarawiyyin or from Dar al-Hadith al-Hassaniyya.[104]

Indeed, Dar al-Hadith al-Hassaniyya itself was also implicated in the reforms of this period. I noted above that the state in 2005 transformed the institution into both an undergraduate and graduate institution, as part of a broader push to gain a measure of control over institutions of higher Islamic learning. The 2005 reform also revised Dar al-Hadith

---

[102] Moroccan Ministry of Pious Endowments and Islamic Affairs, *ʿAshar Sanawat min al-ʿAhad al-Muhammadi al-Zahir: Iʿadah Haykalat al-Haql al-Dini wa Tatwir al-Waqf*, 137.

[103] Ministerial Decision 877.06 of May 3, 2006 (BORM 5449 of August 21, 2006, pp. 2086–7), Articles 2–7.

[104] Ministerial Decision 877.06 of May 3, 2006 (BORM 5449 of August 21, 2006, pp. 2086–7), Articles 8–12.

al-Hassaniyya's curricula to place greater emphasis on foreign language study and training in the social sciences. Although the content of religious subjects did not change significantly, the addition of secular subjects reflected the state's attempt to alter the profile of future religion teachers by broadening their knowledge base.[105]

Finally, the state began incentivizing higher education for mosque-based prayer leaders and educators by offering to pay the salaries of those who passed the ijaza exams at the Qarawiyyin, Dar al-Hadith al-Hassaniyya, or any of the other Moroccan universities. The state also inaugurated a new training program for individuals wishing to work as imam educators. In 2003, the Directorate of Mosque Affairs launched a one-year training program for aspiring imam supervisors (*al-murshidin*). The program, which continues to this day, includes courses in foreign languages, psychology, and group dynamics, in addition to religious topics. All participants must already have a bachelor's degree, either from an Islamic Studies department of a Moroccan university or from the Qarawiyyin. Between 2005 and 2010, the state annually trained 200 imam supervisors, including 50 women (*al-murshidat*). In exchange for receiving a state subsidy, imams were required to meet with one of these supervisors twice monthly.[106]

How to account for these reforms? The regime's governing ideology had not changed in the interim, but in conjunction with shifts in the regime's perception of its opponents and certain bureaucratic expansions, the regime began leaning more heavily on its traditionalism to go after opponents. And along the way, a mildly emboldened set of institutions facilitated changes in the regulation of religion instructors.

Consider the matter of political opposition. A turning point in the Alaouites' perception of its opponents came in the 1980s, when in the wake of the Iranian Revolution and a series of bread riots in 1981 and 1984 that attracted the participation of Islamist movements, Hassan II detected that he faced a new threat in the form of Islamist movements attacking the monarchy's legitimacy. The shift in threat perception had initially prompted the king to pursue *ad hoc* measures aimed at stanching the Islamist tide (to wit: the 1988 informal reinstatement of classical and secular studies at the Qarawiyyin Mosque). But these initial efforts to

[105] Interview with Khalid Saqi and Hssein Khtou, Rabat, December 9, 2013.
[106] Interview with Abdelwahab Bendaoud, Rabat, January 16, 2013; Khtou, "Reforms in the Religious Sphere and Their Educational Repercussions Vis-à-Vis Islamic Schools: The Case of Dar El Hadith El Hassania Institution in Morocco"; Interview with Mohammed Boutarboush, Salé, January 3, 2013.

ious instruction around the country under a measure of state
re no match for the proliferation of unregulated mosques and
hat continued unabated throughout the 1990s.

The terrorist attack in Casablanca of 2003 brought into sharp relief
the stakes involved in poorly managing the religious realm. From the
regime's perspective, there was a direct link between the flourishing of
unregulated religion instructors around the country and the homegrown
religious extremism that had gained momentum in the 1990s and fueled
the 2003 bombings.[107] In response, the monarchy sought to "strengthen
and deepen the institutionalization of Moroccan religious practices" in
ways that the regime could control.[108] The regulations of religion instructors in the 2000s were components of a broader push to regain control of
mosque-based religious instruction and, in so doing, eliminate or at least
mitigate a key source of opposition to Alaouite rule.

The imam training programs were part of this broader push.
Policymakers later recalled that the regime had considered the introduction of female imam instructors a means of fostering a more moderate
religious discourse to counter extremism.[109] More generally, reorienting
the training of imams reflected the regime's broader concern to reshape the
religious discourse emanating from traditional venues of religious learning. In 2013, Abdelwahab Bendaoud, the head of the Religious Affairs
Ministry's Directorate of Traditional Education, recalled the establishment of the new imam training programs a decade prior in this way:

> We're not hiding it: we sought greater and greater control of the mosques because
> it was there that we found so much mayhem and a great many things that were
> counter to the constants of this country. So naturally, we wanted to know what
> was taking place [in the mosques]. Now every imam gets a stipend from the
> Ministry [of Islamic Affairs], in addition to what they earn . . . And in particular,
> they are now trained by ulama, by those we call "imam guides" [al-murshidin]
> and the guides and their trainees meet twice a month, two Saturdays a month, for
> obligatory continuing education courses.[110]

[107] Interview with Abdelwahab Bendaoud, Rabat, January 16, 2013; Interview with
Mohsine Elahmadi, Rabat, January 7, 2013; Interview with Jaafar Kansoussi, Rabat,
January 17, 2013.

[108] Mohammed El Katiri, "The Institutionalisation of Religious Affairs: Religious Reform in
Morocco," *Journal of North African Studies* 18 (2013): 53.

[109] This view was evident in my interviews with Abdelwahab Bendaoud, Jaafar Kansoussi,
and Mohammed Boutarboush. All three had been involved in crafting and/or implementing the reforms of the early 2000s.

[110] Interview with Abdelwahab Bendaoud, Rabat, January 16, 2013.

Bendaoud's reference to "the constants of this country" reflected an important aspect of the regime's attempts to regulate Morocco's religion instructors. In seeking to reorient and standardize their training, the regime repeatedly stressed the need to reestablish the primacy of the Maliki legal school and eliminate competitors that had gained an audience in mosques and Quranic schools around the country, particularly the Hanbali *madhhab* adopted in Saudi Arabia and associated with the more rigid forms of Salafism practiced there. The rhetorical emphasis on a unity of rite was not new. For decades, the monarchy had sought to convey that the Commander of the Faithful derived his legitimacy from his symbolic representation of Moroccans' religious unity. But this legitimacy begins to crumble once the presumption of religious unity falls apart. For the Moroccan regime, the emergence of Islamist movements sympathetic to non-Maliki schools of religious jurisprudence constituted a threat to this unity. In Bendaoud's words, "The most important thing is to have a single rite. It so happens that Moroccans made their choice. They had two rites before the Maliki one, and in the end they chose to adopt only the Maliki rite . . . For me the most important thing is to have a single rite if we are going to achieve a religious peace in this country."[111] Reestablishing this unity of rite would depend on regulating religious instruction, and especially the individuals responsible for this instruction.

To implement the new regulations, the regime would need to employ its administrative apparatus. Whereas the councils of ulama created in the 1980s had remained fairly inconsequential, ensuing expansions in the religious bureaucracy, such as the reorganization of the Ministry of Islamic Affairs in the 1990s to include a new directorate charged with "training of mid- and upper-level religious functionaries, as well as preachers,"[112] and especially the expansions of the early 2000s, meant that by the mid-2000s the regime was in a stronger position to act. The overhaul of the Ministry of Islamic Affairs in 2003 and the injection of funds into its administrative apparatus were noteworthy in this regard. Recall that the 2003 law created two new offices in the Ministry, a Directorate of Traditional Education and a Directorate of Mosque Affairs.[113] These two offices were ultimately responsible for implementing the bulk of the

---

[111] Ibid.

[112] Decree 1-93-164 of November 8, 1993 (BORM 4279 of November 2, 1994, p. 530).

[113] Dahir 1-03-193 of December 4, 2003 (BORM 5174 of January 1, 2004, pp. 105–10); Ministerial Order 2836-09 of January 18, 2010 (BORM 5822 of March 18, 2010, pp. 258–9).

teacher training reforms that followed. The Directorate of Traditional Education, for example, had a mandate to upgrade all schools comprising the system of al-ta'lim al-'atiq (traditional education). This mandate represented a significant increase in state control over institutions of religious learning, and teacher training soon became a component of this control. Likewise, the new Directorate of Mosque Affairs was charged with "bring[ing] all imams under a common line of religious discourse,"[114] and this mandate inspired the one-year training program for imam supervisors. The fact that the budget allocated to the Islamic Affairs Ministry expanded dramatically in this period (from $15 million to roughly $200 million) meant that the state could now offer imams material incentive to upgrade their own education. For example, the growing budget for the Ministry of Islamic Affairs facilitated the regime's offer to pay the salaries of those imams obtaining a bachelor's degree. Bureaucratic improvements permitted the regime to standardize and reorient the training of mosque-based educators in its drive to weaken Islamist opponents.

REGULATING ISLAM IN MOROCCO

The policy decisions I have reviewed in this chapter point to the combined effect of ideological, political, and institutional factors on Morocco's regulation of Islam as played out in the educational realm. When it came to curricula, the Alaouites' traditionalist ideology of legitimation, a comparatively weak institutional endowment, and a preoccupation with undermining the religious nationalists of the Istiqlal Party precluded major changes in the degree of incorporation of Islamic education into the national curricula following independence in 1956. But growing dissent from religious nationalists and ascendant leftist groups in the 1960s and 1970s, coupled with strains on the state's educational bureaucracy, gave the regime incentive to lean on its traditionalist credentials and abandon the stasis of the earlier period in favor of increased Islamic instruction and a reorientation of the content to emphasize the religion's utility in combating unwanted political ideologies. Then, with the help of an expanded religious bureaucracy, and against the backdrop of new opponents in the form of certain Islamist groups, and new alliances with nongovernmental organizations, the regime pursued a second reorientation of the curricula in the 2000s.

---

[114] Interview with Abdelwahab Bendaoud, Rabat, January 16, 2013.

The interplay of ideology, political opposition, and institutional endowment similarly explained the evolving balance between state control and autonomy for institutions of religious instruction. Throughout the reigns of Mohammed V and his son, Hassan II, a traditionalist ideology of legitimation, a political opposition dominated by religious nationalists and leftists, and a weak institutional endowment produced a blend of autonomy and state sponsorship for lower Quranic schools and institutes of higher Islamic learning. Then, against the backdrop of new political challengers in the form of Islamist movements, the regime under Mohammed VI turned to a strengthened religious bureaucracy and invoked its legitimating ideology of religious guardianship to justify greater state control over these institutions.

Lastly, we have seen how an evolving cocktail of ideological, political, and institutional ingredients fueled Morocco's regulation of religion instructors. A traditionalist ideology of legitimation, coupled with efforts to weaken religious nationalist rivals in the Istiqlal, led the regime to neglect the institutions responsible for training future religion instructors and produced a stasis in the state's post-independence treatment of religion instructors. Then, rising tensions with its leftist and religious nationalist opponents, combined with bureaucratic limitations plaguing the education system, led the regime in the 1970s and 1980s to expand the profile of the nation's religion instructors and increase the number of programs devoted to higher Islamic learning for future teachers. When the regime concluded that its primary political challengers could be found in emerging Islamist groups, the monarchy sought to reorient the training of future religion teachers at institutions of higher learning such as Dar al-Hadith al-Hassaniyya, and in this quest it benefited from a strengthened bureaucratic apparatus.

4

The Tunisian Ingredients of Religious Regulation

Turning now to the case of Tunisia, this chapter and the next examine how the combination of ideological, political, and institutional factors I have highlighted accounted for the Tunisian state's regulation of religious education between independence in 1956 and the outbreak of protests in 2010 that would spark a wave of revolts across the region. This chapter sets the stage by reviewing the Tunisian regime's ideology of legitimation, principal sources of opposition, and institutional pillars that jointly contributed to evolving policy decisions in the religious realm, the subject of Chapter 5.

THE TUNISIAN REGIME'S ENDURING NON-TRADITIONALISM

In contrast to Morocco's post-independence monarchs, Tunisia's modern presidents, Habib Bourguiba (r. 1956–87) and Zine al-ʿAbidine Ben ʿAli (r. 1987–2011), relied on non-traditionalist ideologies of legitimation insofar as religion did not feature prominently in their justifications for claiming political power. The Bourguiba and Ben ʿAli regimes did occasionally instrumentalize religion, whether to promote policies that were at odds with traditional religious interpretations or to convey that the leadership was a reflection of Tunisian society. But for both leaders, references to Islam remained peripheral to their self-legitimating strategies.

The non-traditionalism of Bourguiba's ideology was apparent early in his tenure. In speeches and interviews, as well as in official documents of his ruling Neo-Destour Party, Bourguiba promoted a vision for his country that approximated what James C. Scott has called "high-modernist ideology . . . [popular] among those who wanted to use state power to bring about huge, utopian changes in people's work habits, living patterns, moral conduct, and worldview."[1] Bourguiba's high-modernism assumed that human reason was a necessary component of social advancement, and that this reason was at odds with religion. A speech he delivered on February 8, 1961 was exemplary in this regard:

[P]eople who do not believe that reason should be applied to everything in this world and command all human activity; for these people, certain realms – that of religion in particular – should escape the influence of intelligence. But by acting this way, we destroy the very fervor and veneration we owe to all that is sacred ... How can we accept this ostracism against reason?[2]

Central to Bourguiba's high-modernism was the presumption – sometimes implied, sometimes explicitly stated – that his forward-looking outlook would restore Tunisians' dignity and help to put them on a path to economic and social progress. But progress, in turn, depended on state-led social engineering that would reform Tunisians' "naturally conservative" mentalities and "liberate man from prejudice, ignorance, sickness and misery."[3] The language of liberation, which Bourguiba and his allies had previously employed in the struggle for independence from the French, morphed into a discourse of human liberation. Individual enlightenment, presumed to accompany technological and scientific advancements, would ripen Tunisians for modernity and instill in them the "political maturity" required of "authentic democracy." And to achieve enlightenment, citizens would have to shed their retrograde beliefs, superstitions and passions – including those associated with religious practices.[4]

---

[1] James C. Scott, *Seeing Like a State: How Certain Schemes to Improve the Human Condition Have Failed* (New Haven, CT: Yale University Press, 1998), 5.

[2] Reprinted in Franck Frégosi and Malika Zeghal, "Religion et Politique au Maghreb: Les Exemples Tunisien et Marocain," *Policy Paper* 11 (Paris: Institut Français des Relations Internationales, March 2005): 6–7.

[3] The phrasing appeared in Bourguiba's speech before the Union of Industrial Workers in December 1963, reprinted in Roger Le Tourneau, "Chronique Politique," *Annuaire de l'Afrique du Nord* 2 (1963): 225. See also the editorial in *l'Action* of January 19, 1969, cited in Michel Camau, "Le Discours Politique de Légitimité des Elites Tunisiennes [The Political Discourse of Legitimacy among Tunisian Elites]," *Annuaire de l'Afrique du Nord* 10 (1971): 43.

[4] The phrases I cite appeared in Bourguiba's speech, entitled "The Conditions of an Authentic Democracy," delivered to the Central Committee of the PSD on April 26, 1966. More generally, these themes were evident in Bourguiba's speech at the Neo-Destour's Annual Convention of October 19–22, 1964, reprinted in Roger Le Tourneau, "Chronique Politique," *Annuaire de l'Afrique du Nord* 3 (1964): 132; the PSD's political

Importantly, Bourguiba's prescription for modernity did not seek to eliminate religion from the public sphere and it would be a mistake to characterize his worldview as "secular," since he never intended to separate religious and political authority so much as extend state control over the religious realm. Scholars have suggested that Bourguiba's preference for state domination of the religious sphere may have been informed by seventeenth-century Gallicanism, a movement which had transferred control of the French Church from the Holy See to France's monarchs and local bishops.[5] Whatever the inspiration, his drive to establish state domination over religious institutions and practices led Bourguiba to instrumentalize Islam, promoting reformist and often controversial interpretations of religious doctrine to sanction the regime's ostensibly secular policies. The instrumentalization was evident, for example, in attempts to garner support for economic policies by imbuing those policies (and Bourguiba himself) with a religious quality. Consider the language of a 1964 speech:

Among my functions and responsibilities as the Head of State, I am qualified to interpret the religious law ... As the spiritual leader of Muslims in this country, I declare to you that each of you will accomplish an obligation as meritorious [as a religious one] if you donate the equivalent of the cost of one's pilgrimage [to Mecca – one of five religious injunctions in Islam] to social welfare projects or when you invest in industrial businesses of your country, thereby refraining from soliciting foreign lenders.[6]

Bourguiba employed similar tactics when justifying a progressive penal code in 1957 and, as we shall see, when promoting reforms to Islamic education curricula after 1958.

Such attempts to invoke Islam elicited mixed reactions. For Bourguiba's supporters, the effort to lodge policy decisions in an interpretation of the

platform of 1964, reprinted in "Documents," *Annuaire de l'Afrique du Nord* 3 (1964): 656–8; Bourguiba's speech on January 31, 1967 before the PSD Subcommittee on Education, reprinted in "Documents," *Annuaire de l'Afrique du Nord* 6 (1967): 934–6; Minister of Defense Bahi Ladgham's speech in February 1969 to the PSD's university branches, cited in Camau, "Le Discours Politique de Légitimité des Elites Tunisiennes," 44; Ladgham's speech on February 18, 1969 to the Conference of Sahel Executives, cited in Camau, "Le Discours Politique de Légitimité des Elites Tunisiennes," 42; and the PSD Manifesto of October 19, 1969, reprinted in "Documents," *Annuaire de l'Afrique du Nord* 8 (1969): 990–2.

[5] Frégosi and Zeghal, "Religion et Politique au Maghreb: Les Exemples Tunisien et Marocain," 8. For a more recent exploration of this link, see Rory McCarthy, "Re-thinking Secularism in Post-Independence Tunisia," The Journal of North African Studies 19 (2014): 733–50.

[6] The speech is reprinted in Le Tourneau, "Chronique Politique," (1964), 138.

Islamic heritage advanced a worthy goal of demonstrating that Islam contained principles well suited to modern problems and sensibilities. To his detractors, Bourguiba's approach to religion was offensive and masked a desire to marginalize Tunisians' traditional religious identities. It did not endear him to them, for example, when he appeared on television sipping orange juice during the holy month of Ramadan, lamenting that "a modern nation cannot afford to stop for a month every year."[7] Whatever Bourguiba's personal sentiments regarding Islam, he clearly sought to use religion as a tool of social engineering, and the instrumentalization of Islam remained a part of his regime's non-traditionalism.

Bourguiba's successor, who took power in a bloodless coup on November 7, 1987, similarly lacked any religious affiliation that might have afforded him the kind of legitimacy enjoyed by the Moroccan monarchs. But unlike Bourguiba, whose evident impatience with Tunisians' religious sensibilities likely reflected a conviction that religion mostly impeded modernity, Ben 'Ali initially exhibited a more accommodating stance toward religion, rejecting the hostility of his predecessor and reassuring Tunisians that the new regime would embody Tunisians' religious identity and values. If the state under Bourguiba had sought to moralize society, Ben 'Ali promised to usher in a state that would take its cues from society.[8]

The subtle shift was apparent almost immediately. In his November 7, 1987 declaration, Ben 'Ali noted that the new regime would "give *Islamic*, Arab, African and Mediterranean solidarity its due importance," thus prioritizing (at least, rhetorically) Tunisians' religious identity.[9] Two weeks later, the Interior Ministry announced a "morality campaign" aimed at cleansing cafes, commercial centers, streets, and public transportation of individuals engaged in immoral acts. The new regime introduced the call to prayer on the radio, reopened the venerated Zaytuna Mosque-University, created a Presidential Prize to be awarded to those who memorized the Quran, and legalized the student union sympathetic to the country's main Islamist movement at the time, the *Harakat al-Itijah al-Islami* (Islamic Tendency Movement, or MTI by its French acronym). And in contrast to Bourguiba, whose first trip overseas as President had been to the United States, Ben 'Ali's first overseas trip was a pilgrimage to Islam's holy sites in Saudi Arabia.

---

[7] Bouazza Ben Bouazza, "Ex-Tunisian Leader Habib Bourguiba Dies," *The Washington Post* (April 7, 2000).

[8] Asma Larif-Béatrix, "Changement dans la Symbolique du Pouvoir en Tunisie," *Annuaire de l'Afrique du Nord* 28 (1989): 141–2.

[9] Italics mine.

Ben 'Ali's softer stance on religion also made its way into the National Pact of November 7, 1988, a document outlining the principles and values that were purportedly informing the new regime. The National Pact represented a broad consensus insofar as it was signed by all the major political parties and social movements at the time, including the MTI. The first substantive section of the document was devoted to the matter of identity and proclaimed: "The identity of our people is an Arab-Islamic identity." Moreover, under the new regime, "the Tunisian state maintains and reflects the noble values of Islam so that Islam will be a source of inspiration and pride, open to the preoccupations of humanity, to the problems of the age, and to modernity . . ." The document was careful to preserve some of Bourguiba's progressive reforms, such as the Personal Status Code of 1956, but the overall tone of the proclamation suggested religion would enjoy greater accommodation under the new regime.

Rhetorical hints at greater religious accommodation notwithstanding, Ben 'Ali's ideology of self-legitimation remained fundamentally non-traditionalist. His initial overtures to more traditional elements of Tunisian society did not signal a dramatic ideological shift so much as an attempt to distinguish the country's new ruler from his predecessor by conveying that the new regime would be more populist in its orientation. And when it became clear to the new regime that an accommodative stance toward religion in public might offer Islamists a way into the political process, Ben 'Ali shifted tactics and went from promoting Tunisians' religious identities to presenting the state as an authentic "defender" of Islam. This served to continue Bourguiba's practice of extending state control over the religious realm, and to preclude Islamists from competing for this control. As one analyst of Tunisian politics has noted, Ben 'Ali's instrumentalization of Islam ultimately "was intended not to elevate the influence of religion on public life but to minimize it."[10]

Indeed, it did not take long for Ben 'Ali to begin sounding much like his predecessor, prioritizing the country's "modernization" and relegating religion to the margins. His 2004 political platform, released on the eve of the presidential elections, was telling:

Our [political] program prepares Tunisia for tomorrow: the Tunisia of the coming decades, with modern and welcoming cities, a healthy environment, a network of highly developed roads and highways, a large ensemble of means of communication, an upgraded infrastructure . . . Our program aims to prioritize the authentic

---

[10] McCarthy, "Re-thinking Secularism in Post-Independence Tunisia," 11.

values of our society, namely: solidarity, the value of work, and the benefits of participation, voluntarism and associative life.[11]

Notably absent from Ben 'Ali's list of "authentic values of our society" were the religious identities of Tunisians to which he had appealed in his speeches of the late 1980s. The brief period following Ben 'Ali's coup had proved exceptional, and the regime retained a non-traditionalist ideology of legitimation. However, the constancy of the Tunisian regimes' ideology of legitimation contrasted with the changing nature of political opponents lining up to challenge Tunisia's rulers over the years.

THE TUNISIAN REGIME'S POLITICAL OPPONENTS

As in the Moroccan case, three broad clusters of political opponents emerged to challenge the Tunisian regime throughout the period under review. For the first decade and a half after independence, Bourguiba perceived two groups to be his chief detractors: religious nationalists who had been allied with his rival in the Neo-Destour Party, Salah Ben Youssef, and leftist groups frustrated with Bourguiba's tepid socialism. In the 1970s the regime, having largely stamped out the Youssefists, confronted a new challenge in the form of liberals within the ruling party demanding an end to single-party rule. For the remainder of his tenure, Bourguiba viewed these liberals and leftists as his primary foes. Then, in the 1990s and 2000s, Islamists – many of whom Bourguiba had formerly courted to counter his secular opposition – emerged as the leading opponents of Ben 'Ali's regime. Thus, in the early and later periods the regime faced opponents whose demands touched directly on the state's regulation of religion, whereas in the intervening years such demands were largely absent.

(1) 1950s–1960s: Religious Nationalists and Leftists. Following World War I, Tunisia's emerging nationalist movement coalesced around two groups: the *Destour* (Constitution) Party, founded in 1920 and representing a traditional bourgeoisie of large merchant families and landowners, and the syndical movement under the leadership of Mohamed Ali El Hammi. In 1934 these two groups merged to create a broad-based party, the Neo-Destour. Within the Neo-Destour, there emerged a split between a faction drawn to Bourguiba's preference for a negotiated settlement

---

[11] Ben 'Ali's platform is reprinted in Vincent Geisser and Éric Gobe, "Tunisie: Consolidation Autoritaire et Processus Électoraux," *L'Année du Maghreb 2004* (Paris: CNRS Editions, 2006), 329.

with the French, and a group rallying around the party's Secretary General, Salah Ben Youssef, who was calling for a more radical (and, where necessary, violent) approach to defeating the French.[12]

In contrast to the Moroccan experience, the schism within the Tunisian national movement did not merely reflect a difference of opinion concerning the best way to achieve independence. The division also reflected major disagreements over the extent to which religion should inform the institutions of the independent polity. Bourguiba's supporters in the Neo-Destour hailed from the more secular, often bilingual, and self-styled "modernist" elites who had been educated at the Collège Sadiki, a school founded in 1875 by Tunisia's reformist Prime Minister, Khayr al-Din al-Tunisi. These elites were drawn to Bourguiba's emphasis on a *Tunisianness* that trumped individuals' religious or ethnic identities. Ben Youssef's support, by contrast, came from a conservative faction within the Neo-Destour that included lower-class immigrants to the cities, rural tribesmen, and members of the Islamic establishment centered at the Zaytuna Mosque-University.[13]

The polarization between the two camps turned violent even before independence, as Ben Youssef began calling for both armed resistance against the French and attacks against the Bourguibists. At the Neo-Destour's 1955 Congress, Bourguiba orchestrated Ben Youssef's expulsion from the party, and roughly a third of the party defected to join their ousted Secretary General. A crucial factor to tilt the balance in Bourguiba's favor was the decision of the country's main labor union – *al-Ittihad al-Watani al-Tunisi li-l-Shughl* (the National Union of Tunisian Workers, or UGTT by its French acronym) – to throw its support behind Bourguiba's faction within the Neo-Destour. The UGTT's legitimacy and sheer size strengthened Bourguiba's faction considerably, and with the help of French forces still occupying the country, he managed to snuff out Ben Youssef's militias congregating in the southern part of the country.

In his bid for political hegemony after independence, Bourguiba continued to view the Youssefists as a major threat to the regime. Although Ben Youssef fled to Cairo after independence and was mysteriously killed in 1961, a plot to assassinate Bourguiba was uncovered in December 1962 and the regime accused the plotters of being Ben Youssef loyalists. Thirteen of the twenty-six accused plotters were sentenced to death, while the remaining defendants were imprisoned or subjected to forced labor.

[12] Camau, "Le Discours Politique de Légitimité des Elites Tunisiennes," 38.
[13] Charrad, *States and Women's Rights*, 202.

When in December 1966 a series of protests and counter-protests broke out on the part of student opponents and supporters of the regime, the state mouthpiece, *l'Action,* named "Youssefists" as among the instigators of these events.[14]

Joining the remaining pockets of Youssefists in opposition to the regime were Communists and leftist Arab nationalists sympathetic to Egyptian President Gamal 'Abd al-Nasser and the Ba'athists in Syria. In the December 1966 protests, for example, the regime blamed the incident not only on Youssefists but also on "Trotskyists" and "Communists." Similarly, in March 1968, following clashes between the government and students protesting the detention of a theology student who had spoken out against Israel, the ruling party's student wing published a manifesto denouncing the protesters as "enemies of the regime" and accusing them of being Ba'athists. A trial of the protestors in September found 134 individuals guilty of threatening state security and sentenced them to fines, imprisonment, and forced labor. Shortly thereafter, the Neo-Destour (by then renamed the Destourian Socialist Party) published a tract entitled "The Truth about Subversion at the University of Tunis." The text accused three groups of fomenting student unrest since June 1967: Communists, a group calling itself *Perspectives* and allegedly comprising Trotskyists and Maoists, and Ba'athists purportedly working in conjunction with the Syrian embassy in Tunis.[15]

Despite the dubious merits of such claims, Bourguiba continued to perceive radical leftists of various stripes as a menace to his regime. And although he managed to stamp out most Youssefist opposition in the first decade of his tenure, he continued to face leftist resistance throughout his presidency. College campuses in the 1970s and 1980s remained scenes of continued protests by leftist student groups, and relations between the state and the country's dominant labor movement deteriorated. The lowest point came in January 1978, when a nation-wide strike to protest the regime's treatment of the syndicates led to clashes between state security forces and members of the UGTT. Black Friday, as it came to be known, left at least fifty civilians dead and prompted the regime to put most of the labor union's leadership on trial.[16]

[14] Le Tourneau, "Chronique Politique," (1966), 239.
[15] Le Tourneau, "Chronique Politique," (1968), 179–86.
[16] Issa Ben Dhiaf, "Chronique Politique: Tunisie," *Annuaire de l'Afrique du Nord* 17 (1978): 412.

(2) **1970s–1980s: Leftists and Liberals.** In the early 1970s, as he continued to confront leftist opponents, Bourguiba faced a new challenge in the form of liberals within his own ruling party frustrated at his increasingly autocratic tendencies. The liberals' ascension within the Neo-Destour was rooted in an economic crisis that had gripped the country in the late 1960s. In an effort to grow the economy after independence, Bourguiba had sought to streamline agricultural production by bringing some of it under a state-controlled system of farm cooperatives. The government believed these cooperatives would help produce surpluses for export and ensure low prices for commodities at home, dissuading rural migration to the cities. But by 1968, although the cooperatives represented one-third of rural land and implicated a quarter of the rural population, only 15 percent of the lands under cooperatives were operating at a profit and many peasants had actually seen their incomes decline since independence.[17]

Despite these meager results, Bourguiba's Minister of the Economy and National Education, Ahmed Ben Salah, announced in early 1969 that the state would be bringing all lands under collectivization. Ben Salah's announcement sparked a backlash. In January 1969, residents in the village of Ouardanine in the Sahel (east-central) region led protests against the government's plan to collectivize their property, and the state responded with force. Roughly a dozen people were killed in the clashes, and Bourguiba later claimed that the deaths had occurred despite his order that the protestors be allowed to gather peacefully. At the end of 1969, Ben Salah was dismissed from his post and the regime was thrown into chaos.[18]

The loss of lives in Ouardanine and Ben Salah's ensuing dismissal constituted a crisis for Bourguiba's regime because Ben Salah and his collectivization policies had embodied a cornerstone of the regime's *Destourian Socialism*, Bourguiba's term for a mildly socialist framework in which the state assumed a leading role in economic development through central planning while honoring private property and eschewing a more radical redistribution of wealth. The country's first Ten Year Development Plan (1962–71) reflected the tenets of Destourian Socialism, including: state regulation of industry to reduce the country's reliance on imports; bringing foreign-owned businesses under Tunisian ownership; and creating the agricultural cooperatives on lands expropriated from departing

---

[17] For more on the collectivization fiasco, see Kenneth Perkins, *A History of Modern Tunisia* (Cambridge: Cambridge University Press, 2004), 151.

[18] Camau, "Le Discours Politique de Légitimité des Elites Tunisiennes," 56.

Europeans. Bourguiba had conceived of Destourian Socialism as the middle ground between Marxism and capitalism, and the regime consistently portrayed the President as the guarantor of this ideology.[19] The 1964 rebranding of the Neo-Destour as the Parti Socialiste Destourian (PSD) had reinforced this link, making the collapse of the collectivization scheme five years later all the more damaging for the regime.

Following the failure of the state's agricultural collectives in 1969, Bourguiba announced that the state would seek reforms aimed at liberalizing the political system. The economic crisis had evidently demonstrated to him that "the concentration of power in the hands of one person . . . entails some risks," and he would appoint a commission to consult with the public and recommend a series of constitutional amendments devolving some of the Presidency's powers and making the government accountable to both the President and the parliament. The constitutional changes, Bourguiba promised, would enable greater collaboration between the legislative and executive branches. But he maintained his insistence on a single-party system "as the instauration of multiple political parties in the country would expose the nation to the nefarious rifts it experienced for centuries."[20]

In October 1970, the constitutional commission formally presented its recommendations to Bourguiba. The most significant suggestions concerned the separation of powers and the matter of presidential succession. The commission proposed making the Prime Minister accountable to both the President and the legislature (the National Assembly), aiming for a clearer distinction and an equitable distribution of power between the Head of State, the Head of Government, and the National Assembly. The commission also offered an amendment that would create a position of Vice-President or transfer the President's functions to the National Assembly in the event he was forced to give up his post. Later proposals also sought to liberalize the processes by which the PSD elected its main governing bodies, the Central Committee and the Political Bureau. At the PSD's eighth Party Congress in Monastir in October 1971, delegates approved many of these proposals, including the ones aimed at democratizing the party's internal structures. Henceforth, the Central Committee would be elected by PSD congress delegates, rather than chosen from among the President's appointees as had been standard practice since 1956. The 1971 Monastir

[19] Perkins, *A History of Modern Tunisia*, 147.
[20] For these and other excerpts of Bourguiba's June 8, 1970 radio address, see *"Documents – Tunisie," Annuaire de l'Afrique du Nord* 8 (1970): 863–5.

Congress was a turning point insofar as political liberals were elected to lead the Central Committee and emerged in a dominant position.[21]

So convinced was Bourguiba that the party liberals posed a threat to the regime that he spent the next three years rolling back most of their political reforms. On October 20, 1971, merely five days after the eighth Party Congress ended, Bourguiba issued a decree ordering that Ahmed Mestiri, the newly elected head of the Central Committee and a prominent member of the liberal wing, be suspended from the party and appear before a disciplinary hearing on charges of sedition. Two days later, elections were held for fourteen spots on the PSD's Political Bureau from among twenty names submitted by the President – in blatant violation of the revised procedures approved at Monastir – and several liberal members of the Political Bureau were replaced. In April 1973, Bourguiba announced his plans to run for a fourth term and urged the members of the National Assembly to "do a great service to the nation" by proclaiming him President for Life.[22] The final blow came at the PSD's ninth Congress in September 1974, during which most of the liberals who had ascended in 1971 were pushed out, a new Central Committee was elected, and the remaining delegates unanimously elected Bourguiba President for Life.

Four years later, preoccupied with the events surrounding Black Friday, the regime gave little thought to the emergence of a loose coalition of Islamist groups calling itself the Movement of Islamic Renewal (MIR). In 1979, a member group of the MIR called the Islamic Tendency Movement emerged as the dominant representative of the larger coalition. A year later, the MTI unveiled its political platform, calling for an end to the single party system, a rejection of the separation of religion and state, and a "revival of Tunisia's Islamic identity . . ."[23] The group also announced its intention to seek permission from the state to form a political party, a request that was later denied.

The regime initially sought out alliances with the MTI in an effort to counter their shared leftist and liberal opponents. In 1984, for example, leading Islamists were granted private meetings with the Prime Minister. Toward the end of his tenure, however, Bourguiba came to regret these

---

[21] Béatrice de Saenger, "Chronique Politique: Tunisie," *Annuaire de l'Afrique du Nord* 9 (1970): 277.

[22] Michel Camau, "Chronique Politique: Tunisie," *Annuaire de l'Afrique du Nord* 12 (1973): 428.

[23] "Communiqué du 'Mouvement de La Tendance Islamique'," *Le Maghreb* (Tunis: June 13, 1981), 32. For more on the emergence of Islamism in Tunisia, see Susan Waltz, "Islamist Appeal in Tunisia," *Middle East Journal* 40, no. 4 (Autumn 1986): 653.

overtures and began seeking to repress the group, often through violent means. As Bourguiba's Minister of State for the Interior and then his Interior Minister, Ben Ali was intimately involved in the regime's efforts to repress the MTI and affiliated groups. The experience convinced him repression alone was not effectively undermining the group's potency.[24]

Indeed, following the soft coup in 1987, there was a brief reconciliation in the regime's relations with Islamists. In the early days of his administration, Ben Ali granted amnesty to several thousand exiled opponents and political prisoners of the former regime, including many Islamists rounded up in the waning years of Bourguiba's presidency. After several years in which thousands of Islamist activists had been jailed, exiled, and killed, the coup and attendant release of Islamist prisoners was welcome news for the MTI. Upon meeting with Ben Ali in November 1988, MTI leader Rached Ghannouchi declared that his movement rejected violence, sought a constructive relationship with the new regime, and was ready to participate in the political system since "the defeat of the tyrant who had fought Islam."[25] The MTI's willingness to sign the National Pact suggested it was dropping, or at least setting aside, its long-stated demand that the state annul the Personal Status Code.

At the same time, the MTI interpreted Ben Ali's initial efforts at greater religious accommodation and political liberalization to mean that the Islamist movement would now be a full participant in the emerging political system. In 1989 the MTI tested out this assumption by participating in legislative elections. To get around the prohibition on religiously based parties, the group changed its name to *Ennahda* (Renaissance). When the state still refused to grant the group formal status, Ennahda fielded candidates as independents in twenty-two of the country's twenty-five electoral districts, and captured 15 percent of the overall vote.

(3) 1990s–2000s: Islamists. The success of Ennahda Party members in the 1989 elections led Ben Ali to conclude that they posed a threat to his regime, and he soon abandoned his accommodative stance in favor of repression. Violent confrontations ensued. Within weeks of the legislative elections, the regime had arrested hundreds of Ennahda members. In February 1991, three Islamist activists burned down a Tunis office of Ben Ali's ruling party, the Rally for a Constitutional Democracy (RCD), killing

---

[24] Frégosi and Zeghal, "Religion et Politique au Maghreb: Les Exemples Tunisien et Marocain," 25.

[25] Ghannouchi's statement is cited in Asma Larif-Béatrix, "Chronique Tunisienne," *Annuaire de l'Afrique du Nord* 27 (1988): 748.

one security guard and injuring another. Ennahda condemned the attack and claimed the perpetrators were not part of the movement, but the regime evidently remained unconvinced. In July 1992, a series of mass trials took place in which Ennahda members were accused of terrorism. Up to 30,000 Islamists were jailed during this period and some were tortured. Others, including Ghannouchi, fled as the movement was formally outlawed. The regime continued to portray Islamists as religious fanatics throughout the 1990s and early 2000s, arguing that only the state could "defend" Islam and represent its authentic form.[26] In contending with his Islamist opponents, Ben 'Ali benefited from a comparatively robust institutional apparatus, the roots of which stretched back to the pre-independence era.

THE BLESSINGS OF A ROBUST INSTITUTIONAL ENDOWMENT

After Bourguiba became President in 1957, the regime solidified its grip on the emerging institutional structures of the state, foremost among them a hegemonic political party. The President's rhetoric of legitimation implied that, just as the masses had followed his lead in achieving independence from the French, they ought to follow him along a path toward economic prosperity. For now, that path was being forged by a single party, the Neo-Destour. Bourguiba's preoccupation with unity was a legacy of the violent clashes that had broken out between various factions of the Neo-Destour around independence, and it translated into an insistence that the state could only achieve its aims via a single-party system.[27] Thus, Bourguiba succeeded where the Istiqlalians in Morocco failed, creating a political system in which the dominant nationalist party became synonymous with the state.

The hegemony of the ruling party after independence was evident in the Neo-Destour's high rate of membership, its penetration into Tunisian society, and the ideological cohesion of its leadership. In 1962, Clement Henry Moore reported that party membership stood at roughly 250,000–300,000 out of an adult male population of just a million. So pervasive was the party apparatus that, with nearly 1,000 branches around the

---

[26] McCarthy, "Re-thinking Secularism in Post-Independence Tunisia," 13.
[27] Bourguiba and his closest supporters contended that the one-party system was only transitory until economic development could be secured, at which point political pluralism would emerge. Such pluralism never arrived, as the intra-party schisms of the 1970s would show. See Camau, "Le Discours Politique de Légitimité des Elites Tunisiennes," 55; Charrad, *States and Women's Rights*, 210.

country, "virtually all provincial officials, whether in the party or in the government, [we]re either Neo-Destour militants or former militants, brothers in the same cause."[28] The contrast with Morocco's leading nationalist party, the Istiqlal, was stark: the latter faced steep opposition among rural tribes, preventing it from becoming a mass-based party and achieving the Neo-Destour's level of societal infiltration.

Key decisions throughout the first fifteen years of Bourguiba's tenure brought the state and the party closer together. From the outset, leading members of the Neo-Destour's Political Bureau (the executive body) served as ministers in Bourguiba's governments, and Bourguiba's constant reshuffling of the Political Bureau gave its members incentive to continue supporting the President's initiatives, thereby minimizing ideological dissent at the top. At the Neo-Destour's 1964 Congress, in which the party renamed itself the Destourian Socialist Party to emphasize Bourguiba's economic agenda, the party adopted a series of structural changes that severely limited the independence of national organizations and further tied the party and state together. For example, the delegates approved a measure requiring members of labor unions, youth organizations, and other nominally independent groups to join the PSD as individuals, rather than through their affiliation with the national organizations, as they had in the past. This effectively stripped these organizations of the ability to pressure the party by threatening to withdraw their members. And whereas up to that point, regional and local offices of the PSD had remained independent of the government, delegates to the 1964 Congress decided that henceforth regional governors would represent both the PSD and the state.[29]

Two years later, the parliament approved a revision to the constitution which implicated procedures for replacing the President of the Republic. The 1959 constitution had stipulated that in the event of the President's untimely death or forced resignation due to illness, the cabinet would choose one of its members to serve as Interim President until the parliament could elect a candidate fulfilling the constitutionally mandated requirements. With the 1966 revision, the Interim President would instead be chosen from among a Council of the Republic comprising cabinet members and members of the PSD's Political Bureau. As Kenneth Perkins

---

[28] Clement Henry Moore, "The Neo-Destour Party of Tunisia: A Structure for Democracy?" *World Politics* 14 (April 1962): 467, 469, and 471.

[29] Ibid., 476; Clement Henry Moore, *Tunisia Since Independence: The Dynamics of One-Party Government* (Berkeley, CA: University of California Press, 1965), 94; Perkins, *A History of Modern Tunisia*, 147.

noted in his political history of the country, such measures produced a system in which "the party act[ed] as the agent of impulsion, the state the agent of execution [and] the Parti Socialiste Destourien emerged . . . with a tighter grip on the state and its citizens than ever before."[30]

However, beginning in the late 1960s, key developments began weakening the ruling party. The first sign of this weakening followed the 1969 collectivization debacle. Although the PSD retained a sizeable membership – Hermassi reported that in the early 1970s the figure had grown to 380,000, or one-third of adult males over the age of twenty[31] – there were indications of decreasing support among the populace. For example, between 1969 and 1974 voter participation in local elections dropped from 91 percent to 79 percent, and voter abstention rates for legislative elections continued to rise in the 1970s and 1980s, reaching 25 percent by 1989.[32] Growing public frustration with the party and the regime fueled numerous manifestations of social strife in this period, not least the bloody confrontation between state security forces and the UGTT in 1978 that left between fifty and 200 dead, an armed uprising in Gafsa in 1980 that claimed the lives of forty-eight Tunisians and left over one hundred injured, and a series of riots in 1984 that left eighty-nine dead and hundreds more injured.[33]

There was also a marked retreat in the party's penetration of associational life during this period. Hmida Ennaifer, a public intellectual from a prominent Tunisian family of religious notables, later recalled: "After the miserable experiment in socialism, we felt less of a hegemonic presence of the modern state, of the Bourguibist state."[34] The party's loosening grip on public life was reflected in the emergence of unaffiliated organizations such as the Tunisian League of Human Rights in 1976. Whereas in the earlier period, associations had been nonexistent outside the Neo-Destour/PSD, the regime's formal, if grudging, recognition of the League of Human Rights a year later reflected an emerging space in civil society over which the party

---

[30] Perkins, *A History of Modern Tunisia*, 147.

[31] Hermassi, *Leadership and National Development in North Africa*, 161.

[32] Voting and abstention rates are drawn from Béatrice de Saenger, "Chronique Politique: Tunisie," *Annuaire de l'Afrique du Nord* 11 (1972): 337; Lise Storm, *Party Politics and the Prospects for Democracy in North Africa* (Boulder, CO: Lynne Rienner Publishers, 2014), 92.

[33] These figures are drawn from John P. Entelis, *Comparative Politics of North Africa* (Syracuse, NY: University of Syracuse Press, 1980), 141; Issa Ben Dhiaf, "Chronique Politique: Tunisie," *Annuaire de l'Afrique du Nord* 19 (1980): 578; Jean-Philippe Bras, "Chronique Politique: Tunisie," *Annuaire de l'Afrique du Nord* 23 (1984): 970.

[34] Interview with Hmida Ennaifer, Tunis, September 19, 2012.

no longer commanded a firm hold. By 1985 the League's membership had grown to 3,000.[35]

The ideological cohesion among party leaders also began to show signs of cracking. This unity had characterized the PSD through the first fifteen years of Bourguiba's tenure, and it had permitted bold policy shifts such as the adoption of the socialist economic model in 1964. But after the collectivization scandal, the ruling party succumbed to internal schisms (as evidenced by the emergence of the liberal wing discussed above), and divisions even emerged within Bourguiba's inner circle. These schisms led to numerous embarrassing about-face decisions on the part of the regime, as in 1981 when Bourguiba rescinded a decree of his Prime Minister that had banned the sale of alcohol and ordered cafes closed during the month of Ramadan. (The Prime Minister in question, Mohamed Mzali, would also come under fire for policies he pursued as Education Minister, a development to which I will return in Chapter 5.) Also in 1981, the Ministry of Education banned the veil in public schools, a decision that would be overturned three years later.

Still, such examples of internal fragmentation, and the more general public disenchantment with the ruling party during this period only mildly reduced the regime's institutional strength, and the PSD continued to dominate the political arena. Even when Bourguiba experimented with limited party pluralism in 1981, allowing smaller parties to participate in legislative elections for the first time, the election results confirmed the PSD's enduring supremacy. That year, 85 percent of the electorate granted the PSD 95 percent of the parliament's seats, while independents and new parties such as the liberals' *Mouvement des Démocrates Socialistes* only mustered a combined 5 percent. Between 1981 and 1986, PSD membership actually *increased*, and the number of party branches rose from forty to sixty for every 100,000 inhabitants.[36]

The new regime that assumed power in 1987 initially hinted that it would continue liberalizing the political arena by laying the groundwork for democratic, multiparty elections and enshrining greater individual freedoms and associational rights for civil society. In his November 7 speech to the parliament, Ben 'Ali described the regime change in this way:

---

[35] Susan Waltz, *Human Rights and Reform: Changing the Face of North African Politics* (Berkeley, CA: University of California Press, 1995), 134–9.

[36] Issa Ben Dhiaf, "Chronique Politique: Tunisie," *Annuaire de l'Afrique Du Nord* 20 (1981): 618–19; Clement Henry Moore, "Political Parties," in *Polity and Society in Contemporary North Africa*, ed. William I. Zartman and William Mark Habeeb (Boulder, CO: Westview Press, 1993), 53–4.

Our people has reached a degree of responsibility and maturity where every individual and group is in a position to constructively contribute to the running of its affairs, in conformity with the republican idea which gives institutions their full scope and guarantees the conditions for a responsible democracy, fully respecting the sovereignty of the people as written into the Constitution . . . Our people deserves an advanced and institutionalized political life, truly based on the plurality of parties and mass organizations.[37]

The November 7 declaration also announced several major legal reforms, including a planned constitutional revision to eliminate the Presidency for Life, a new law regulating political parties, and a more liberal press code. All signs pointed to a break from the former regime.

To reinforce the new regime's orientation, the PSD in February 1988 changed its name to the Rally for a Constitutional Democracy, and a series of seemingly liberal reforms followed that year. On July 12, 1988, for example, the Chamber of Deputies (the upper house of parliament) amended the constitution, eliminating the Presidency for Life, doing away with automatic succession by the Prime Minister, and limiting the number of presidential terms to three. That same day, the parliament adopted two laws, one liberalizing the press code and another relaxing restrictions on civil society organizations. Later that month, the President handed down a new election law – favorably received by numerous opposition groups – that would regulate the presidential and legislative elections scheduled for 1989. And in November, the National Pact decried the "one-party system, the marginalization of institutions, the personalization of power, the monopolization of authority [and] other practices contrary to the country's constitution" that had been "the cause of numerous crises." The document went on to announce that in place of such practices, the new regime would govern in accordance with "the aspirations of the Tunisian people for liberty, sovereignty and justice, and its . . . attachment to the rules of democratic governance and the principles of human rights."

Still, even as the new regime took initial steps toward a multiparty system, it pursued measures aimed at controlling such openings. Already in 1988 there were signs that Ben 'Ali might not be as eager to fully embrace the political liberalization for which many were clamoring. For example, when the PSD changed its name in February 1988, Ben 'Ali saw to it that the party's newly constituted Central Committee retained several figures closely associated with the old regime, avoiding the more radical purge

[37] Ben 'Ali's speech is available at http://al-bab.com/documents-section/tunisia-overthrow-bourguiba.

some were demanding. Months after Ben 'Ali had released thousands of Islamists imprisoned under Bourguiba, the new regime passed a law prohibiting political parties from forming on the basis of religion, a clear attempt to keep groups such as the MTI out of the electoral system. And whereas the secular opposition parties had initially welcomed the electoral law of 1987, by February 1988 they were crying foul over what they saw as the RCD's attempts to monopolize the political realm and limit the effectiveness of competitors through new laws regulating electoral lists in the run-up to the 1989 legislative elections.[38]

By the early 1990s it had become clear that the new President had no intention of dismantling the one-party system. On the contrary, the RCD emerged from the 1989 legislative elections (widely deemed fraudulent) in firm control. Although Ben 'Ali did allow several opposition parties to join the parliament in ensuing years, their presence remained a cosmetic feature of an increasingly autocratic single-party system. The party's hegemony was apparent in several respects. Voter turnout for parliamentary elections, which had dipped in the preceding decades, rebounded from 76 percent in the 1989 elections to 95 percent and 91 percent in the 1994 and 1999 elections, respectively. Between 1987 and 1989 alone, membership in the party rose by 50 percent, to roughly 1.5 million. By the mid-1990s student membership in the party had risen to 8,000 (up from a few hundred in 1987) and total party membership hovered around 1.7 million, a considerable number in a country of roughly 10 million inhabitants. The RCD extended its control through 6,713 branches (more than four times as many as in the 1970s) and 300 associations scattered around the country, staffed by some 55,000 citizens. In 1993 more than 83,000 individuals ran as candidates for local branch positions within the Party. The party's reach was simply no match for opposition parties or civil society groups, Islamist or otherwise.[39]

In his bid for political control after the 1989 elections, Ben 'Ali also benefited from a bureaucracy Béatrice Hibou later described as a

---

[38] Larif-Béatrix, "Chronique Tunisienne," (1988), 746; Zakya Daoud, "Chronique Tunisienne," *Annuaire de l'Afrique du Nord* 28 (1989): 681–2.

[39] Moore, "Political Parties," 53; Larbi Sadiki, "Ben 'Ali's Tunisia: Democracy by Non-Democratic Means," *British Journal of Middle Eastern Studies* 29 (May 2002): 62. These figures should not be taken to reflect public support for the party. In such a repressive political environment, party membership was likely seen as a means of securing access to patronage and other benefits presumably unavailable to those remaining outside. But precisely because the public evidently perceived such membership to come with benefits, the increasing number of individuals joining the PSD reflected the party's success in convincing citizens they faced no alternative institution in the political landscape.

"well-organized structure [with] cadres who are often competent."[40] In fact, both Ben ʿAli and Bourguiba were blessed with a comparatively robust bureaucracy, reflected in its centralized nature and the skilled personnel therein. Even before the Protectorate, the central state exerted administrative control over the vast majority of Tunisian territory through the work of roughly sixty governors (qayids) dispersed throughout the country collecting taxes and performing other regulatory functions. In contrast to Morocco's quasi-independent governors, Tunisia's qayids were appointed directly by the monarchy (the institution that ruled prior to the French invasion in 1881). Under these governors, an additional layer of local state representatives and nearly 2,000 religious figures liaised between the population and the state administration.[41]

In addition to its centralized nature, the Tunisian bureaucracy was staffed by a highly skilled cadre of civil servants. Theda Skocpol, Dietrich Rueschemeyer, Peter Evans and others have singled out the creation of well-trained elites and an *esprit de corps* among civil servants as crucial components of a robust bureaucracy. Early on, Tunisia's bureaucracy enjoyed both, thanks largely to the Collège Sadiki. Since 1875 – significantly, before the French incursion – this prestigious school had been educating Tunisians, in French and Arabic, in subjects ranging from Islamic law to history to physics. Most graduates of Sadiki went on to a higher education in France before returning home to work in the higher echelons of public administration. In the 1970s, Hermassi observed that Sadiki's "graduating classes have formed a network of enduring relationships covering professional, familial, and political spheres, from which has emerged a genuine *esprit de corps*. This *esprit de corps* continues, today, to influence and weld together the political elites."[42]

If Bourguiba inherited a relatively robust bureaucratic apparatus, his regime also made several key decisions in the early post-independence years that spared the country many of the bureaucratic challenges confronting Morocco around the same time. For example, consider the matter of teacher shortages. The 1958 school reform did not make schooling mandatory for all children, instead stipulating only that children were guaranteed *the right* to a free education. And since the Tunisian regime did not pursue full-scale Arabization, it did not have to purge hundreds

---

[40] Béatrice Hibou, *The Force of Obedience: The Political Economy of Repression in Tunisia* (Cambridge: Polity Press, 2011), 116.
[41] Hermassi, *Leadership and National Development in North Africa*, 25.
[42] Ibid., 121.

of French-speaking teachers and find immediate replacements, as in the Moroccan case. In the late 1950s, the government shortened the number of weekly hours of primary school to fifteen for the first two years and twenty-five for the last four years, which meant that two classes could work back to back in the same room.[43] This not only reduced the demand for new buildings but also reduced the demand for new teachers because a single teacher could now teach both classes. Such decisions enabled the Tunisian state to avoid the crippling teacher and classroom shortages seen in Morocco during this period. Indeed, while Tunisian Education Ministry reports in the late 1950s and 1960s did make occasional references to teacher shortages, the needs paled in comparison to the Moroccan case, and they disappeared entirely from these reports by the 1980s.

Alternatively, consider the matter of educational inspectors. Modeled on the French system, Tunisia's and Morocco's inspectors were trained and paid by their respective education ministries to monitor teachers and ensure their professional development over the years. The comparatively robust nature of Tunisia's bureaucracy was apparent in the consistently higher number of educational inspectors. By the 1970s, for example, whereas the ratio of Moroccan inspectors to primary school teachers stood at one inspector for every 218 teachers, the ratio in Tunisia was already down to 1:68.[44]

In addition to a relatively strong educational bureaucracy, Tunisian policymakers developed a centralized religious bureaucracy much earlier than their Morocco counterparts. In 1962, for example, Bourguiba created the post of Mufti of the Republic, the highest religious figure in the country, who would be appointed by the President and whose functions included issuing certificates of conversion to Islam, answering questions relating to Islam, and advising the government on "schoolbooks and on all documents and studies in connection with the Islamic religion."[45] Furthermore, the independent regime early on developed a civil service of religious functionaries on the government payroll, one that continued to expand over the years. A 1966 decree created two new positions: a Preacher

---

[43] Ahmed Abdesselem, "Tunisia," *Yearbook on Education* (International Bureau of Education, 1959): 414.

[44] Moroccan Ministry of Education, *Le Mouvement Educatif au Maroc, 1973–1974 et 1974–1975*, 21 and 23; Tunisian Ministry of Education, *Rapport sur le Mouvement Éducatif en Tunisie* (Tunis, 1977), 15–16.

[45] Decree 62–107 of April 6, 1962 (Journal Officiel de la République Tunisienne [JORT] 19 of April 6–10, 1962, p. 390).

of the Governorate (*wa'iz al-wilaya*) and a Preacher of Delegation (*wa'iz mu'atamidiyya*). In Tunisia, whereas the term *imam* had traditionally designated the man who led a congregation in prayer, the *wa'iz* offered a lesson after the prayers to those gathered in the mosque. In the new parlance, the wa'iz al-wilaya was the upper-most religious functionary below the Mufti of the Republic, to whom he reported, and he oversaw the activities of the wa'iz mu'atamidiyya, who in turn supervised religious instruction in the mosques and occasionally served as an imam himself. Both the wa'iz al-wilaya and the wa'iz mu'atamidiyya received salaries and benefits according to the same pay scale as teachers falling under the purview of the Ministry of Education.[46]

In 1967 the regime established a Directorate of Religious Affairs within the State Secretariat of the Presidency. The Directorate was charged with handling matters "related to the construction, administration, and upkeep of Muslim places of worship as well as problems related to the nomination and compensation of associated employees." A decade later the state developed a corps of Religious Inspectors tasked with overseeing the Preachers of the Governorates and lower-level imams. Inspectors were principally recruited from among Preachers of the Governorates who had been serving for at least five years, and they reported to the Directorate of Religious Affairs (which, in 1970, was transferred from the Presidency to the Prime Minister's Office). The inspectors' salaries and advancement followed the same pay scale as employees of the Office of Pedagogy in the Ministry of Education.[47]

Expansions in the religious bureaucracy continued in the ensuing decades.[48] In one of his last acts as President, Bourguiba in 1986 transferred the Directorate of Religious Affairs from the Prime Minister's office to the Interior Ministry. A year later Ben 'Ali decreed that all religious functionaries had to be approved by the Interior Ministry before coming on the government payroll. When the Directorate of Religious Affairs became

---

[46] Decree 66–151 of April 8, 1966 (JORT 17 of April 8–12, 1966, p. 602–4).

[47] Decree 67–345 of October 5, 1967 (JORT 43 of October 6–10, 1967, p. 1252–3); Decree 77–938 of November 17, 1977 (JORT 77 of November 22–25, 1977, p. 3224–5).

[48] See, for example: Decree 86–532 of May 6, 1986 (JORT 30 of May 9, 1986, p. 580) and Decree 87–664 of April 22, 1987 (JORT 31 of April 28–May 1, 1987, p. 575–6); Decree 89–1690 of November 8, 1989 (JORT 77 of November 17–21, 1989, p. 1805–6); Decree 93–1952 of August 31, 1993 (JORT 74 of October 1, 1993, p. 1645–7); Decree 94–558 of March 17, 1994 (JORT 23 of March 25, 1994, p. 494–5); Decree 95–993 of June 5, 1995 (JORT 46 of June 9, 1995, p. 1264–5); Decree 2003–2411 of November 17, 2003 (JORT 96 of December 2, 2003, p. 3489).

TABLE 4.1 *Legitimating ideology, political opposition, and regime endowment in Tunisia, 1956–2010*

Time period (Approximate)	Legitimating ideology	Primary political opponents	Institutional endowment
1956–1960s		Religious nationalists + Leftists	Strong
1970s–1980s	Non-traditionalist	Leftists + Liberals	Mixed
1990s–2010		Islamists	Strong

the Ministry of Religious Affairs in 1993, it assumed responsibility for regulating holy sites and overseeing all religious personnel, which now included imams, preachers, those who issued the call to prayer, reciters of the Quran, and teachers of the Quranic preschools, the latter of whom had become civil servants and begun receiving a monthly government salary in the late 1980s. The new ministry also began monitoring instruction in the Quranic preschools and Quranic associations. All personnel in the religious realm now had to be approved by the Minister of Religious Affairs, from the Religious Inspector on down to the building guard of a mosque. As Chapter 5 demonstrates, the early creation and ensuing expansion of a religious bureaucracy in Tunisia facilitated key regulations concerning religious education.

Before turning to those regulations, I offer a summary of the ideological, political, and institutional developments reviewed above (Table 4.1).

5

Balancing Muhammad and Montesquieu in Tunisia

On a crisp day in February 2015, I ventured into the old city, or *madina*, of Tunis and walked down a central artery of the market toward the Zaytuna Grand Mosque. The 1,300-year-old structure sits roughly in the middle of the madina, and although I had circled it many times previously, on this particular day I had an invitation to enter the mosque. My contact led me up a narrow staircase, through a dark corridor to one side of the main prayer hall, and into a small office with high ceilings and walls lined with books. A few moments later, in walked Hussayn al-ʿAbidi, the self-proclaimed Shaykh of the Grand Mosque, for our scheduled interview. A diminutive figure with a square jaw and graying hair, al-ʿAbidi had attracted a torrent of negative press for his incendiary sermons denouncing Shiites and calling for the death of blasphemers. For many in the Tunisian religious establishment, al-ʿAbidi – whose formal theological training was questionable, at best – had become an embarrassment, and by the time we met in February 2015, Tunisian authorities had repeatedly threatened to remove him from his post.

The confrontation between al-ʿAbidi and the state had been brewing for nearly three years. Following the 2011 uprising in Tunis that sparked what came to be known as the Arab Spring, a group of Tunisian citizens petitioned and won the right to reopen the Zaytuna Grand Mosque after decades of inactivity. In May 2012, the government produced a document formally recognizing the reestablishment of the Zaytunian education system and affirming the institution's independence from state interference. A short time later, al-ʿAbidi, evidently taking advantage of the Zaytuna's immunity from state regulation, installed himself as Shaykh of the Grand Mosque. But in June 2012 he called for the killing of two artists whose works were appearing in a nearby gallery, and over the next three years al-ʿAbidi's rhetoric grew increasingly inflammatory. The government, wary of sparking a public backlash and reluctant to renege its own promise to maintain the Zaytuna's independence, repeatedly tried and failed to evict him from the mosque.

It was this institutional independence that al-ʿAbidi appeared most intent on conveying to me that day in February. Pulling out a copy of the relevant inter-ministerial agreement from a folder on his desk, al-ʿAbidi directed me with his index finger to the precise wording of the relevant article: "You see?" he said, practically shouting, "Here, right here in Article One, it states that 'The Zaytuna Grand Mosque is an INDEPENDENT, Islamic educational institution!'" Furthermore, he noted, Article Three stipulated: "The Shaykh of the Grand Mosque is the only legitimate representative of the institution." From al-ʿAbidi's perspective, the state's efforts to evict him from the mosque were not only morally objectionable but also illegal. One month later, al-ʿAbidi was forcibly removed from the Zaytuna, ending a three-year saga but leaving the debate over state control of religious institutions largely unresolved.

* * * * * * *

This chapter delves into Tunisia's evolving regulation of religious education from independence in 1956 to the onset of the Arab Spring in late 2010. I begin with an examination of curricular reforms, focusing on how and why the country's leaders pursued a contraction and reorientation of religious instruction throughout the 1950s and 1960s, shifted gears to expand and reorient the relevant curricula in the 1970s and 1980s, and once again sought a contraction and reorientation in the 1990s and early 2000s. On the matter of state control versus autonomy, the relevant institutions in Tunisia came under nearly total state control in the 1950s and 1960s, then experienced a mix of control and autonomy throughout the 1970s and 1980s, and were once again subject to increasing state control in the 1990s and 2000s. Finally, the chapter explains and analyzes the Tunisian state's evolving approach to regulating religion instructors. The training and licensing procedures for teachers and mosque-based educators were standardized in Tunisia much earlier, and to a greater degree, than in Morocco. But beginning in the 1970s, the state relaxed its professional requirements for these individuals, broadening the pool of prospective religion instructors. In the 1990s and 2000s the state once again sought to reorient the profile of religion instructors by reforming their training and issuing stricter licensing procedures. The chapter demonstrates that these policy changes resulted largely from the evolving interplay of the Bourguiba and Ben 'Ali regimes' ideological orientations, political opposition, and institutional resources at their disposal.

CRAFTING CURRICULA

(1) **1956–1969: Contraction and Reorientation.** During the French Protectorate (1881–1956), Tunisian Muslim children who attended school were required to take classes in Quranic instruction, but the post-independence curricula reduced the amount of Islamic education in the public schools and presented religious teachings almost exclusively in relation to the regime's policy goals.[1] Unlike in Morocco, where the reforms of the early state-building period were largely *ad hoc,* the Tunisian regime under Bourguiba promulgated a comprehensive reform in 1958 that sought to unify the various educational tracks of the Protectorate and bring them under state control.[2] The 1958 law came to be known as "Messadi's law," so-named for Mahmoud Messadi, Bourguiba's Minister of Education and a leading architect of the legislation. To appreciate the curricular changes Messadi's law inspired, it is worth reviewing what the new curricula replaced.

The education system inherited by the independent Tunisian regime in 1956 consisted of various types of schools, some of which predated the Protectorate and some of which had emerged under French rule. Before the arrival of the French, schooling for Tunisian Muslim children was available at traditional Quranic schools, or *kuttabs* (sing. *kuttab*) as they are known in Tunisia. These schools extended from the primary to the secondary level and fed into the Zaytuna Mosque-University in Tunis. The kuttab curriculum focused on Quranic memorization and Arabic grammar, and occasionally the traditional schools offered lessons in math, history, and other nonreligious subjects. Beginning in 1875, a second option

---

[1] The contrast between the amount of time devoted to Islamic instruction in Tunisia and Morocco was most glaring at the primary school level. By the 1967–8 school year, Moroccans in their first year of primary school were spending 16.3 percent of weekly hours on religious lessons as opposed to 8.6 percent in Tunisia. In the fifth year of primary school the difference was even greater: 13.3 percent in Morocco compared to 1.2 percent in Tunisia. See Noureddine Sraieb, "Politiques culturelles nationales et unité Maghrébine," *Annuaire de l'Afrique du Nord* 9 (1970): 108.

[2] Law 58-118 of November 4, 1958 (JORT 89–102 of November 7, 1958, p. 1056).

emerged with the establishment of the bilingual Sadiki School (Collège Sadiki), where students could study subjects such as math and geography as well as religious subjects such as Islamic theology and jurisprudence. The presence of the Sadiki school – which had no equivalent in Morocco – would have significant implications for the independent state's regulation of religious education.[3]

When the French arrived in 1881, they left the kuttabs and Sadiki in place, reasoning that the authorities would be less likely to encounter resistance if traditional educational institutions – and especially religious instruction – continued functioning as before. But the colonial administrators established a competitor to these traditional schools in the form of public elementary and secondary "Franco-Arabic" schools. The Franco-Arabic schools were open to Tunisian and European children, and instruction was bilingual (though French took priority as the language of instruction for 21 out of 30 hours per week). The curriculum of the Franco-Arabic schools largely mirrored that of public schools in France, with two noteworthy modifications: children of European settlers were required to take a course on the Tunisian Arabic dialect, and Tunisian Muslim students took classes on the Quran and classical Arabic. By the end of the Protectorate, whereas roughly 36,000 Tunisian children were still attending kuttabs, roughly 138,000 Muslim children were enrolled in Franco-Arabic schools, representing over three-quarters of the Muslim students learning in non-kuttab schools on the eve of independence.[4]

Beginning in 1907, a fourth option emerged in the form of "modern Quranic schools" founded by members of a burgeoning nationalist movement known as The Young Tunisians. These schools, which were initially funded by private donations and administered by the Authority

3 Information on precolonial schooling in Tunisia was drawn from Mokhtar Ayachi, *Écoles et Société en Tunisie 1930–1958* (Tunis: Cahiers du Centre d'Études et de Recherches Economiques et Sociales, 2003), 288; Noureddine Sraieb, "L'idéologie de l'école en Tunisie coloniale (1881–1945)," *Revue du monde musulman et de la Méditerranée* 68–9 (1993): 239.

4 Many kuttabs were transformed into modern Quranic schools throughout the 1930s and 1940s, but I was unable to find reliable data on the number of students enrolled in these schools on the eve of independence. In addition to the Franco-Arabic schools, there were also twelve private elementary schools: one Catholic, two Protestant, two French-Jewish, four Muslim/Quranic, and three secular schools. The information I cite here on kuttabs and the Franco-Arabic schools of the Protectorate is drawn from Sraieb, "Mutations et réformes de structures de l'enseignement en Tunisie," *Annuaire de l'Afrique du Nord*, 6 (1967), 47; Sraieb, "L'idéologie de l'école en Tunisie coloniale (1881–1945)," 244–9; Ayachi, *Écoles et Société en Tunisie 1930–1958*, 289–90.

of Pious Endowments (*Jami'at al-Habous*), devoted more time to instruction in Arabic and taught "principally the Quran, Islamic culture, [and] Arabic literature, in addition to the French language, math, history, and geography."[5] The modern Quranic schools were similar to the Free Schools that emerged in Morocco during the Protectorate, and as in Morocco, they became centers of nationalist resistance.

However, unlike the Moroccan Free Schools, Tunisia's modern Quranic schools followed a curriculum more closely mirroring that of the French Protectorate public schools, and they came under state control well before independence. From the colonial administration's perspective, regulating these schools offered a chance to limit their growth and thereby contain the political impact of these institutions. For their part, teachers in the modern Quranic schools saw formal affiliation with the state as a means of gaining access to positions within the colonial administration that had remained closed to Muslims. On the eve of independence, there were 290 modern Quranic schools educating around 36,000 Muslim children, corresponding to roughly 20 percent of Muslim children enrolled in non-kuttab schools at the time. Still, the overall percentage of Tunisian Muslim children enrolled in school by the end of the Protectorate remained paltry. For example, by 1956 only 3 percent of Muslim Tunisian children aged from fifteen to twenty were enrolled in secondary schools.[6]

Such were the contours of the educational landscape that the Bourguiba regime inherited in 1956. Messadi's law defined secondary education as three years of middle school followed by three years of high school, and religious instruction would be taught in the first five years of secondary school. The subject was coupled with civic education and designated as "Religious and Civic Education" (*al-Tarbiyya al-Diniyya wa-l-Wataniyya*). In the last year of high school it was replaced by a course entitled "Philosophy and Islamic Thought" (*al-Falsafa wa-l-Tafkir al-Islami*).

Following the adoption of the 1958 law, "religious and civic education" was allotted 1 hour per week in the first three years of secondary school. This translated into roughly 3 percent of students' weekly hours on the subject – and, therefore, presumably less on exclusively religious topics. In the high school years, students were divided into five

---

[5] Decree of June 28, 1938, cited in Ayachi, *Écoles et Société en Tunisie 1930–1958*, 314.
[6] These enrollment figures are drawn from Sraieb, "L'idéologie de l'école en Tunisie coloniale (1881–1945)," 249; Carl L. Brown, "Tunisia: Education, 'Cultural Unity,' and the Future," in *Man, State, and Society in the Contemporary Maghrib*, ed. William I. Zartman (New York: Praeger Publishers, 1973), 365.

tracks: modern letters, classical letters, science, math, and what was known as the common (*normal* in French) track for future primary school teachers. Depending on the track, students were spending anywhere from 1 to 3 hours per week (3–7 percent) on religious and civic education. In the last year of high school, students in the classical letters, modern letters, and common tracks were spending between 2 and 3 hours per week (7–10 percent) in the "Islamic Thought" course. The baccalaureate exam included a section on "religious and civic education," but non-Muslim students were exempt from the religious education section.[7]

In terms of curricular content, Islam was most often presented in the service of the regime's ostensibly secular aims. For example, the 1959 secondary school religious education curriculum noted that "[religious] instruction must establish the link, in studying these subjects, between Muslim law and modes of its practical application in the Republic of Tunisia."[8] Four years later, the "religious and civic education" curriculum for the first year of high school included lessons on "the organization of the state in Islam, the foundations of government according to Islam, the social contract (*al-takaful al-ijtima'i*), consultation (*al-shura*), justice ... [and] the role of the judge in Islam."[9] In 1968 the Education Ministry noted that "religious and civic education" curricula should foster students' attachment to Islam by "presenting [the religion] in all its purity, liberated from the sclerotic shackles that corrupted the faith throughout centuries of ignorance, decadence and under-development . . ." The curricula sought to impress upon students that religion did not merely consist of beliefs or principles but "reunited belief, science and action that, collectively, constitute elements of efficiency in the life of man."[10]

Thus, the curricula of the post-independence Tunisia carved out minimal space for religion, and the regime sought to reorient religious

[7] Lelong, "Le Patrimoine Musulman dans l'Enseignement Tunisien après l'Indépendance," 82–3 and 227. Students in the math and science tracks were not taught Islamic Thought.
[8] Tunisian Ministry of Education, *Programmes Officiels de l'Enseignement Secondaire Fascicule VI: Instruction Civique et Religieuse* (Tunis: Ministry of Education, 1959), 11; Sraieb, Colonisation, Décolonisation et Enseignement: L'Exemple Tunisien [Colonization, Decolonization, and Education: The Tunisian Case], 119.
[9] Lelong, "Le Patrimoine Musulman dans l'Enseignement Tunisien après l'Indépendance," 246.
[10] Tunisian Ministry of Education, *al-Ahdaf al-'Ama li-l-Tarbiyya al-Islamiyya [General goals of Islamic education]* (Tunis: Tunisian Ministry of Education, 1968), cited in Lelong, "Le Patrimoine Musulman dans l'Enseignement Tunisien après l'Indépendance," 249.

instruction to emphasize links between religious teachings and secular policies. Undoubtedly these decisions were partly motivated by the regime's non-traditionalist ideology. As Chapter 4 demonstrated, Bourguiba and his allies in the Neo-Destour/Destourian Socialist Party (PSD) clearly believed that traditional religious practices were impeding modernization. And although the President's prescription for modernity did not eliminate religion from the public sphere, Bourguiba consistently emphasized that Tunisia's march toward modernity would require citizens to embrace interpretations of their religion that were more in line with the exigencies of "modern" life. The curricular reorientation partly reflected the regime's fervent non-traditionalism.

Still, if ideological convictions explained why Bourguiba sought to reorient the curricula after independence, they cannot fully account for why he succeeded. Here we need to consider the array of opponents facing the young regime and the Bourguibists' superior institutional endowment. Charrad has convincingly shown how the crushing of the religious nationalists allied with Ben Youssef in the years surrounding independence meant that members of the traditional religious establishment were largely absent from the policy-making apparatus of the independent state, leaving Bourguiba virtually unchallenged in his first decade of rule.[11] Blessed with a strong institutional endowment, as reflected in the hegemonic party and a comparatively robust bureaucracy over which he and his allies presided, Bourguiba's faction enjoyed considerable control over the state's administrative apparatus without needing to expend political capital bringing rival power centers under control – in stark contrast to the predicament of the Alaouite monarchs at the time. Such conditions enabled the regime to easily implement reforms, including in the educational realm, that reflected the ideological persuasions of the mostly bilingual, Sadiki-trained elites surrounding Bourguiba.

For the Sadikians, the state had to take a leading role in developing the Tunisian economy, and economic development could only come with improvements in the education system. Since the state had to lead the way in matters of economic development, and since economic advancement depended on educational improvements, the state had to regulate educational content so as to ensure that students' knowledge and skills would further the goal of economic development. The school, in other words, had to become a vehicle of modernization. This was not a new idea in

---

[11] Charrad, *States and Women's Rights*, 210.

Tunisia. The nineteenth-century reformers congregating around Khayr al-Din al-Tunisi had believed a school such as Sadiki – with its bilingual education and blend of religious and secular courses – would prepare Tunisia to compete with a rapidly modernizing Europe. Bourguiba's allies presented their reforms as a rejection of the Protectorate policies and a resumption of the reformist trends begun *prior* to the French invasion.[12]

The tactic reflected an important historical contrast with Morocco, where bilingual education had been introduced *after* the French incursion and so the burden on policymakers to justify bilingualism (and a concomitant reduction in religious instruction) after independence was heavier. Given the French administrators' expansions in Arabic and religious instruction for most Tunisian Muslim students during the Protectorate, the Bourguibists' desire to apply the *pre-Protectorate* Sadiki model to the entire public school system after the French withdrawal amounted to a contraction and reorientation of Islamic education curricula. And unlike their Moroccan counterparts, Tunisian elites could reasonably claim that such a move reflected a return to a more authentic educational system untainted by the innovations of the French.

Still, the policy decision was not uncontested. In 1957, the Ministry of National Education, then under the leadership of Lamine Chebbi, appointed a commission to devise a comprehensive reform of the education system. Among the members of the commission, two competing visions emerged. The first, promoted by Minister Chebbi and his chief of staff, Mohamed Mzali, called for continuing the Arabization of elementary schools launched during the Protectorate under the auspices of the *Direction d'Instruction Publique,* the main administrative body responsible for education policy. On the other side, men like Messadi, the Ministry's Director of Secondary Education at the time, argued that the independent state should break from the French policy and adopt a bilingual system that would reserve Arabic instruction for religious education and classical studies, while reintroducing French for subjects like math and science (as had been the case at Sadiki). When Bourguiba was asked to weigh in, he sided with Messadi and installed the latter as Minister of Education.[13]

---

[12] For more on the regime's efforts to convey its historical continuity with Khayr al-Din's generation, see Mohamed Mzali, *Un Premier Ministre de Bourguiba Témoigne* (Paris: Jean Picollec, 2004), 295–6; Abdelkader Zghal, "Le retour du sacré et la nouvelle demande idéologique des jeunes scolarisés," *Annuaire de l'Afrique du Nord* 18 (1979): 44.

[13] Mzali, *Un Premier Ministre de Bourguiba Témoigne,* 296.

Messadi exemplified the elites in Bourguiba's inner circle after independence. Born in 1911, when the country was still under French rule, Messadi attended a kuttab as a young boy and later matriculated into Sadiki. As Education Minister, he was intent on rolling back the colonial administrators' curricular innovations which he had encountered as a Sadiki student. In a report he wrote while serving as Minister, entitled *A New Conception of Tunisian Education*, Messadi explained that the 1958 reform reflected the independent regime's conviction that "Our schools have remained too strongly marked by the French tradition . . . This is why it was necessary to break with this foreign tradition . . . and to give our education [system] another orientation." At the secondary school level, Messadi's curricular reorientation meant that

Arabic literature and language, civic and religious education, study of Islamic thought, the history and geography of Tunisia, the Maghreb, and the Muslim world, scientific knowledge, through natural history and the physical sciences . . . will now have the proper place in the training of our youth.[14]

Messadi's report thus suggested the 1958 law's marginalization of Islamic education was no accident, but rather part of a conscious effort to re-prioritize the subjects Tunisian students would study. The ordering of Messadi's wording was telling: students would first learn the history and geography of Tunisia, then broaden their view to North Africa, and only thereafter consider the Muslim world. This spoke to a belief among many of Bourguiba's partisans that the Tunisian national identity should be a territorial one. The Youssefists, by contrast, had maintained that one's *Tunisianness* was informed not merely by one's attachment to Tunisia's geographical boundaries, but by one's Arab and Muslim heritage – a heritage shared by people well beyond Tunisia's borders. Messadi's wording reflected the victory of one ideology over another. With little opposition standing in his way, he could easily implement curricular reforms reinforcing the regime's non-traditionalist viewpoints.

(2) 1970–1988: **Expansion and Reorientation.** Beginning in 1970, what had been a state-led effort to minimize Islamic instruction gave way to an expansion and reorientation of religious lessons, as reflected in an increasing amount of Islamic instruction, greater curricular emphasis on Muslim philosophers at the expense of Western thinkers, and a growing

---

[14] Mahmoud Messadi, *Nouvelle Conception de l'Enseignement en Tunisie* (Tunis: Tunisian Ministry of Education, October 1958), 66–7.

space for religious practices in the schools. The first sign of change came on May 7, 1970, when the newly installed Minister of Education, Mohamed Mzali, held a press conference to explain that "[i]n the new educational policy of the country, we will seek to strengthen the authentic, national character of our educational methods, without compromising their modern virtues. The Arabic language, Islam, and the inculcation of patriotic values should take on greater and greater importance in our education system . . ."[15]

Curricular reforms ensued. In 1970 the government increased the number of weekly hours allotted to the sixth-year Islamic Thought course from two to seven. A year later, the Education Ministry added 1 hour of weekly Islamic instruction to the first three years of secondary school, and in 1974 the government doubled the number of weekly hours devoted to the subject, heeding recommendations of a consultative body known as the High Council on National Education. The early part of the decade also saw the addition of a secondary school track preparing students for university studies in theology. And in 1981 two new subjects – "Islamic Thought" and "Theological Studies" – were added to the baccalaureate exam, though they remained optional.[16]

In addition to regulations increasing the amount of religious education, a key change came with the Ministry's 1976 decision to Arabize the high school philosophy course. Since the country's independence, students in their last year of high school had been required to take a "Philosophy and Islamic Thought" course. The philosophy course had always been taught in French, and focused on Western works by Plato, Rousseau, Kant, Hegel, and Marx, with an occasional sprinkling of lessons on Islamic thinkers. Early on, Ministry officials expressed concern that the mandate to teach both Western and Islamic philosophy would

---

[15] Mzali, "Les Nouvelles Options de Notre Enseignement" (Tunis: Tunisian Ministry of Education, 1970).

[16] For the curricular shifts of this period, see Tunisian Ministry of Education, *Programmes Officiels de l'Enseignement, Fascicule No. 13: Philosophie et Pensée Islamique* (Tunis: Tunisian Ministry of Education, 1970b), 5–7; Michel Lelong, "Les évolutions récentes de l'enseignement islamique en Tunisie" in *Communiqué Presenté au XXIXe Congrès des Orientalistes* (Paris, 1973), 181 and 229; Mohamed Charfi and Hamadi Redissi, "Teaching Tolerance and Open-Minded Approaches to Understanding Sacred Texts," in *International Perspectives on the Goals of Universal Basic and Secondary Education*, eds. Joel E. Cohen and Martin E. Malin (New York: Routledge, 2010), 168; Frégosi and Zeghal, "Religion et Politique Au Maghreb: Les Exemples Tunisien et Marocain," 20; Ordinance of April 16, 1981 (JORT 28 of April 24, 1981, p. 904–9).

present teachers with difficult choices and perhaps even contradictory lessons. A 1963 directive, for example, noted that whereas secular philosophy in the tradition of the European Enlightenment tended to be organized around ahistorical topics, Islamic thought had to be taught through a historical, contextualized lens, and the government encouraged teachers to familiarize themselves with both subjects so as to "harmonize" the two. Up until 1976, high school philosophy teachers were most often Sadiki alumni with advanced degrees from the social science departments of Tunisian and French universities.[17]

The 1976 decision to Arabize the philosophy course led to a rewriting of the textbooks in circulation. Consequently, the number of hours devoted to Western philosophy was reduced and the hours dedicated to Islamic philosophy increased. The policy change also meant that a new cadre of teachers – those capable of teaching in Arabic – would replace the French-speaking teachers. Since individuals with the strongest Arabic skills were most often graduates of the traditional Zaytuna system and largely unfamiliar with Western philosophy, recruiting them to teach philosophy in the high schools brought about not only a linguistic shift but a shift in content as well. The experience of Hamadi Ben Jaballah is instructive. A journalist who went on to earn a doctoral degree in philosophy at the University of Tunis (where he wrote his dissertation on Kant), Ben Jaballah taught high school philosophy courses from 1974 to 1978. When the Ministry circulated a new, Arabic-language textbook in 1976, he found that many of the Western, particularly leftist, thinkers had been removed. He refused to abandon the texts or the methodology he had been using, and his protest did not go unnoticed. Minister Mzali himself visited one of Ben Jaballah's classes and later sent him a letter informing him that since the town in which Ben Jaballah resided considered the philosophy he was teaching "atheistic," the Ministry would be transferring him to another school. Ben Jaballah was shuffled around three times in as many years. By the 1980s the high school philosophy textbooks were dominated by Muslim thinkers, and as late as 1988 some

---

[17] Tunisian Ministry of Education, *Programmes Officiels de l'Enseignement Secondaire, Fascicule XIV: Philosophie et Etude de la Pensée Islamique* (Tunis: Ministry of Education, 1963), 20; Tunisian Ministry of Education, *Programmes Officiels de l'Enseignement du Second Cycle, Fascicule No. 6: Philosophie et Pensée Islamique* (Tunis: Ministry of Education, 1969); *al-Baramij al-Rasmiyya li-l-Ta'lim al-Thanawi: al-Tarbiyya al-Islamiyya wa-l-Wataniyya* [Official High School Curricula: Islamic and Civic Education] (Tunis: Tunisian Ministry of Education, 1970); Lelong, "Les évolutions récentes de l'enseignement islamique en Tunisie," 183–5.

texts were explicitly dismissing non-Muslim thinkers and urging students to avoid reading them.[18]

Finally, beginning in the 1970s, the state became more receptive to societal demands for prayer in the schools and gender segregation in the classrooms, both of which contributed to an increasingly religious atmosphere in the schools. High school teachers increasingly encountered students in newly designated prayer rooms, where students and teachers could pray together three times a day. The students' growing desire to pray was a bottom-up development, but the state encouraged it as well. A 1972 Education Ministry report, for example, instructed teachers of Islamic and civic education to lead their students in prayer so that the students might gain familiarity with the daily prayers. The same report urged teachers to make use of religious rituals to "instill feelings of faith and ignite the spark of national sentiment" among the students.[19]

Such changes – the increasing amount of Islamic instruction in the schools, a reorientation of the curricula to emphasize Islamic think-ers, and an encouragement of religious activity in the public schools – occurred despite the fact that the dominant ideology of the regime had not changed. Bourguiba was still President, and there is no evidence to suggest he had experienced a change of heart concerning religion and its purported incompatibility with modernization. On the contrary, through-out this period he continued to express a mild disdain for religion, as when he told members of parliament in 1975 that

Providence has given us a Tunisian State of flesh and blood in which the Tunisian chooses his governor and where the law cannot be modified without the approval of representatives of the Tunisian people. Not even Islam could achieve this, as [the religion] did not foresee a Constitution regulating the succession of the Head of State. The Prophet did not leave behind a Constitution. After his death, the community of Muslims knew only polemics and division into clans and factions . . .[20]

[18] Interview with Hamadi Ben Jaballah, Tunis, October 12, 2012; Charfi and Redissi, "Teaching Tolerance and Open-Minded Approaches to Understanding Sacred Texts," 168. For more on the change to the philosophy curricula, see a brief essay by Ali Chennoufi, a philosophy professor and member of the commission responsible for revis-ing the philosophy textbooks, reprinted in "Etudes: l'Enseignement au Maghreb," *Revue Maghreb Machrek* 78 (1977): 67.

[19] Tunisian Ministry of Education, *al-Taqrir al-Niha'i 'an I'mal al-Lajna al-Qarah li-l-Falsafa al-'Ama wa-l-Falsafa al-Islamiyya [Final report of the working group on general and Islamic philosophy]* (Tunis: Ministry of Education, 1972).

[20] As reprinted in *La Presse*, March 20, 1975.

Bourguiba's impatience with religion was similarly apparent in 1981, when he rescinded an order by the Prime Minister outlawing the sale of alcohol during the month of Ramadan and closing all bars and restaurants during the daytimes of the holy month. The expansion and reorientation of religious education and related curricula could not have resulted from a change in ideology at the top. So what happened?

Recall that with the 1969 collapse of the agricultural collectives, Bourguiba's regime had suffered a blow to its legitimacy as the ruling party began splintering and a liberal faction emerged in opposition to Bourguiba's governance. In his efforts to contain the fallout stemming from the collectivization disaster, Bourguiba embarked on a controlled (and, as it turned out, short-lived) process of political liberalization. The brief political opening afforded by the 1969 crisis facilitated changes to the religious education curricula because the state's decision to open up the political process to public debate suddenly provided a forum for the airing of societal preferences concerning education. For example, the public consultations launched in 1970 to amend the constitution revealed widespread support for the reestablishment of the Zaytunian educational system the regime had shut down after independence. Similarly, the High Council on National Education, the consultative body Bourguiba had created to bring greater public representation to the decision-making process, ended up recommending those "emergency" measures increasing the amount of Islamic education in 1974.[21]

Heeding such recommendations offered Bourguiba a way to shore up badly needed support in the wake of the 1969 disaster, especially when it became clear he was no longer willing to fulfill his promise of more far-reaching political liberalization. On the eve of the PSD Congress in 1974, at which most of the liberal reforms were to be canceled, the High Council on National Education met and ordered a doubling of the number of hours of Islamic education in the secondary schools. The timing was not coincidental. Bourguiba and his allies knew they risked antagonizing liberals in the party by renouncing the reforms of 1971. Increasing Islamic education in the schools would throw a bone to the party rank and file – many of whom were products of a traditional education – and thereby undermine their potential alliance with the liberals in Ahmed Mestiri's camp. Although the liberal party elites in Tunis were mostly

[21] Noureddine Sraieb, "Chronique Sociale et Culturelle: Tunisie," *Annuaire de l'Afrique du Nord* 9 (1970): 417; Taoufik Monastiri, "Chronique Sociale et Culturelle: Tunisie," *Annuaire de l'Afrique du Nord* 10 (1971): 424.

Sadikians, many of the local branches of the PSD at this time were being run by teachers and other professionals with a more traditional background. Increasing religious education offered Bourguiba a way to neutralize his opponents.[22]

But the curricular shifts of this period also flowed from a certain weakening of the ruling party. As we saw in Chapter 4, the 1969 collectivization failure had brought to the surface ideological divisions among senior party officials that ultimately seeped into Bourguiba's administrative apparatus. The appointment of Mohamed Mzali as Education Minister in the 1970s was a case in point. As early as November of 1969 (the same month in which Bourguiba dismissed his Minister of Economy and National Education, Ahmad Ben Salah, over the collectivization disaster), the President convened an intergovernmental commission to assess problems in the education system and suggest reforms. The commission's meetings throughout the spring of 1970 revealed deep concerns over the "authenticity" (*al-asala*) of the education Tunisian children were receiving. The commission's proposals, issued in May of that year, maintained an important place for French in the primary schools but listed as one of its three main recommendations "the 'Tunisification' . . . of the child." Following up on the work of the commission, Mzali delivered his speech indicating that the country's new approach to its education system would "seek to strengthen the authentic, national character" of the schools.[23]

Such nationalist overtones also increasingly colored Bourguiba's rhetoric. In August 1970, as his constitutional commission was undertaking consultations, the President stressed in a speech that more education on Tunisia's national identity would foster a national unity the country badly needed in order to move beyond the economic crisis. "The knowledge of [Tunisia's] national history is the foundation of our personality," Bourguiba said, encouraging the state to create "new curricula . . . and charge our teachers with instructing students on Tunisian history from Antiquity to today." The Education Ministry, meanwhile, outlined four

---

[22] Ali Mahjoubi, "La réforme de l'enseignement en Tunisie (1989–1994)," *Attariq Aljadid* 183–4 (June 5, 2010), accessible at http://ettajdid.org/spip.php?article531; Mohamed Charfi, *Islam and Liberty: The Historical Misunderstanding* (London: Zed Books, 2005), 146.

[23] Summaries of the meeting, as well as sections of the commission's proposals, are reprinted in Sraieb, "Chronique Sociale et Culturelle: Tunisie," 400–32. For Mzali's comments, see Mzali, "Les Nouvelles Options de Notre Enseignement."

principles upon which the education system would rest: "democracy, efficiency, *authenticity*, and openness."[24]

But talk of a national character raised the question of what constituted
this character. What did it mean to be "authentically" Tunisian? Identity
debates were not new to Tunisia, as the Bourguibist-Youssefist split of the
1950s had made clear. This time, however, the 1969 economic disaster and
the regime's crisis of legitimacy worked to the advantage of those advocating an "authenticity" based on Tunisia's Islamic heritage. Bourguiba
himself adopted a discourse of morality and values that (intentionally or
not) invited greater talk of religion. In his speech launching the process
of political consultations, for example, he framed the future reforms as
part of a broader push to facilitate "the renaissance of moral values at
the heart of the Party and the government, as it is on these values that the
prestige of the State rests." In the months that followed, members of parliament stressed that reinvigorating Arabic and Islamic instruction would
restore the "moral values" to which Bourguiba had alluded.[25]

There had always been voices in parliament and elsewhere calling for
greater attention to Islamic education. Now these voices could anchor
their demands in Bourguiba's own rhetoric of morality, values, and
national identity – a rhetoric he and his allies were employing principally
to stir up nationalist fervor and undermine opposition among leftists and
liberals. But by portraying them as misguided delinquents bent on sowing
chaos and dividing the nation, Bourguiba opened up a discursive space
for proponents of *religious* morality, *religious* values, and Tunisians' purported *religious* authenticity.[26]

---

[24] The text of Bourguiba's 1970 speech is reprinted in Sraieb, "Chronique Sociale et
Culturelle: Tunisie," 419. The Education Ministry's reform is cited in Monastiri,
"Chronique Sociale et Culturelle: Tunisie," 424. Italics mine.

[25] Bourguiba's speech referencing the "renaissance of moral values" is reprinted in
"Documents – Tunisie," 863–4. For the relevant debates in parliament, see the comments
of Youssef Rouissi on December 26, 1970, reprinted in Sraieb, "Chronique Sociale et
Culturelle: Tunisie," 417–18.

[26] For earlier examples of parliamentarians bringing attention to the matter of Islamic
education, see the debates in the National Assembly in December 1961, cited in Lelong,
"Les évolutions récentes de l'enseignement islamique en Tunisie." The regime's rhetorical
attacks against the leftists and liberals in Bourguiba's midst appeared in the Communiqué
of the Parti Socialiste Destourien Political Bureau following Mestiri's expulsion from
the party in Tunis, January 21, 1972; Bourguiba's speech to a gathering of university
deans and professors, April 17, 1972; and Hédi Nouira's speech on the student protests, July 2, 1976. See "Documents: Tunisie," *Annuaire de l'Afrique du Nord* 11 (1972):
819–30; Issa Ben Dhiaf, "Chronique Politique: Tunisie," *Annuaire de l'Afrique du Nord*
15 (1976): 386.

One such proponent was Mohamed Mzali, the former Education Ministry official who had disagreed with the orientation of Messadi's 1958 reform. A graduate of Sadiki and the Sorbonne, Mzali later became Secretary General of the PSD and served as Bourguiba's Prime Minister in the early 1980s before falling out of favor with the regime and exiling himself to France in 1986. His most widely recognized, and controversial, achievements were in his capacity as Education Minister throughout the 1970s, when he spearheaded changes to religious education and related curricula.

Mzali's entry into the highest positions of state power exemplified the breakdown in the ruling party's ideological cohesion. Although he shared his boss's conviction that education was the best means of producing a morally righteous citizenry infused with a sense of civic duty, Mzali deviated from Bourguiba in repeatedly stressing that citizens' morals should be anchored in their Arab-Muslim identities. In the press conference of May 7, 1970, at which he unveiled the state's new education policy, Mzali linked the inculcation of morals to an increase in religious education:

Education must . . . produce individuals . . . imbued with the authentic values of their country, abiding by principles of morality, civic [duty] and patriotism . . . The subjects taught up to now have not always adhered to the spirit of a true Tunisification of education that must guide the conception of all curricula . . . The emphasis will be placed on Arabic and Arab-Muslim civilization, [and] civic, moral and religious education . . .

In Mzali's estimation, the curricula that grew out of Messadi's 1958 reform had not accurately reflected Tunisians' ethnic and religious identities; they had not been sufficiently "authentic." To the extent that the new curricula would correct this deficiency by placing greater emphasis on Tunisians' Arab and Muslim identities, Mzali's proposals rested on the more fundamental assumption that to be authentically Tunisian was to be Arab and Muslim.

Strengthening religious education would also protect students against the intrusion of competing and dangerous ideologies. Mzali's rhetoric took on an increasingly defensive tone, much like that of Hassan II around the same time. On June 18, 1976, for example, Mzali described the "Tunisification" of the education system thus:

We must understand education to include the youth's moral and spiritual formation, and the consolidation of his attachments to his surroundings and to the Tunisian, Arab-Muslim personality. This has been neglected and [the neglect] has

instilled in our youth a lack of rootedness and feelings of detachment, plunging
them into doubt and a spiritual and ideological void. As for [the students'] attachment to the religious values of Islam, it is practically nonexistent – causing the
void they are suffering and rendering them more receptive to imported ideologies
and foreign traditions . . . This reform of our education system should permit us
to anchor our youth in their milieu and to instill Arab-Islamic values in them.[27]

It was in the vein of using Islamic education to combat unwanted political ideologies that the philosophy curricula became a target of reform.
At a meeting of the PSD's Political Bureau in June 1974, then-Minister
of Education Driss Guiga (Mzali had stepped down) read aloud the titles
of several recently approved philosophy doctoral dissertations that allegedly revealed sympathy for Marxist and other leftist currents traversing
the university campuses, and he urged that the philosophy curricula be
Arabized in an effort to counter such ideologies.[28] Two years later, Mzali
lent credence to the idea that the state was revising the philosophy curriculum to push back against unwanted political ideologies in an editorial
he penned for the journal *al-Fikr* (The Idea):

The proponents of certain doctrines contrary to our national options and incom-
patible with our cultural values take advantage of education generally and of
certain "sensitive" subjects specifically – principally history and philosophy in its
various forms – to spread their theories and preach their convictions. They similarly take advantage [of the teaching of such subjects] to sap the cultural model
to which a majority of our students belong, to destroy the national framework of
which our youth are proud, and to lead them to doubt the social and moral values
at the heart of an eternal Tunisia and inspired by the Arab and Islamic heritage.[29]

That Mzali could implement these curricular changes throughout the
1970s spoke to the ideological fragmentation crippling Bourguiba's rul-
ing party. By the mid-1980s Bourguiba seemed keen to reverse the trend.
In 1987, to his newly appointed Education Minister, Mohamed Sayah,
Bourguiba expressed his growing concern over the long-term impact of
Mzali's curricular changes: "I named you [Education Minister] so that
you can undo what Mohamed Mzali did. For ten years he marginalized
French [instruction]. But it's thanks to the French language that we had

---

[27] Abdelaziz Dahmani and Souhayr Belhassen, "Interview with Mohamed Mzali," *Jeune
Afrique* (May 30, 1979): 71–7.
[28] Mzali, *Un Premier Ministre de Bourguiba Témoigne*, 319–20.
[29] Mzali, "A propos de l'enseignement de la philosophie," *Al-Fikr* 21 (February 1976).
Translated into French and reprinted in Chennoufi, "Etudes: l'Enseignement au
Maghreb."

access to science. Thanks to French, we studied Montesquieu. *Without Montesquieu, this regime would lose its legitimacy."*[30]

The statement reflected the strong association in Bourguiba's mind between his education policies and his regime's legitimacy, and it highlighted the ruler's inability to contain the ideological divisions that had afflicted his own administration. The crisis of 1969 had introduced new political opponents and punctured the regime's institutional strength, facilitating curricular changes Bourguiba evidently came to regret.

(3) **1989–2010: Contraction and Reorientation.** Two years after Bourguiba's plea to bring back Montesquieu, a new Education Minister, Mohamed Charfi, announced plans for a comprehensive reform of the education system. This ushered in a contraction and reorientation of the religious education curricula, in which the state reduced the amount of Islamic instruction, separated religious education from civic education, reinstated non-Muslim thinkers to the high school philosophy curricula, and expanded lessons on Muslim reformist thinkers and ethical principles in Islam compatible with pluralism, toleration, democracy, and human rights.

The centerpiece of Charfi's reforms was a 1991 law, the state's most comprehensive education legislation since 1958. Whereas the 1958 law had made no mention of religion (save one reference to Islamic education in the classical letters track of secondary schools), the 1991 law addressed the matter on numerous occasions. Primary education, for example, would "contribute to the development of [the student's] religious and civic education." And the preface to Charfi's law noted that Tunisia's education system was based on "the national Tunisian identity and adherence to the Arab-Muslim civilization."[31] The "and" linking the two concepts was significant: whereas Mzali and his supporters had conveyed that Tunisian identity was synonymous with citizens' Arab-Muslim heritage, Charfi now distinguished between the two.

The 1991 law restructured the education system to comprise nine years of primary and middle school, and four years of secondary school. At the middle school level, Islamic education was reduced to 1.5 hours per week (5 percent) in the first year and 1 hour per week (3 percent)

---

[30] Italics mine. Sayah was a former Director of the PSD and a minister in numerous Bourguiba governments, including Education Minister from May to November 1987. The recollection is drawn from an interview Sayah gave to Michel Camau and Vincent Geisser in 2002. See Michel Camau and Vincent Geisser, eds., *Habib Bourguiba, la Trace et l'Héritage* (Paris: Karthala, 2004), 643.

[31] Law 91-65 of July 29, 1991 (JORT 55 of August 6, 1991, p. 1398), Section II, Article 8 and Section I, Article 1. Italics mine.

in the second and third years; in the high schools, it was replaced by a course on Islamic thought and was reduced to between 1 and 1.5 hours per week (3–6.5 percent), depending on the year and the track of study. In terms of content, Islamic instruction was separated from civic education, and the former was taught for 1 hour per week in every year of school except the final year of high school, when it was replaced by the philosophy course.[32]

The separation of religious and civic education was significant for two main reasons. The first had to do with the evolving profile of the teachers. As the schools had been progressively Arabized in the decades after independence, teachers of "religious and civic education" were increasingly those trained in religious studies, with little knowledge of civic education as Messadi conceptualized it in 1958. Critics of the Tunisian education system in the 1980s and 1990s argued that civic education had been stripped of substance and almost entirely replaced by religious instruction, in part because the teachers were not trained to teach civic education.[33] Charfi's decision to separate the two subjects meant that religion teachers would no longer be teaching civic education. Instead, he began recruiting graduates of law, history, sociology, and other social science and humanities faculties to teach the civic education course, thus removing it from the purview of those trained in religious subjects.

The decision to separate religious and civic education was also significant from a conceptual standpoint. To the extent that civic education aimed to form good citizens, distinguishing it from an education that sought to form good Muslims implied the two were distinct. Charfi was keen to convey through his reform that there was a religious realm separate from the profane. But this was a point of contention, even among members of his own team. Hmida Ennaifer, the public intellectual mentioned previously and a scholar of Islamic and Western philosophy whom Charfi recruited to help revise the religious and civic education curricula, later quit in protest over the decision to separate the two subjects and assign civic education to social scientists. "What I objected to," Ennaifer explained, "was the notion that civic education had no connection whatsoever to religious education. It's as if religion and civic life are completely separate. For me, it was necessary, on the contrary, to demonstrate that human history, human rights, all of this is constitutive of religious

---

[32] Decree 92-1180 of June 22, 1992 (JORT 41 of June 26, 1992, p. 810); Decree 92-1183 of June 22, 1991 (JORT 41 of June 26, 1992, p. 813).
[33] Mahjoubi, "La réforme de l'enseignement en Tunisie (1989–1994)."

education. We shouldn't create a rupture between these two concepts."[34] Despite such objections, the separation of religious and civic education became a key component of Charfi's reforms.

The reforms stemming from the 1991 law also initiated a shift in content away from theological aspects of Islam toward ethical teachings of the religion compatible with pluralism, human rights, and other widely recognized ingredients of a liberal democracy. Moncef Ben Abdeljelil, a philosophy professor at the University of Sousse whom Charfi recruited to revamp the religious education curricula after Ennaifer left, described the shift thus:

This dogmatic attitude [permeating the earlier textbooks] that is based on a non-critical spirit is . . . the main thing that should be tackled through education itself so that you can create a different way of thinking, a different mindset. And you need to maybe rethink the whole religious phenomenon and in particular the whole Muslim heritage so that Islamic education could be given in a different way and [from] a different perspective. In so doing, you are [helping] to create what might be called at that time "civil society," which means a society where religion plays a different role. Instead of playing a theological role, it plays an ethical role.[35]

As Malika Zeghal has noted, new textbooks disseminated during Charfi's tenure reflected this shift by "insisting on the renewal (*al-tajdid*) of Islamic thought and emphasizing the aims (*al-maqasid*) of Islamic law rather than Islam's rituals and legal norms," presenting Islam "as a religion embedded in history and as a tradition of change . . . [urging that] it is necessary to adapt religious references to the changing realities of the world." In an effort to stress the religion's applicability to modern realities, the curricula also emphasized reformist Muslim intellectuals.[36]

In some cases, Charfi's team did not even write new textbooks so much as resort to textbooks that had been in circulation immediately after independence. In the initial years of his tenure, for example, Charfi replaced two religious education textbooks with one from the early 1970s entitled "Independent Reasoning and Renewal in Islam" (*al-Ijtihad wa-l-Tajdid fi-l-Islam*). Ultimately, two new texts were written – one for Islamic

---

[34] Interview with Hmida Ennaifer, Tunis, October 11, 2012.

[35] Interview with Moncef Ben Abdeljelil, Sousse, October 23, 2012.

[36] Zeghal, "Public Institutions of Religious Education in Egypt and Tunisia: Contrasting the Post-Colonial Reforms of Al-Azhar and the Zaytuna," 118. Specifically, Zeghal cites a 1997 eleventh-grade textbook entitled *Kitab fi-l-Tafkir al-Islami* [Textbook for Islamic Thought].

education in grades one to ten and another for Islamic Thought in the last two years of high school.[37] Additionally, the Islamic Thought course was separated from the philosophy course, which was reinstated in the last year of high school and revised to focus once again on Western thinkers.

Why did the state embark on such a radical reform of the religious education curricula in the early 1990s? The crucial development here was Ben ʿAli's determination that Islamists constituted the greatest threat to its survival, not the leftist groups or liberals his predecessor had feared. The regime's shifting perception of its political opponents after the soft coup prompted Ben ʿAli to seek alliances with many of the liberals Bourguiba had previously alienated, and this alliance ultimately facilitated the curricular changes.

Recall that Ben ʿAli's initial hints of an inclusive political process faded in 1989, when the regime invalidated the results of the legislative elections and excluded Islamists from the political process. But in the aftermath of the fraudulent 1989 elections, Islamists were not the only ones angered at being shut out of the political sphere: liberal groups such as Ahmed Mestiri's Movement of Socialist Democrats (or MDS by its French acronym) and other smaller independent parties were equally incensed at the RCD's unwillingness to cede political space. Liberal and Islamist opponents of the ruling party joined forces to denounce the results of the legislative elections. The day after the results were announced, Ennahda leader Rached Ghannouchi and MDS head Ahmed Mestiri held a joint press conference condemning the irregularities and voter fraud the RCD had committed. If the new regime was going to capitalize on the authority of its newly consolidated party, it would have to break the emerging alliance between Islamist and secular activists who had been dismayed by the election results.

Doing so turned out to be relatively easy. Indeed, despite the appearance of a unified front, the alliance between Islamists and liberal opponents of the regime had begun to fray even before the elections. In parallel with the new regime's tendency to undermine its own rhetoric of liberalization by limiting implementation of its initial promises, Ennahda during the first two years of Ben ʿAli's presidency undercut its own credibility by sending mixed signals about its intentions in the emerging system. For example, even as it agreed to sign on to the National Pact, Ghannouchi stressed that the Personal Status Code – cherished by many liberals – could not

---

[37] As recounted in "Interview with Mohamed Charfi," *Jeune Afrique* (April 30, 1990); Interview with Hamadi Ben Jaballah, Tunis, October 12, 2012.

be considered "sacred" and thus should periodically be reevaluated and, if necessary, revised.[38] Likewise, in the 1989 legislative elections the campaign rhetoric of many candidates running as independents but known to be affiliated with Ennahda often contradicted the principles laid out in the National Pact. While Ennahda officially denied sanctioning such rhetoric, campaign slogans criticizing the Personal Status Code left many of Ennahda's secular cosigners of the National Pact increasingly suspicious of the movement's true intentions.[39]

Thus, by the time the election results were announced, Ennahda had alienated many of its liberal friends among the opposition. Ben ʿAli took advantage of this alienation and wasted little time: less than a week after the election, he appointed a new cabinet that included a prominent leader of the MDS as Minister of Health and a leading human rights advocate – Mohamed Charfi – as Education Minister, leaving the Islamists increasingly isolated. When Ennahda once again applied for and was denied a permit to form a political party, a disgusted Ghannouchi exiled himself in Paris, warning that "[u]ntil now, we sought only a shop and we did not get it. Now it's the whole *souk* (marketplace) we want."[40]

From the regime's standpoint, appointing Charfi as Education Minister fulfilled two key imperatives: mitigating blowback from secular factions angry about a resurgent RCD, and peeling away liberal factions from their alliance with Ennahda, thereby dividing and weakening the regime's most formidable opponents at the time. The dynamics surrounding Charfi's appointment after the 1989 legislative elections were strikingly similar to Bourguiba's political maneuvers following the liberals' ascension at the Monastir Congress in 1971. Both preceded important changes in religious education curricula, with one crucial difference: the regime's perception of its most threatening adversaries. Whereas Bourguiba had seen leftists and liberals in his own party as the opponents to crush in the 1970s, Ben ʿAli perceived the Islamists as a threat both to the new regime and to their secular liberal allies who were increasingly dismayed by his unwillingness to follow through on the basic promise of political liberalization. Charfi's appointment, and the changes to religious education curricula that ensued, were by-products of the regime's survival strategy.

---

[38] Elbaki Hermassi, "L'État Tunisien et le Mouvement Islamiste," *Annuaire de l'Afrique du Nord* 28 (1989): 303.

[39] Abdelkader Zghal, "Le Concept de Société Civile et la Transition vers le Multipartisme," 210.

[40] Perkins, *A History of Modern Tunisia*, 190.

BALANCING AUTONOMY AND STATE CONTROL

(1) **1956–1969: State Control.** In contrast to the Moroccan regimes of Mohammed V and Hassan II, the independent Tunisian state under President Habib Bourguiba established formal state control over nearly all institutions of religious learning, eliminating formerly autonomous schools and consolidating and integrating the remainder into the emerging system of public education. The fates of the traditional Quranic schools (kuttabs) and the Zaytuna Mosque-University spoke to this control.

Earlier, I noted that by the time the country had gained its independence, the preceding decline of the kuttabs had convinced officials in Bourguiba's regime that these schools were headed for extinction. Mahmoud Messadi, the minister who had authored a comprehensive education reform in 1958, took it as given that "traditional education [in the kuttabs and the Grand Mosque] . . .the fundamental character of which is unsuited to aptitudes, to current conditions and needs . . . will disappear in its current form."[41] The 1958 education reform did not explicitly do away with the kuttabs; in fact, the law did not even mention them. But in a sense, it did not have to. The growing number of public elementary schools attracting children and their families, coupled with the state's expropriation of the pious endowments which had funded the kuttabs, diminished the institution after independence. The few kuttabs remaining after 1956 were mostly limited to preschools attended by children for one or two years prior to entering the public elementary schools. Insignificant from a numerical standpoint, they received no financial support from the state and would not be subject to government regulation until the early 1980s.

The more dramatic development concerned the Grand Mosque of Zaytuna, its annexes, and the Zaytuna-affiliated lower schools for primary and secondary school-aged children. Like the kuttabs, the Zaytuna had been subject to government regulation even before the Protectorate, undergoing state-sponsored reforms as early as 1842. In 1875, Khayr al-Din had pioneered curricular reforms introducing courses in history and mathematics. However, during the Protectorate, the Zaytuna largely escaped state sponsorship (in contrast to the Qarawiyyin), and this autonomy would have important implications for its treatment after independence.

---

[41] Messadi, *Nouvelle Conception de l'Enseignement en Tunisie.*

At independence there were around 25,000 students studying in the Zaytuna system, of whom roughly 12,000 were at the Grand Mosque and its annexes.[42] The first sign of change came with a decree of October 13, 1955 bringing the Grand Mosque and its annexes under the administrative purview of the Ministry of Education. Five months later, the newly independent state reorganized the system to distinguish between a higher education track and "Zaytuna secondary schools" that became part of the new public school system under the Education Ministry, which appointed their directors. A decree of April 26, 1956 transformed the Grand Mosque into the "University of Zaytuna," an institution offering master's degrees in Arabic language and Islamic sciences, and consolidated its annexes into three Zaytuna secondary schools. And in 1961, a decree closed the Grand Mosque and reorganized the University of Zaytuna as the Zaytuna Faculty of Theology and Religious Sciences, a department attached to the new University of Tunis and housed in a building separated from the ancient mosque. In remarkably little time the Grand Mosque was stripped of its educational identity and a centuries-old system of religious learning was transformed into an appendage of a public university.[43]

At the secondary school level, instruction in the Zaytuna schools initially proceeded in the classical model of the Grand Mosque and its affiliates. In the mid-1950s these schools had attracted around 11,000 Tunisians, nearly half of the 22,600 secondary school students at the time of independence. Most students in the Zaytuna secondary schools were permitted to continue studying until they obtained their high school diplomas. But over the next decade, these schools were gradually eliminated. The last Zaytuna secondary school in the capital city, the Ibn Khaldoun School, closed its doors at the end of the 1964–5 academic year, after which Zaytuna education ceased to exist in the country and the properties of these schools were nationalized.[44]

[42] Mahmoud Abdel Moula, "L'université Zaytounienne et la Société Tunisienne," PhD dissertation (La Sorbonne, 1967), 168; Noureddine Sraieb, "Mutations et réformes de structures de l'enseignement en Tunisie," 51.

[43] Decree of March 29, 1956 (JORT 27 of April 3, 1956, p. 497–8); Decree of April 26, 1956 (JORT 34 of April 27, 1956, p. 592); Decree 61-110 of March 1, 1961 (JORT 9 of March 3–7, 1961, p. 354).

[44] For information on secondary schooling at the Zaytuna, see: Tunisian Ministry of Education, "Statistique au 15 Novembre 1956: Tableau récapitulatif général" (Tunis: Ministry of National Education, 1956); Asma Nouira, "*al-Mu'asasat al-Islamiyya al-Rasmiyya fi Tunis min 1956 ila al-Yawm* [Institutions of Official Islam in Tunisia from 1956 to the Present]," PhD dissertation (University of Tunis, 2008), 89.

Thus, the Bourguiba regime established state sponsorship of virtually all institutions of religious learning from the outset, in contrast to the Moroccan monarchs' decision to leave some of these institutions alone. As we shall see, the President's motivation to establish state domination over these institutions stemmed from his ideological convictions concerning religion and a concomitant concern to eliminate certain political rivals, while his success reflected the relatively strong institutional endowment he inherited.

A consistent theme of Bourguiba's speeches and interviews, as well as the official documents of his ruling Neo-Destour Party, was the belief that traditional religious practices were contrary to human reason and thus impeded modernization. He was similarly clear in his promotion of an *étatist* ideology, according to which a strong state would lead the way in modernizing not only society, but religion itself. As he noted in a 1964 speech, "What good would prayers and fasting accomplish if the State was reduced to weakness and disintegration? The State comes first! For, without the State, religion would be in danger."[45] From such convictions, it followed that the state should formally sponsor, and thereby control, institutions of religious learning.

Still, Bourguiba's push to establish state control over these institutions was only partly a matter of ideology. An equally salient factor fueling Bourguiba's policies during this period was his desire to undermine and punish factions that had rallied around his main rival at independence, Salah Ben Youssef. Many of Ben Youssef's strongest supporters hailed from traditional religious circles affiliated with the Zaytuna. Whereas in earlier decades, the nationalists in the Neo-Destour (and even Bourguiba himself) had found it politically advantageous to adopt Zaytunian rhetoric promoting the preservation of Tunisia's traditional identity in the face of French aggression, many in the Neo-Destour came to view a close association with the Zaytuna as a liability when independence appeared within reach. By the early 1950s, when the Neo-Dustur was negotiating the country's independence from France, Zaytunian opposition to the government increasingly amounted to Zaytunian opposition to the Neo-Destour. When Bourguiba orchestrated his rival's expulsion from the party in 1955, Ben Youssef reached out to Zaytunians and quickly found allies. Indeed, he delivered one of his earliest speeches denouncing

---

[45] Frégosi and Zeghal, "Religion et Politique Au Maghreb: Les Exemples Tunisien et Marocain," 17.

Bourguiba's policies at the Zaytuna Mosque, reinforcing the political identity that institution had assumed on.[46]

The Zaytunians would suffer for their association with Ben Youssef, as Bourguiba's radical restructuring of the institution after independence made clear. In 1960, for example, Bourguiba approached Abdelaziz Djait, a Zaytunian who was then serving as the country's Grand Mufti, in hopes of obtaining a fatwa sanctioning the President's insistence that fasting on Ramadan should no longer be an obligation for Muslims. When Djait issued a religious edict maintaining the injunction to fast during the holy month, Bourguiba dismissed him from his post, along with several other Zaytunians he had initially courted. Meanwhile, Zaytunian students continued to demand that the state grant their diplomas equal status to those of the students coming out of Sadiki and the new secular university. Going after the Zaytuna was as much about crushing a group of elites who had sided with Ben Youssef and removing a thorn in Bourguiba's side as it was about implementing a particular ideological vision.[47]

In his drive to eliminate his political opposition, Bourguiba benefited from an institutional endowment his rivals lacked, one that enabled him to push through reforms with virtually no resistance. A key factor working in Bourguiba's favor was the comparatively robust and centralized bureaucracy he inherited. Even prior to the French arrival in 1881, Tunisia had undergone a considerable degree of bureaucratic centralization, which not only made it easier for the colonial authorities to govern the country but also later made Bourguiba's task of consolidating power after independence less taxing than the one facing the Moroccan sultans at the time.

The relative ease with which Bourguiba could centralize power was evident in the educational realm: for example, since most of the Quranic schools had already come under a degree of state control in the Protectorate administration, it was not difficult for the independent state to assume administrative oversight of these institutions and transform them into public schools or eliminate them altogether. Nor did the Tunisian education system suffer from the kinds of bureaucratic limitations plaguing the Moroccan system around the same time. For example,

---

[46] Moore, *Tunisia since Independence: The Dynamics of One-Party Government*, 63.

[47] Frégosi and Zeghal, "Religion et Politique Au Maghreb: Les Exemples Tunisien et Marocain," 11. Many Zaytunians did, however, find jobs in lower-level bureaucratic posts. For more on this aspect of the legacy of the Bourguibist-Youssefist split, see Charrad, *States and Women's Rights*, 210.

because the regime initially (and, as it turned out, wisely) refrained from making public education compulsory for all children, Tunisia never faced the kind of demographic pressures plaguing Morocco's education system. And because Tunisia maintained a more thoroughly bilingual system, the state did not need to purge large numbers of French instructors from the ranks of its teaching corps, so the regime never faced the formidable teaching shortages confronting its Moroccan counterpart. The absence of such strains on the Tunisian education system meant that Bourguiba enjoyed a relatively strong and coherent administrative apparatus through which he could impose his political will.

Still, dismantling an institution like the Zaytuna was not a foregone conclusion. But here, Bourguiba profited from the divisions among the Zaytunian ulama. We have seen that prior to independence, some Zaytunians had urged modernizing reforms to the institution, while others opposed changes they viewed as overly Westernizing. Such disagreements precluded major reforms and left the Zaytuna increasingly weak, especially when compared to the Sadiki school, which could boast the prestige of having produced many of the nationalists involved in expelling the French. After independence, the schisms among the Zaytunian ulama persisted, informing their reactions to the 1961 reform which brought the institution under the Education Ministry's control.

On one end of the spectrum were those Zaytunians who rejected any state sponsorship of the institution, urging that the institution retain its fiscal and pedagogical autonomy. In January 1961, for example, rioting erupted in Kairouan after the government transferred an imam out of the city following his public denunciations of Bourguiba's reforms. The imam had been a respected scholar at the Zaytuna prior to the state's take-over of the institution, and after publicly criticizing the regime's handling of the university, the governor of Kairouan had him removed. On the opposite end of the spectrum were reformists like Fadhl Ben ʿAchour, who welcomed state sponsorship on the assumption that it would bring a much-needed upgrade to the curricula and greater financial security once the institution could access state coffers. Finally, there emerged a third group of ulama, represented by figures such as Chadhly Ben al-Qadi, who accepted the Ministry of Education's administrative control but urged the regime to let the institution remain pedagogically independent.[48]

---

[48] Nouira, 95.

Such divisions were a gift to Bourguiba. He could appoint someone like Ben ʿAchour as Dean of the Zaytuna Faculty and later Mufti of the Republic, even as he was losing the support of many other Zaytunians angered by the destruction of their institution and their marginalization more generally. Bourguiba's grip on power was simply no match for his opponents, who remained internally divided and institutionally weak. The success Bourguiba enjoyed in defeating his Youssefist opponents, coupled with his command of a robust bureaucratic apparatus, enabled him to lock in state control of most institutions of religious learning with minimal resistance.

(2) **1970–1986: State Control and Autonomy.** In the 1970s there was a subtle but significant shift in the balance between state-controlled and autonomous institutions of religious learning. The Tunisian state's control of most institutions in the previous decades gave way to a mix of control and autonomy, as the state's grip on institutions of religious learning loosened. Two developments reflected the increasing space for autonomous instruction. The first was the creation of the Quranic Preservation Society in 1970. This was a loosely organized, independently financed association promoting cultural and religious activities revolving around knowledge of the Quran. Though state officials attended the Society's inaugural event, and the regime was keen to ensure that the organization did not spread negative views of Bourguiba's policies, it did not come under state control until the late 1980s.[49]

The second development was a rise in the number of autonomous kuttabs throughout the 1970s. Precise data for this period was difficult to obtain, but the trend was evidently significant enough to warrant a new law in 1980 designating kuttabs as a form of private education and placing responsibility for the schools under the Directorate of Religious Affairs, a division of the Prime Minister's office. All new kuttabs, which would be open to children beginning at age four, had to obtain a permit from the Directorate; the schools were required to teach the Quran, basic Islamic precepts, and the beginnings of Arabic grammar; and *"those kuttabs already in existence"* had one year to comply with the new regulations.[50]

The 1980 law regulating the kuttabs implied that Messadi's prediction of the imminent demise of traditional education had not come to

[49] Interview with Hmida Ennaifer, September 19, 2012.
[50] Order of the Prime Minister of 6 September 1980 (JORT 51 of September 16, 1980, p. 2237–8). Italics mine.

pass. Indeed, by 1987, the first year for which data is available, the state reported that there were at least 378 kuttabs under formal state control. Between 1987 and 2009, the number of kuttabs in Tunisia continued to rise – from 378 to 1,186 – and the number of children attending them increased by 400 percent. Many of these schools – whether attached to mosques, Sufi lodges, or pious endowments the state had nationalized – came under some form of state sponsorship, as the state assumed fiscal responsibility for their equipment and upkeep. However, the number of private and informal kuttabs also grew throughout this period, and contemporary analysts noted that the exponential growth in kuttabs far surpassed the number of official permits granted, suggesting many kuttabs continued to escape formal state regulation.[51]

Given Bourguiba's enduring aversion to religion in public life, a flourishing of relatively autonomous groups such as the Quranic Preservation Society and the increasing number of unregulated kuttabs during this period must find explanation elsewhere. Indeed, a clearer picture emerges when we consider the evolving nature of Bourguiba's political opposition and the concomitant diminishing hegemony of his ruling party.

In the 1960s and 1970s Bourguiba identified the greatest threats to his rule in leftist groups and liberals calling for democracy and an end to single-party rule. To counter those threats, the regime began employing a nationalist rhetoric emphasizing notions such as "authenticity" in a bid to reestablish the ruling party's legitimacy, and the discourse of authenticity created opportunities for traditionally oriented members of the Neo-Destour and its successor PSD to play up citizens' religious identities. At the same time, the regime's institutional endowment had taken a hit following the collapse of a national agricultural collectivization program in 1969. Thereafter the PSD fell prey to internal schisms, growing popular disdain, and a retreat from associational life. These developments facilitated the decline in state sponsorship for institutions of religious learning.

Consider the creation of the Quranic Preservation Society. After the collectivization debacle of 1969, liberal and leftist opponents of the

[51] For the figures on the kuttabs, see Aida Talmoudi, "*Min al-Katatib ila Riyad al-Aftal: Tatawur Mu'asasat Tarbawiyya ma Qabl al-Madrasiyya* [From kuttabs to daycare centers: the development of preschool education in Tunisia]" Master's thesis (University of Tunis, 2013), 22; Nouira, 22–8 and 161; Jeanne Ladjili-Mouchette, "Le Kuttab et le Jardin d'Enfants en Tunisie," in *Les Institutions Traditionnelles dans le Monde Arabe*, ed. Hervé Bleuchot (Paris: Karthala, 1996), 140.

regime were ascendant. In an effort to blunt their momentum, Bourguiba began reaching out to more traditional circles for support. In this vein, the regime in 1970 gave its blessing to the formation of a Quranic Preservation Society, in hopes that the group's activities would counter the domination of the leftist and liberal groups on college campuses. The strategy worked, though perhaps too well, as many of the individuals who were active in the Quranic Preservation Society (including Rached Ghannouchi, who gave lessons in mosques) later emerged as the country's leading Islamists – and the regime's most ardent opponents.

Alternatively, consider the rise in the number of unregulated kuttabs. The growing visibility of these schools in the 1970s and 1980s flowed naturally from the heightened rhetoric of authenticity and identity politics the regime itself was promoting in the aftermath of the 1969 disaster. And it was no coincidence that the growing presence of traditional kuttabs accompanied the ruling party's retreat from associational life. Even in the 1950s and 1960s, there had been a considerable gap between the more secularist tendencies of the PSD's leadership and the party's rank and file. Clement Henry Moore observed in the 1960s, for example, that while many local PSD branch leaders shared Bourguiba's impatience with traditional religious practices, they refrained from imposing their views on local party members for fear of alienating the PSD's base.[52] With the blow to the party's legitimacy after 1969, these branch leaders faced a greater burden to advocate on behalf of Bourguiba's non-traditionalist ideology. While the number of PSD branches did not decline markedly in this period, their ability to mobilize the masses took a hit, as evidenced by Ennaifer's comment about the decline of "the hegemonic presence of the modern state, of the Bourguibist state."

The retreat of this "hegemonic presence" provided fertile ground for the rising number of traditional Quranic schools. As suggested by the 1980 law seeking formal state sponsorship of the schools, the citizenry's souring on the PSD had facilitated a growing space for these unregulated schools to flourish. But if this bottom-up Islamization of Tunisian society had initially worked to the regime's advantage in countering leftist opposition, by the early 1980s the regime seemed to be playing catch-up. Bourguiba's preoccupation with undermining political opposition, coupled with his weakened institutional endowment, had evidently reduced the state's control over institutions of religious learning.

---

[52] Moore, *Tunisia since Independence: The Dynamics of One-Party Government*, 133.

(3) **1987–2010: State Control.** Whereas in the 1950s and 1960s Bourguiba had sought formal state sponsorship of these institutions by eliminating autonomous ones and consolidating the remainder within the emerging public education system, his successor in the late 1980s began encouraging a proliferation of new, albeit state-controlled, institutions. Two developments exemplified this shift: the opening of a new Zaytuna University and affiliated institutes, and the creation of a state-sponsored League of Quranic Associations to facilitate religious instruction through schools and informal settings at the regional and local levels.

In 1987 Ben ʿAli created Zaytuna University, comprising three institutions: the High Institute for Theology in Tunis, the High Institute for Islamic Civilization in Tunis, and the Institute for Islamic Studies in Kairouan. The first two institutions offered four-year bachelor's degree programs in theology and related subjects to Tunisian and foreign students, respectively, while the center in Kairouan was devoted to training future prayer leaders (imams) and promoting Islamic culture in Tunisia and throughout Africa. Tellingly, the Grand Mosque was not incorporated into the new university, and in this way Ben ʿAli maintained the physical (and conceptual) separation between Zaytuna the mosque and Zaytuna the educational institution.[53]

The regime placed the new university under the administrative and fiscal control of the Ministry of Higher Education and Scientific Research (henceforth, "Ministry of Higher Education"), cementing the state's sponsorship of the institution. The 1988 state budget allocated 177,000 Tunisian dinars (roughly $206,000 at the time) to the institution, representing 96 percent of the institution's total funding for that year (and a mere 1.1 percent of the state's higher education budget). Ensuing laws stipulated that the governing councils of the university's institutes had to include a representative of the Prime Ministry's Directorate of Religious Affairs, and all non-state sources of funding for the university had to be submitted to the Ministry of Higher Education for approval.[54]

---

[53] Law 87-83 of December 31, 1987 (JORT 91 of December 29–31, 1987, p. 1637), Article 96; Decree 95-865 of May 8, 1995 (JORT 40 of May 19, 1995, p. 1136-7). In 1988 the regime reopened the Grand Mosque and permitted the creation of a Scientific Council of Zaytuna to oversee lessons on preaching and guidance there, lessons which attracted considerable public interest. Within two years, however, the project was aborted and the scientific council was dissolved. For more on this episode, see Nouira, 96.

[54] Law 87-83 of December 31, 1987, Annex A (JORT 91 of December 29–31, 1987, p. 1660-1); Decree 90-578 of March 30, 1990 (JORT 26 of April 17, 1990, p. 515-17), articles 6 and 10.

The controlled proliferation of religious institutions was also apparent in less formal realms of religious learning. In 1988 the Quranic Preservation Society – the loosely organized, financially independent association created in 1970 to promote cultural and religious activities around knowledge of the holy text – was reconfigured into a new, state-sponsored League of Quranic Associations (*Rabitat al-Jam'iyyat al-Quraniyya*) under the auspices of the Prime Ministry's Directorate of Religious Affairs. A Zaytuna-trained scholar presided over the League, which boasted regional and local branches tasked with supervising the education taking place in kuttabs, opening new Quranic schools in Kairouan, and arranging local and national Quranic memorization competitions.[55]

To account for the shift in the Tunisian state's approach to these institutions beginning in the late 1980s, we must once again consider the combined effect of the regime's non-traditionalist legitimating ideology, the nature of its primary political opponents, and a comparatively robust institutional endowment. By the time Ben 'Ali assumed the presidency in 1987, the regime's perception of its greatest threat had shifted decisively from the leftist and liberal movements of prior decades to the Islamists rallying around the MTI. To deal with the threat, Ben 'Ali pursued a two-pronged strategy. On the one hand, he sought to distinguish himself from his predecessor by encouraging a proliferation of religious institutions, thereby demonstrating that the Islamists were not alone in their desire to see religion gain a more prominent place in the public sphere. Hence the decision to (re)open the Zaytuna in 1987. On the other hand, Ben 'Ali invoked the non-traditionalist themes of his predecessor to insist that the state regain the monopoly on religious discourse and practice it had lost in the previous decades. Since the emergence of Islamist movements in the late 1960s, the mosque had been a key locus of Islamist activity and the MTI had appropriated the Friday sermon (*al-khutbah*) and other mosque-based lessons as a vehicle of social activism. Indeed, the MTI's presence throughout the mosques had led Rached Ghannouchi to declare by 1980 that "the mosques have become centers of Islamic acculturation and Islamic education," in implied contrast to the country's schools.[56]

---

[55] Nouira, 164–5.

[56] Ghannouchi's interview is reprinted in Christiane Souriau, "Quelques Données Comparatives sur les Institutions Islamiques Actuelles du Maghreb," *Annuaire de l'Afrique du Nord* 18 (1979): 378. For more on the MTI's growing presence in the mosques, see Tozy, "Islam et État au Maghreb," 40.

A decade later, Ben 'Ali's regime calculated that it would need to fight the Islamists' fire with fire, promoting religious education while ensuring that the state recapture control of the process. Hence the decision to reconstitute the Quranic Preservation Association as a state-run organization that would regulate the content of religious education disseminated in mosques and Quranic schools. The extent to which the regime viewed institutions of religious learning as potential political threats was evident in the shifting administrative jurisdiction of the kuttabs. In 1986 the Directorate of Religious Affairs, under whose purview the kuttabs fell, moved from the Prime Minister's office to the Interior Ministry, where it remained for the next seven years. This meant that the kuttabs were being managed by the same agency responsible for state security. When in the 1990s the Directorate was reorganized into its own ministry, Ben 'Ali's Minister of Religious Affairs reiterated in an interview that the state's insistence on formally sponsoring Quranic schools stemmed from a concern that the schools had become a breeding ground for religious movements opposed to the regime:

The ministry [of religious affairs] does not want there to be any ambiguity surrounding the role of the Quranic school: the kuttab should teach exclusively the Quran and hadith. The ministry will grant permits to open kuttabs only to those men and women who wish to accomplish this task. But it refuses to allow the kuttab to become a refuge for a certain discourse, a discourse of hate . . .[57]

REGULATING TEACHERS OF ISLAM

The elimination of most traditional religious schools after independence meant that religious instruction thereafter took place in public schools and in mosques. From independence to the late 1960s, Bourguiba's ideology of legitimation – particularly his conviction that the state ought to control the religious realm – and his drive to weaken his political opponents affiliated with the prestigious Zaytuna Mosque-University, fueled a standardization of Tunisia's religion instructors. In the 1970s and early 1980s, faced with new political challengers and a diminished institutional endowment, the state shifted course and encouraged a reorientation and relaxation in training and licensing regulations. Then, from the late 1980s onward, the emergence of Islamists as the regime's new prime enemy prompted a reorientation in the training of religion instructors in the

---

[57] As cited in Ladjili-Mouchette, "Le Kuttab et le Jardin d'Enfants en Tunisie," 142.

schools, and a reliance on a comparatively robust religious bureaucracy to more heavily regulate mosque-based educators.

(1) **1956–1970: Standardization.** In the first fifteen years of Bourguiba's administration, the regime sought to standardize the profiles of school- and mosque-based religion teachers, respectively, though each in different ways. Religion teachers in the schools were recruited from the Zaytuna, and for these individuals the regime reduced their training to a curriculum emphasizing classical religious subjects. By contrast, for those wishing to work as mosque-based educators, the state developed new training programs blending secular and religious subjects. We shall see how these policies reflected a mix of ideological, political, and institutional considerations.

With the reorganization of the Zaytuna in 1961, the state began recruiting individuals who had attained the 'alimiyya (university-level) diploma at the Grand Mosque to work as Islamic education (and Arabic) teachers in public secondary schools. In a speech in June 1961, Bourguiba stressed that he was looking to these Zaytuna graduates to "contribute to form the youth according to renovated Islamic principles."[58] Open to students who had attained the *tahsil* (Zaytuna's equivalent of the high school diploma) and to those who had passed the baccalaureate exam at a public high school, the Zaytuna faculty of theology would train future religion teachers and began offering two bachelor's degree programs: one in Islamic law (sharia) and one in theology.[59] In both programs, the required courses focused on Quranic studies, the Sunna (the body of Prophetic sayings and actions that comprise a source of Islamic law), and Islamic jurisprudence. The emphasis on classical religious subjects would remain in place until the mid-1980s.[60]

At the same time, the state began developing new training programs for those destined to disseminate religious instruction in the mosques. In the early 1960s, alongside its bachelor's degree programs, the Zaytuna faculty of theology began offering a three-year course of study leading to a Certificate in Preaching and Guidance (*shahadat al-wa'iz wa-l-irshad*). The program was designed as a transitional course of study for former Zaytuna secondary school students who had not attained the high school (tahsil) diploma but wished to pursue a career in the

---

[58] Bourguiba's speech of June 29, 1961 is cited in Moore, *Tunisia since Independence: The Dynamics of One-Party Government*, 54.

[59] Decree 61-357 of October 27, 1961 (JORT 46 of October 27–31, 1961, p. 1388–9); Ministerial Order of March 25, 1963 (JORT 15 of March 26–9, 1963, p. 365–9).

[60] Lelong, "Le Patrimoine Musulman dans l'Enseignement Tunisien après l'Indépendance," 96.

religious realm. In contrast to the Zaytuna faculty's bachelor's degree programs, which continued to emphasize study in religious topics, the new certificate program blended religious and secular topics, requiring courses in traditional subjects such as Quranic recitation and interpretation, preaching, and religious philosophy alongside courses in a foreign language, history/geography, and the administrative organization of the Tunisian Republic.[61] And in 1967, the state created the Islamic Institute of Kairouan, where holders of a Certificate in Preaching and Guidance could pursue additional studies. Courses at the Kairouan Institute lasted three years, and covered religious subjects as well as math, Arab literature, natural sciences, and French language. Graduates who successfully completed these requirements obtained a diploma permitting them to become imams, further standardizing the training for these individuals.[62]

The state's standardization of school-based and mosque-based religion instructors during this period, no less than the creation of new training programs and institutes during this period – with all the inherent start-up costs – resulted principally from three developments. First, as we saw in Chapter 4, Bourguiba's non-traditionalist ideology of legitimation dictated that the state assert control over the religious realm. Standardizing the training of religion instructors (whether they were destined for schools or mosques) flowed naturally from this broader ideological orientation. Second, Bourguiba was concerned in this period to eliminate political opposition from religious nationalists sympathetic to his main rival at the time, Salah Ben Youssef. As many of Ben Youssef's allies were centered around the Zaytuna – Tunisia's leading repository of future religion instructors – going after these opponents amounted to going after the country's educators. Third, we have seen that the Tunisian regime was quick to establish a civil service of religious functionaries, in line with its drive to bring the religious realm under state control. The new training programs for mosque-based religion instructors were partly an attempt to create a new pool of individuals who could staff this nascent bureaucracy. Thus, Bourguiba's ideology of legitimation, the nature of his political opponents, and the regime's expanding bureaucratic apparatus jointly contributed to the regulation of the nation's religion instructors during this period.

---

[61] Decree 61-357 of October 27, 1961 (JORT 46 of October 27–31, 1961, p. 1388–9); Ministerial Order of March 25, 1963 (JORT 15 of March 26–9, 1963, p. 370–72).

[62] Lelong, "Le Patrimoine Musulman dans l'Enseignement Tunisien après l'Indépendance," 96.

Consider the decision to hire Zaytuna alumni as religion teachers in the schools. Bourguiba's negative views of religion and his belief that the state should assert hegemony over the religious realm alienated many traditionally oriented Tunisians and translated into policies that granted preferential treatment to Sadiki graduates and increasingly excluded Zaytunians from the emerging structures of state power. For example, Sadikians ran the elite ministries of foreign affairs, interior, agriculture, and industry, while not a single Zaytunian featured in the upper echelons of the state bureaucracy. This exclusivity fueled growing frustration and anger among many ulama, and the regime's decision to hire Zaytuna graduates as religion and Arabic teachers in the emerging public schools was partly an attempt to blunt their opposition.[63]

A blend of ideological and political considerations similarly explained the decision to reduce the Zaytuna Grand Mosque and its affiliated institutions to a faculty of theology focusing on religious studies. Unlike in Morocco, where the Qarawiyyin Mosque-University had resisted attempts at curricular and pedagogic reform prior to independence, the Zaytuna had actually undergone several curricular innovations during – and, more importantly, prior to – the Protectorate. For example, at the level of higher Islamic learning, the Zaytuna was already offering courses in nonreligious subjects before 1956. Given Bourguiba's ideological aversion to religion, it stood to reason that the independent regime would continue to develop the Zaytuna's secular courses of study and marginalize the institution's religious courses of study. Yet, the 1961 reform effectively reversed this trend by reducing the Zaytuna to a small faculty focused largely on imparting knowledge of Islamic law and other religious domains. To understand why, it is necessary to recall the political importance of the Zaytuna.

The regime's main political opponents at the time included partisans of Ben Youssef, the pan-Arabist, pan-Islamic ideologue whom Bourguiba had expelled from the Neo-Destour in 1955. Though institutionally weak, the ulama still enjoyed what the Tunisian political scientist Asma

---

[63] A similar desire to co-opt frustrated ulama motivated Bourguiba to hire them as judges in the emerging court system. See Charfi and Redissi, "Teaching Tolerance and Open-Minded Approaches to Understanding Sacred Texts," 166.

Nouira has called an "ideational and spiritual hegemony over society."[64] In his quest to eliminate the Youssefists as a political threat, Bourguiba similarly sought to break this hegemony. Narrowing the scope of the Zaytuna curricula to encompass strictly religious subjects reinforced a philosophical argument underpinning the regime's legitimating ideology, namely that the religious had to be separate from the profane. But this idea was anathema to many Zaytunians, so reducing their institution to one engaged principally in religious studies served the regime's broader goal of enfeebling Bourguiba's opponents, undermining their "ideational and spiritual hegemony over society," and reducing their political salience.

Likewise, creating new programs such as the Certificate in Preaching and Guidance, and investing in new institutions such as the Islamic Institute of Kairouan (despite the attendant costs), made sense in light of the regime's non-traditionalist ideology and its desire to weaken political opponents. In contrast to the mostly religious curricula at the Zaytuna, these new programs blended secular and religious subjects, thereby ensuring that future mosque-based educators on the government payroll would receive training more closely reflective of the regime's reformist (if, for some, hostile) approach to religion. From a state-building perspective, the strategy seemed to work insofar as most graduates of the program in preaching and guidance went on to work as Preachers of Governorates and Preachers of Delegation, the two upper-level civil service positions created in 1966.

(2) **Mid-1970s–mid-1980s: Reorientation and Relaxation.** In the 1970s, the regime's approach to the country's Islam instructors shifted. Two changes were noteworthy. First, the state began requiring a greater amount of religious knowledge on the part of future public school Arabic language and Islamic education teachers, as reflected in changes to the civil service exams for prospective secondary school teachers. Up until the mid-1970s, future teachers of Arabic who took the civil service exam had to demonstrate knowledge of "the history of Islamic civilization" by answering questions on the institutions of the Umayyad Caliphate in southern Spain, and "sociological questions" on "Reformism in [Islamic] Thought." A 1973 civil service exam for prospective Arabic teachers, for instance, included written questions on "the history of Islamic thought and civilization" and an oral exposé on the same subject. In 1976,

---

[64] Nouira, 104.

however, the civil service exam for prospective Arabic teachers began requiring a formal Quranic narration.[65]

Likewise, up until the mid-1970s those wishing to become secondary school teachers of "civic and religious education" were required to demonstrate knowledge of topics drawn from the 1959 middle school "religious and civic education" curriculum, and from the 1963 high school "civic and religious education" curriculum. These curricula had emphasized lessons linking religious concepts to contemporary Tunisian life (e.g., imploring students to consider connections "between Muslim law and modes of its practical application in the Republic of Tunisia"), and the civil service exam for future teachers of the subject largely mirrored the topics appearing in the secondary school curricula.[66]

In 1981, the exam for those wishing to teach "religious and civic education" in the secondary schools included three times as many questions as in the previous period, shifting the emphasis from questions on the history and sociology of Islam to questions testing explicitly religious knowledge. For example, the 1981 exam required prospective teachers to give a Quranic exegesis, and tested their knowledge of works addressing the Prophetic tradition (the Sunna), sources of Islamic jurisprudence, and movements of reform in Islamic thought. A comparison of the exam requirements in the earlier and later periods, as shown in Table 5.1, is instructive.[67]

The increase in religious knowledge required of prospective Arabic and religion teachers in the schools partly reflected the curricular changes taking place at the primary and secondary school level. The expansion of Islamic education in the primary and secondary school curricula required the state to ensure that future teachers could demonstrate a greater amount of religious knowledge. Insofar as the curricular reorientation of the period was a by-product of Bourguiba's efforts to shore up support among more traditional circles to counterbalance the liberal and leftist groups threatening the regime, adjusting the teacher training requirements was a second-order result of the regime's attempt to undercut its opposition.

---

[65] Ministerial Order of June 6, 1973 (JORT 116 of June 8–12, 1973, p. 918–20); Ministerial Order of October 30, 1976 (JORT 67 of November 5, 1976, p. 2656–7).

[66] Tunisian Ministry of Education, *Programmes Officiels de l'Enseignement Secondaire Fascicule VI: Instruction Civique et Religieuse.*

[67] Ministerial Order of August 9, 1965 (JORT 41 of August 6–10, 1965, p. 986–7); Ministerial Order of April 21, 1981 (JORT 29 of April 28–May 1, 1981, p. 941–3).

TABLE 5.1 *Exam requirements for future religion teachers, 1965 and 1981*

1965 Civil service exam requirements	1981 Civil service exam requirements
Subject related to a question included in the middle school civic and religious education curriculum or from the first three years of high school. *See*: (1) Official middle school curricula (1959) for Civic and Religious Education and (2) Official high school curricula (1963) for Civic and Religious Education.	(1) The Quran. Exegesis of the *al-maʾidah* sura: linguistic and religious analysis; recitation and [derivative] legislation; (2) The Prophetic tradition. Works addressing the *Sunna*: genres and specificities; (3) Muslim jurisprudence: its sources and its practices; and (4) Movements of renovation and reform in Islamic thought: the reformist ideas of Muhammad ʿAbduh and Jamal al-Din al-Afghani and others.

A second change in the training of religion instructors came alongside the emergence of autonomous organizations such as the Quranic Preservation Society. These groups, which began cropping up in the 1970s, encouraged Islamic instruction around the country in mosques and informal settings. The expanding spaces for religious instruction in Tunisian society amounted to a relaxation in the training standards for religion instructors outside the schools because those wishing to give lessons under the auspices of groups such as the Quranic Preservation Society did not have to present any credentials to do so. Indeed, one suspects Bourguiba later regretted the state's lack of supervision over the lessons being given by men like Rached Ghannouchi, an active member of the Quranic Preservation Society and future Islamist ideologue.

Finally, as we saw in Chapter 4, after the 1969 collectivization scandal, the ruling party retreated somewhat from associational life. The creation of organizations such as the Quranic Preservation Society spoke to this retreat. These groups largely escaped state regulation because the ruling party at the time was no longer in a position to exert the kind of hegemony it had enjoyed in previous decades. The relaxation in standards for religion instructors, particularly outside the schools, thus resulted partly from the regime's weakened institutional endowment during this period.

(3) **Late 1980s–2010: Reorientation.** Beginning in the late 1980s, Tunisia implemented sweeping changes to the training and licensing

procedures for religion teachers. Key reforms altered the curricula of the institutions responsible for teaching future religion instructors, incorporating a greater emphasis on social sciences and secular subjects. We have seen that as a result of Mohamed Charfi's overhaul of the public education system in his capacity as Minister of Education, religious and civic education in the secondary schools became two distinct subjects. While the state began recruiting civic education teachers from among graduates of the social science and humanities faculties, Islamic education remained the purview of Zaytuna graduates. However, two sets of reforms altered the education of these Zaytunians. First, for individuals already working as middle and high school religion teachers, Charfi's team established mandatory continuing education workshops in the summer months. Participants attended a series of lectures by university professors in the humanities, sessions which introduced them to the study of religion from sociological and historical perspectives. They also spent time working with educational inspectors and advisers (many of whom were not religion scholars) to address challenges arising in the classrooms, especially potential problems surrounding the introduction of the new textbooks.[68]

The second set of reforms took aim at the Zaytuna theology department. In 1995, the state reoriented the training of future religion teachers (and ulama more generally) by revising the Zaytuna's degree programs. Recall that Ben 'Ali had (re)created Zaytuna University in 1987, merging the High Institute for Theology in Tunis, the High Institute for Islamic Civilization in Tunis, and the Institute for Islamic Studies in Kairouan. Whereas the 1956 decree reorganizing the Zaytuna Grand Mosque had noted that "education at the Grand Mosque and its annexes aims to conserve the sciences of the Religious Law and of Arabic Letters, and to give students a modern instruction," the preamble to the 1995 decree stated that the Zaytuna University sought "to guarantee a scientific training enabling the student to discover that which, in the values of Islam as a dogma, a school of thought and a civilization, [promotes] the human being as a free and responsible person . . . and to ally one's fealty to the aims of the religion with the need to respond to the demands of [modern] life."[69]

The newly articulated institutional purpose informed ensuing curricular changes. Studies at Zaytuna were reorganized into four

---

[68] Interview with Moncef Ben Abdeljelil, Sousse, October 23, 2012.
[69] The 1987 regulation is Law 87-83 of December 31, 1987 (JORT 91 of December 29–31, 1987, p. 1637), Article 96. For the 1995 reform, see Decree 95-865 of May 8, 1995 (JORT 40 of May 19, 1995, p. 1136-7).

tracks: (1) Islamic knowledge, defined to include Islamic law and other religious subjects, (2) the history of religions, including non-Abrahamic faiths, (3) humanities, in which religion would be studied as a sociological and anthropological phenomenon, and which now included courses in Western and non-Western philosophy, and (4) languages, both as applied to Islamic sciences (Latin, Syriac, Aramaic, Greek, and Hebrew classes would enable students to access texts written by the first Muslims) and modern foreign languages such as French, English, German, Spanish, and Italian.[70]

In line with this broader reorganization, the High Institute of Theology began offering a four-year bachelor's degree for Tunisian students in "theology and Islamic thought," replacing the former ijaza degrees in sharia and Islamic Sciences. In contrast to its predecessors, the new degree program required courses in the sociology of religion, social science research, comparative religion, the history of medieval philosophy, and a second foreign language. For those wishing to pursue advanced religious studies, the reforms of 1995 also created doctoral programs requiring the study of human rights law, the history of scientific advancement in the Muslim world, and a second foreign language. The regime invited professors from the humanities and social science faculties to teach these courses, marking the first time scholars of nonreligious fields were teaching at Zaytuna. This meant that future religion teachers would no longer receive their training exclusively from classically trained religion scholars.[71]

There were also important changes to the training requirements for imams. In 2003 the state for the first time opened its Religious Inspector corps to non-Zaytuna graduates, meaning that individuals without a background in religious scholarship would be training and supervising mosque-based educators. A separate 2003 law stipulated that inspectors would be teaching and supervising imams through weekly (and eventually, daily) visits to mosques. This was in contrast to their predecessors in earlier decades, whose responsibilities never extended to such supervision.

---

[70] Moncef Ben Abdeljelil, "al-Taʿlim al-Dini bi-Jamiʿat al-Zaytuna Hadiran [Religious Education in the Modern Zaytuna University]," in *Kayfa Yudarris al-Din al-Yawm? [How Do We Teach Religion Today?]* (Casablanca: King Abdul-Aziz Al Saoud Foundation for Islamic Studies and Human Sciences, 2003), 20.

[71] Ministerial Order of November 3, 1995 (JORT 92 of November 17, 1995, p. 2150–4); Ministerial Order of February 6, 1996 (JORT 13 of February 13, 1996, p. 331–4); Interviews with Hamadi Ben Jaballah, Tunis, October 12, 2012; Iqbal Gharbi, Tunis, October 30, 2012; Moncef Ben Abdeljelil, Sousse, October 23, 2012; Mokhtar Ayachi, Tunis, October 18, 2012.

New regulations also sought to incentivize and reorient the education of future mosque-based educators. For example, the state now delineated the pay scale of imams and preachers according to their level of education, granting those who had received a bachelor's degree in theology or Islamic sciences a higher salary than those who had not. Through these reforms, the state sought to reshape the profile of the mosque-based instructor to include those who had received an education that blended religious and secular subjects.[72]

The state's shifting regulation of religion instructors during this period – the curricular changes at the Zaytuna University from 1995 onward, new regulations aimed at monitoring the training of imams and other mosque-based educators, and the state's decision to open up posts in the religious bureaucracy to individuals with little background in religious knowledge, thereby ensuring that religion instructors would report to individuals with dubious religious knowledge – resulted from the blend of ideological, political, and institutional factors that should by now be familiar to the reader.

The confrontation between the Ben ʿAli regime and the Islamists of Ennahda following the disputed 1989 legislative election had marked a turning point insofar as the new regime's conciliatory stance toward the Islamists gave way to a policy of repression after Ennahda's strong showing at the polls. Buoyed by the resurgent strength of his ruling party, Ben ʿAli cultivated alliances with liberals such as his new Education Minister, Mohamed Charfi in an effort to counterbalance the Islamists, setting the stage for ensuing changes to religious and civic education curricula at the primary and secondary school levels. These same alliances ultimately produced the changes to the system of higher Islamic learning for future religion instructors. Indeed, it was a member of Charfi's inner circle who devised and implemented both the continuing education programs for public school religion teachers and the curricular changes to the Zaytuna in 1995.

In 1989 Charfi asked Moncef Ben Abdeljelil to join his team and advise the Ministry on reforming the primary and secondary school curricula. Ben Abdeljelil held advanced degrees in Arabic Studies and

---

[72] Nouira, 171. See also Decree 2003-2082 of October 14, 2003 (JORT 84 of October 21, 2003, p. 3146–50); Decree 2003-2082 of October 14, 2003 (JORT 84 of October 21, 2003, p. 3146–50); Decree 2008-3542 of November 22, 2008 (JORT 96 of November 28, 2008, p. 4001–2).

Islamic Civilization from Tunisian universities. Prior to joining Charfi's team he had spent a year on a Fulbright fellowship at Princeton University, where he had studied under Clifford Geertz and Lawrence Rosen, scholars whom he later credited with expanding his interests beyond "orthodox studies" in Arabic language and literature to include the study of Islam from anthropological and sociological perspectives. "I came to rethink the whole Islamic phenomenon," Ben Abdeljelil later recalled. "I put myself between what I call an historian of Islam and an anthropologist of the Muslim world."[73] When Charfi left his post in 1994 after a falling out with Ben 'Ali, Ben Abdeljelil stayed on as an advisor to Charfi's successor and turned his attention to reforming the Zaytuna curricula.

In his capacity as the lead architect of the Zaytuna curricular reforms in the mid-1990s, Ben Abdeljelil sought to shift the teaching of Islam from a theological enterprise to one that conceived of Islam as a sociological and historical development. The injection of courses on the anthropology and sociology of Islam at the Zaytuna reflected Ben Abdeljelil's preference for approaching religion through the lens of social science. There was a deeper philosophical debate at play here, and in Ben Abdeljelil's drive to reframe the way Tunisians studied Islam he encountered resistance from colleagues on Charfi's cabinet who agreed on the need for reform but preferred to maintain the emphasis on Islam's core theology.

Ben Abdeljelil wanted students at the Zaytuna to move away from purely theological studies and gain a greater understanding of how Islam had evolved and functioned in Tunisian and other societies over time. Such a desire also fueled his design of the summertime continuing education workshops for Tunisia's religion teachers, particularly the lectures that focused on imparting to teachers a set of skills that would enable them "to connect ideas and sociological contexts."[74] Against the backdrop of an ascendant RCD, Ben 'Ali's push to undermine his Islamist opponents ended up inviting into the policy arena liberal elites with particular views on the nature of religious inquiry and the relationship between religion and state more broadly. These views ultimately made their way into the reforms regulating religion instructors.

[73] Interview with Moncef Ben Abdeljelil, Sousse, October 23, 2012.
[74] Ibid.

REGULATING ISLAM IN TUNISIA

As in the Moroccan case, ideological, political, and institutional considerations jointly fueled Tunisia's approach to regulating Islam through its education system. On the matter of curricula, Bourguiba's non-traditionalist ideology of legitimation, his concern to obliterate opposition among the religious nationalist factions loyal to Ben Youssef, and the blessing of a hegemonic party and highly centralized bureaucracy, produced the contraction and reorientation of the curricula we saw in the first fifteen years of Tunisia's independence. With the emergence of new political enemies and a ruling party weakened by ideological fragmentation – two results of the 1969 economic debacle – the Tunisian state began increasing the amount of Islamic instruction and reorienting its content to focus on more heavily dogmatic aspects of the religion that could combat purportedly dangerous, mostly leftist, ideologies. When the regime ultimately calculated that its most formidable opponents were no longer leftists and liberals but rather the Islamists of Ennahda, Tunisia embarked on yet another reorientation of the curricula to counter the threat.

Alternatively, consider the shifting balance between state control and autonomy for Tunisia's institutions of religious learning. A non-traditionalist ideology of regime legitimation, coupled with the threat of religious nationalist opponents and the regime's comparatively strong institutional endowment, enabled Bourguiba to establish state sponsorship of nearly all Quranic schools and the country's leading institution of higher Islamic learning in the early post-independence period. But with the emergence of liberal opponents in the 1970s, and a damaged ruling party in retreat, there was a shift toward greater autonomy for these institutions as the regime struggled to rebound from a crisis of legitimacy. Then, the rise of Islamists as the regime's primary opponents in the late 1980s prompted Ben 'Ali to rely on strengthened party and bureaucratic apparatuses to increase state control over these institutions.

Lastly, we have seen how regulating the training and licensing of future religion instructors were similarly inspired by a blend of ideological, political, and institutional considerations. In the 1950s and 1960s, the regime's non-traditionalist ideology of legitimation, Bourguiba's desire to stamp out Youssefist opposition centered around the main institution responsible for teaching future religion instructors, and the imperative to fill positions in the state's emerging bureaucracy of religious functionaries led the regime to standardize the training of religion teachers in the schools and in mosques. It did this by reducing the Zaytuna to an institution focused almost exclusively on religious subjects, and by creating new programs for mosque-based educators that blended secular and religious subjects. Then, throughout the 1970s and 1980s, a weakened ruling party and the emergence of liberals and leftists as the regime's principal challengers incentivized both a reorientation in the licensing requirements for future religion instructors in the schools, and a relaxation in the training standards for the nation's religion instructors outside the schools, particularly in informal settings and in mosques. When in the late 1980s and early 1990s the regime's primary political opposition emerged among the Islamists of Ennahda, Ben 'Ali's efforts to isolate his political adversaries produced a reorientation in the training procedures for religion instructors in the schools and for future graduates of the Zaytuna more generally.

6

Regulating Islam after the Spring

The policy decisions coursing through this book challenge a prevailing narrative in the literature on Middle East politics that has pitted "secular" states against "religious" societies and opposition movements. A closer examination of the politics of religious regulation in Arab countries not only blurs the line between notions of "religious" and "secular" but also demonstrates the extent to which authoritarian regimes in the region have been more nimble in their responses to societal pressures than previously thought, a finding with potentially important implications for scholars of authoritarian governance and resilience.

To varying degrees, the "Arab Spring" uprisings that broke out in 2011 tested that resilience. Some regimes, such as that of Morocco's Alaouite monarchy, emerged from the storm intact. Others, such as Tunisia's autocracy under Ben ʿAli, crumbled beneath the weight of unprecedented societal pressures. Insofar as the fall-out from the uprisings carried implications for the regimes' ideological underpinnings, political opponents, and institutional endowment – i.e., the three ingredients of religious regulation – the post-Spring trajectories of these states offer a useful test of my main argument. If, as I have sought to demonstrate, religious regulation in these countries has stemmed from the interplay of ideology, political opposition, and institutional endowment, then continuity in these three factors should spell a continuity in the state's religious regulation. By contrast, we would expect changes in any of these ingredients to produce shifts in a state's regulations of religious institutions and discourse. The post-Spring Moroccan and Tunisian experiences largely support this basic premise.

In the kingdom on the western edge of the Arab world, the Alaouite regime's response to the outbreak of protests in 2011 ultimately reinforced the monarchy's legitimating ideology, solidified the landscape of political opposition, and strengthened key pillars of the regime's institutional endowment. As a result, the state has been able to continue implementing and building on the education reforms of the prior decade and a half. Plans to continue cleansing religious education curricula of extremist teachings, legislation further centralizing state control over institutes of higher Islamic learning, and expansions in the state's imam training programs speak to this continuity. In Morocco, the events of 2011 did not fundamentally alter the ingredients of religious regulation, and so regulating Islam after the Spring has looked much as it did before the Spring.

In Tunisia, the picture is more complicated. The Jasmine uprising birthed a process of democratization that maintained the non-traditionalist ideological underpinnings of the governing system but reshaped the configuration of regime support and opposition, and significantly weakened the institutional structures upon which the *ancien regime* had relied to enact policies. One immediate effect of these changes was a greater autonomy for religious institutions, and the adoption of a new constitution produced a new legal template for the regulation of religious institutions that suggested policy shifts would ensue. Yet, instabilities borne of the democratic transition, coupled with the fact that decisions about religion and state for the first time entered the realm of democratic politics, ultimately halted the shift toward greater autonomy and stalled reforms implicating curricula and religion instructors. The Tunisian democratic experiment remains in its early stages, but the country's trajectory since 2011 suggests that even if a process of democratization alters the salient factors accounting for religious regulation in an authoritarian context, that same process can produce externalities that undermine or at least delay the predicted changes in religious regulation.

In this concluding chapter, I explore the evolving nature of religious regulation in Morocco and Tunisia since the Arab Spring, assess the extent to which my overarching theory has held up against developments in these countries since 2011, consider questions emanating from the book that merit further research, and offer some concluding observations about religious regulation in a post-Spring Arab world.

EXTENDING THE REFORMS: MOROCCO SINCE 2011

At a meeting of his Council of Ministers on February 6, 2016, King Mohammed VI noted the importance of religious learning in the kingdom and instructed the government to continue reforming the religious education curricula and textbooks in the public, private, and ʿatiq systems with a view to "emphasizing in this education the values of tolerant Islam, in the framework of the Sunni Maliki rite, which advances moderation, tolerance, and coexistence with different cultures and civilizations."[1] Four days later, the cabinet announced that French instruction would be reintroduced in the first year of primary school, and mathematics and science courses would henceforth be taught in French. This meant effectively reversing a thirty-year process of Arabization in the public schools, a decision that provoked the ire of PJD leaders who believed increasing French instruction would only serve to entrench the country's traditional, secular elite. (The dominant Islamist party was not opposed to children learning non-Arabic languages, *per se*. PJD leaders such as Abdelilah Benkirane and Lahcen Daoudi, who became Minister of Higher Education, had publicly called for greater English language instruction.) The tumultuous events of the Arab Spring had not reduced the regime's penchant for identity bargaining. On the contrary: the political upheaval that threatened Morocco in 2011 ultimately reinforced the very conditions that had facilitated a series of reforms implicating the curricular incorporation of Islam, the balance between autonomy and state control of religious institutions, and the training of the country's religion instructors since the late 1990s. To understand how, it is worth reviewing the events of 2011 and their aftermath.

Morocco's comparatively tame variant of an Arab Spring began on February 20, 2011 when 150,000–200,000 protesters poured into the streets of fifty-three cities and towns across the kingdom demanding an end to corruption, greater limits on the king's power, and heightened government attention to poverty and youth unemployment. Like its peer social protest movements throughout the region, Morocco's "February 20 Movement" remained largely leaderless and attracted a broad swath of the population. It was joined by what had remained the country's largest informal and anti-regime Islamic movement, al-ʿAdl wa-l-Ihsan, and by a host of smaller leftist political parties. The February 20 Movement also garnered the support of ostensibly state-linked human rights organizations such as the Moroccan Human Rights Association and the Moroccan Organization for Human Rights. But unlike its peers in

---

[1] Muhammad al-Ashhab, "*al-Maghreb Yuqar Khitat li-Islah al-Taʿlim wa Istratejiyya li-l-Tanmiyya fi-l-Sahra*" [Morocco announces an education reform plan and development strategy in the Sahara], *Al-Hayat*, February 8, 2016. The king's speech was also reprinted on the Islamic Affairs Ministry's website.

Tunisia, Egypt, and elsewhere, the protest movement in Morocco by and large retained a commitment to the overarching system of government, allowing the monarchy to avoid the crisis of legitimacy that accompanied uprisings in other Arab states. Indeed, the slogan most heard in the streets during those heady days in February was *al-shaʿb yurid al-dustur al-jadid* (the people want a new constitution), not the ubiquitous *al-shaʿb yurid isqat al-nizam* (the people want the fall of the regime) heard in Egypt and elsewhere.[2]

The king responded swiftly and, it turned out, astutely to the protests. On 21 February he announced the creation of an Economic and Social Council, chaired by a former interior minister, to offer recommendations to the government in the context of a broader endeavor to "develop . . . a new social charter based on major contractual agreements that create the right environment to meet the challenge of revamping the economy, boosting competitiveness, promoting productive investment and encouraging public involvement to achieve development at a faster pace." Then on 3 March, the king announced the creation of a National Human Rights Council to replace the Consultative Council on Human Rights (CCHR). The latter had been established in 1990 and later assumed a leading role in Mohammed VI's transitional justice initiative of the early 2000s, in which the state compensated victims of human rights abuses committed during his father's reign. In contrast to the CCHR, the new National Human Rights Council would not include members of the government and would, therefore, presumably enjoy greater independence in its mandate to "monitor and assess the human rights situation, blow the whistle and enrich rights-related debate . . . examine any violations or alleged violations of human rights and conduct appropriate inquiries."[3]

Less than a week thereafter, on 9 March, the king announced his intention to amend the constitution and submit it for approval in a popular referendum. A blue-ribbon commission led by Abdelatif Menouni, a law professor at Mohammed V University, was appointed to draft the new foundational law, and political parties, business representatives, labor unions, and other stakeholders in civil society were invited to submit amendments. Notable changes in the final text included recognition of the Berber community's native language, Tamazight, as an official

---

[2] Mohamed Madani, Driss Maghraoui, and Saloua Zerhouni, "The 2011 Moroccan Constitution: A Critical Analysis," *Institute for Democracy and Electoral Assistance* (2012): 10.

[3] Dahir 1.11.19 of March 1, 2011 (BORM 5922 of March 3, 2011, p. 260–6).

language alongside Arabic; expanded legislative prerogatives for the parliament; a new requirement that the king appoint a prime minister from the party obtaining the greatest number of seats in parliament; the promotion of human rights, including the right to privacy and the right to a fair trial; equality between men and women (so long as said equality did not contradict the "permanent characteristics of the kingdom"); and steps toward an independent judiciary. The new text maintained the king's sole authority over foreign affairs, the religious realm, and national security; and although it referred to Morocco as "a constitutional monarchy, democratic, parliamentary, and social," the revised constitution did not subject the monarchy to legal constraints.[4] On July 1 over 70 percent of the electorate reportedly turned out to vote on the constitution, and 98 percent of the voters approved of the new text. Evidently, most of the Moroccan public and the major political parties perceived the proposed constitution as an important step in Morocco's gradual transition toward democracy.

How did the outbreak of protests and the regime's response implicate the ideological, political, and institutional factors driving religious regulation in the kingdom? Consider first the matter of ideology. Menouni's first draft hinted at a potential shift in the legitimating ideology of the regime, insofar as it declared Morocco to be "a modern state with the Islamic religion," referred to the king as a "citizen monarch," erased reference to the king's sacred status as the nation's religious leader, and introduced a clause guaranteeing freedom of conscience and belief. The PJD strenuously objected to the proposed language implicating the state's Islamic nature and establishing a freedom of belief, and Benkirane threatened to encourage his supporters to reject the text in the impending referendum if it included such language.

The commission over which Menouni presided ultimately incorporated the leading Islamist party's objections into the final document, preserving the designation of Morocco as an Islamic state, retaining the king's status as the nation's religious leader, and granting the state authority to regulate religious activity.[5] Article 41 of the new constitution reaffirmed that Islam is "the religion of the state," retained the state's longstanding motto of "God, Country, King," and identified the king as "the Commander of the Faithful, who rules in respect of Islam [and] guarantees the free exercise of religion." The king's guardianship of the religious realm was preserved

---

[4] Madani, et al., "The 2011 Moroccan Constitution: A Critical Analysis," 18.
[5] Buehler, "The Threat to 'Un-moderate': Moroccan Islamists and the Arab Spring," 252-4.

insofar as the new constitution stipulated that "the king exercises by *dahir* religious prerogatives, inherent to the institution of the Commandership of the Faithful, which are conferred to him exclusively . . . " And while the text removed reference to the king's "sacred" status, Article 46 held that "the person of the King is inviolable, and to him respect is due." Thus, the 2011 constitution ultimately reinforced the traditionalist basis of the monarchy's legitimacy to reign and govern.

Consider next the degree to which developments in 2011 affected the constellation of political opponents confronting the regime. At first, the alliance between the February 20 Movement, the anti-monarchy Islamists of 'Adl wa-l-Ihsan, a host of smaller leftist parties and labor unions, and state-linked human rights organizations suggested the monarchy faced a new and potentially formidable configuration of challengers. But by getting out in front of the protests and quickly announcing steps toward reform, the king undercut this emerging bloc of opponents. When parliamentary elections were scheduled for the fall, the February 20 Movement announced it would boycott the vote, but by then it had lost steam due to internal fragmentation and the success of the referendum. Meanwhile, its main ally, al-'Adl wa-l-Ihsan, joined in the boycott but was ultimately sidelined following the PJD's decision to endorse the new constitution and participate in the legislative elections a few months later.

Those elections took place on November 25, 2011 and were considered largely free and fair by domestic and international observers. The Interior Ministry reported a voter turnout of 45 percent, up from 37 percent in the 2007 legislative elections. The PJD, thirteen years after formally entering the political system, won 107 of the 395 seats, followed by the center-right Istiqlal Party with sixty seats. True to the letter of the new law, the king named PJD leader Abdelilah Benkirane as Prime Minister, or "head of government" in the new locution. Benkirane quickly demonstrated an eagerness to avoid any confrontation with the palace, assuring the public that his party intended to work constructively with the king, and generously doling out nineteen of the thirty-one ministerial portfolios to independents and members of the PJD's coalition partners in the Istiqlal, the Popular Movement (MP by its French acronym), and the leftist Party of Progress and Socialism. The Islamist party evidently chose to prioritize maintaining good ties with the Palace, even at the risk of eliciting criticism from its base of supporters. Far from posing a threat to the monarchy, then, the PJD's ascension facilitated the monarchy's goal of a divided Islamist opposition. The radical, anti-regime Islamists of al-'Adl wa-l-Ihsan emerged from the Moroccan Spring ever more isolated, and the death of the movement's leader in 2012 further weakened the movement. With the PJD integrated into the political process, the most outspoken pockets of opposition to the monarchy were reduced to the radical Islamists of al-ʿAdl wa-l-Ihsan and a smattering of liberal youth groups that had joined the February 20 Movement but proved unable to coalesce around a unified political platform. The basic constellation of regime opposition and support thus survived the Moroccan Spring.

Finally, it is worth examining the extent to which the events of 2011 and their aftermath affected the monarchy's institutional resources, particularly the political party and bureaucratic structures at the regime's disposal. The Moroccan Spring propelled the PJD into a leadership position in the national legislature, and local elections in 2015 saw the PJD sweep the major cities. (It remains unclear to what degree political authority will devolve to local and regional councils, as stipulated in the new constitution.) Still, the basic landscape of political parties did not radically change. As in the earlier periods, the post-Spring Alaouite regime continued to turn the lack of a hegemonic party into an asset by leaning on various palace-friendly factions to counteract the PJD – principally, the PAM, the MP and the RNI – and by establishing alternative institutional mechanisms for securing power. The constitutional provisions concerning the relationship between royal and governmental authority were pertinent in this regard.

Although the 2011 constitution implied that political parties would take on greater significance through the expanded powers of the elected parliament, the new text also checked those powers by delineating clear boundaries between the purviews of the Council of Government (to be chaired by the head of government) and the Council of Ministers (to be chaired by the king); by reinforcing the immunity of the royal decree (*dahir*) from government input or veto; and by enshrining the king's leadership over bodies with little to no government oversight, such as the Security Council, the Supreme Council of the Magistracy, and – most importantly for our purposes – the High Council of Ulama. We saw in Chapter 2 that the High Council had undergone a restructuring in the early 2000s, but 2011 marked the first time the institution was constitutionally mandated to serve as the country's only legitimate source of religious guidelines (*fatawa*). Moreover, the new constitution stipulated that the High Council, under the king's leadership, would issue these guidelines on the basis of "the tolerant principles, rules and aims of Islam," reflecting language which had appeared in earlier education reforms and which the king would use in his address to his Council of Ministers in early 2016.

Beyond the institutional tools enshrined in the new text, the monarchy found additional ways to make up for the lack of a hegemonic party. Within days of the PJD's victory in the 2011 national election, the king began appointing economic, trade, and constitutional law experts to a new royal advisory council. As Benkirane spent the month of December struggling to form a government – a process many criticized for taking too long, fueling the perception of inept political parties – the king's cabinet grew to include former ministers and political figures openly hostile to the PJD. Arguably the most controversial appointment was that of Fouad Ali al-Himma, a former classmate of the king who had founded the PAM in 2009 and was an outspoken critic of Benkirane's party. In the context of the PJD's strong showing in the legislative elections, many interpreted al-Himma's appointment to the royal council as a check on the Islamists and the institutional resources their victory could bring them in light of the new constitution.

Consider now the monarchy's bureaucratic tools. In Chapter 3, I highlighted several instances in which the regime's approach to religious education – such as its encouragement of the msids in the 1960s and its tacit blessing of private institutes of Quranic instruction throughout the 1970s and 1980s – partly reflected unrelated bureaucratic constraints such as the lack of classrooms and qualified teachers to staff the public schools. In key respects, Morocco's educational bureaucracy has scored important gains in recent years. Primary school enrollment, for example, reached 96 percent in 2014, reflecting the state's success in narrowing the gap between the number of school-aged children and the available teachers and classrooms to accommodate them.[6] But in other respects, the state has continued struggling to meet the needs of its educational system. Teacher shortages have been especially acute at the level of higher education. In 2015, nearly 700,000 students were enrolled in universities, a 10 percent increase over the previous year and a jump from 433,000 in 2010.[7] As we shall see, the lack of qualified professors at the university level has contributed to policies implicating institutions of higher Islamic learning in post-Spring Morocco.

---

[6] The World Bank, "Education Development in Morocco: Enhancing Educating Quality and Governance," April 15, 2014. Accessible at www.worldbank.org/en/results/2014/04/15/education-development-in-morocco.

[7] Ursula Lindsey, "Private Universities in Morocco Aim to Fill Gap between Higher Education and Job Market," *Financial Times*, November 23, 2015.

On the other hand, the religious bureaucracy has seen ongoing enhancements since 2011. Previously, I noted that Ahmed Toufiq's reorganization of the Ministry of Islamic Affairs, begun in 2003, was accompanied by a dramatic increase in budgetary investments to this bureaucracy. Those investments have only continued to grow: the Ministry's operating budget went from $203 million in 2012 to $294 million in 2016 (a 46 percent increase when adjusted for inflation), with an additional $162 million going toward "capital investments" such as the building and refurbishing of mosques and community centers. Consequently, the Ministry's budget for "developing 'atiq education" grew from $18 million in 2013 to over $21 million in 2016 (a 16 percent increase when adjusted for inflation).[8] These figures suggest a strengthened religious bureaucracy, although when juxtaposed alongside the bureaucratic strains in Morocco's educational system and the continuing lack of a hegemonic party, the resulting picture arguably remains one of a "mixed" institutional endowment for the regime.

The ongoing traditionalism at the heart of the regime's self-legitimation, the increasing isolation of radical, anti-monarchy Islamists as the only serious source of opposition to the regime, and the persistently mixed institutional endowment for the regime have enabled the monarchy to solidify its control over religious institutions and continue the reform process begun before the Arab Spring with little standing in the way.

This has been evident in the matter of curricula. By granting the PJD its constitutionally mandated authority in government in 2011, the regime increased the chances that Islamists in power would now be held to account for their governance. The king seized on this liability by pushing for a series of reforms, including proposed changes in the educational realm. In his annual Throne Speech of 2013, for example, Mohammed VI publicly criticized the Islamist-led government for purportedly failing to address persistent problems in the educational system, including the poor quality of instruction for those without means and the mismatch between the educational system and the needs of the labor market. In light of parliament's inability to act, the king announced, he would take it upon himself to follow through on the promises of the new constitution regarding the educational system, including the creation of a permanent

---

[8] The figures for the Ministry's operating budget are drawn from annual reports issued by the Ministry between 2012 and 2016. For the figures on traditional education specifically, see the 2013 report entitled "al-Ta'lim al-'Atiq" [Traditional Education], and the 2016 report, "Mashru' al-Mayzaniyya al-Far'iyya li-Sannat 2016" [Draft Budget for 2016].

High Council of Education that would evaluate and offer recommendations on reforming the education system.[9]

In a similar vein, the Minister of Education, Rachid Belmokhtar, bypassed the parliament when in December 2015 he submitted a proposal for a comprehensive education reform to the royal cabinet. That proposal urged that courses in math and science be taught in French rather than Arabic, partly to make it easier for high school graduates to pursue studies in the scientific disciplines at the university level, where the relevant courses had continued to be taught in French. Belmokhtar, an independent with close ties to the Palace, submitted the proposal unbeknownst to Benkirane, prompting the head of government to publicly reprimand his Education Minister and express his opposition to the move away from Arabization.[10] But by then it was too late, and in a matter of days the king indicated he would accept the proposal and support its implementation.

It was in this context that Mohammed VI announced to his Council of Ministers – a body consisting of the head of government and his cabinet – the forthcoming curricular changes in the religious education courses and textbooks of the public, private, and ʿatiq systems. In the regime's latest identity bargain, the king invoked his religious bona fides to promote religious education even as he was set to reduce Arabic instruction, benefiting from political and institutional conditions that the Moroccan Spring had reinforced. Secondary schools have continued to devote 2 hours per week to Islamic instruction,[11] and the king's February 2016 speech to his Council of Ministers suggested the drive to reorient the content away from extremist teachings would proceed much as before the Spring. Indeed, in the months following that speech, a royal commission led by Ahmed Abbadi, the head of the League of Moroccan Ulama, was convened to begin scrubbing the textbooks of references to religious teachings deemed violent or extremist.[12]

The trend toward increasing state control over institutions of religious learning has also continued much as before. A 2015 royal decree bringing all institutes of higher Islamic learning under the umbrella of the

[9] King's speech of August 20, 2013. Accessible at www.map.ma/fr/discours-messages-sm-le-roi/sm-le-roi-adresse-un-discours-la-nation-loccasion-du-60eme-anniversaire-.

[10] Omar Brouksy, "Le Maroc enterre trente ans d'arabisation pour retourner au français," *Le Monde*, February 19, 2016.

[11] International Bureau of Education, "Maroc," *Données Mondiales de l'Education* 7e édition (2010/2011), 20.

[12] Omar Brouksy, "La fausse réforme de l'éducation islamique enseignée aux enfants marocains," *Le Monde*, July 15, 2016.

state-run Qarawiyyin system was exemplary in this regard.[13] In addition to consolidating state control over these institutions, the 2015 law highlighted the recent creation of new institutions aimed at further expanding and reorienting the training of religion instructors. In 2013, for example, the state opened the Mohammed VI Institute for Quranic Readings and Studies, offering undergraduate and master's degree programs in Quranic readings and Quranic studies. A mix of bureaucratic and political considerations were behind the creation of this institute. In part, the institute was designed to produce graduates who will work as professors of Islamic Studies in the public universities, where demand for Islamic Studies courses has continued to rise despite chronic teacher shortages.[14] But the design of the curricula at the new institute also reflects the monarchy's efforts to push back against ideologies popular among jihadi groups. Students in the readings track take courses in the art of Quranic recitation, mastery of which is presumed to shield against erroneous – and extremist – interpretations of the text. The Quranic studies track requires 5 hours per week of English instruction, as well as classes in history, humanities, and logic alongside courses in Quranic exegesis that similarly treat the problem of extremism as fundamentally a problem of ignorance.[15]

Expansions in the religious bureaucracy and concerns to counteract extremist groups similarly fueled continued investments and reorientations in imam training. We saw in Chapter 3 that between 2005 and 2010 the state had trained 250 Moroccan imam supervisors annually, including women (murshidat), in hopes of regaining some measure of control over the religious sphere and producing religion instructors who could push back against extremist tendencies that had mushroomed in the preceding decades. In 2015, against the backdrop of the growing threat of the so-called Islamic State (IS) in the Levant and in Libya, terror attacks in Europe, and a subdued but latent Al-Qaeda in the Islamic Maghreb (AQIM) in Mali, the Ministry of Islamic Affairs took advantage of its expanding budget to inject $20 million into a new training facility in Rabat to accommodate a growing number of foreign students, principally from West Africa but also from Europe.[16] In addition to the 250 Moroccan students (of whom one hundred were

---

[13] Dahir 1.15.71 of June 24, 2015 (BORM 6374 of July 2, 2015, p. 3710–14).
[14] Interview with Khalid Saqi, Rabat, October 6, 2015.
[15] Decree 1.13.50 of May 2, 2013 (BORM 6153 of May 20, 2013, p. 4196–8).
[16] Dahir 1.14.103 of May 20, 2014 (BORM 6268 of June 26, 2014, p. 5470–3).

women), the 2015–16 cohort included one hundred students from Côte d'Ivoire, 120 from Guinea (among whom twenty murshidat), 111 from Mali, thirty-seven from Tunisia (among whom four murshidat), and twenty from France. While the program remains a one-year course of study for Moroccans and Tunisians, the West African students follow a two-year course of study and the Europeans will spend three years in the program, principally to devote additional time to learning Arabic. The foreign students in the murshidin/murshidat program report that they plan to return to their home countries and hope to work as preachers in mosques, schoolteachers, or other religious functionaries of the state.[17]

The classes at the imam training academy are divided into an Islamic law track, a humanities track (including courses on the history of Islam, the history of the countries from which the students hail, comparative religion, general philosophy, and Islamic philosophy), and vocational training. Reflecting the kingdom's broader reform agenda, religious studies courses at the imam training academy stress Malikism, Ash'arism, and the Junayd Sufi tradition,[18] and administrators of the program report that the assumption informing the Islamic law curricula is that extremism throughout the region stems from an ignorance and misunderstanding of the relevant texts. As such, courses in sharia focus on the Sunna (the sayings and behavior of the Prophet) as a model of behavior, and include lessons debunking *takfir*, the practice popular among jihadi groups of labeling individuals as unbelievers. The long-term impact of such initiatives remains to be seen, but in the meantime the kingdom appears poised to continue implementing reforms in the religious realm much as it did before the Arab Spring. And so long as the ideological, political, and institutional factors I have highlighted remain largely unchanged, there is little reason to expect drastic shifts in the kingdom's approach to regulating religious instruction.

---

[17] As recounted to the author by a group of students during a visit to the academy on October 8, 2015.

[18] Junayd al-Baghdadi was a ninth-century Sufi ascetic credited with developing one of the more orthodox schools of Islamic mysticism. His proximity to the earliest generation of Muslims has endeared him even to Salafists, who generally exhibit disdain for Sufi scholars and practices that emerged later. See, for example, www.youtube.com/watch?v=YakXuCAlCoY.

REGULATING RELIGION IN A DEMOCRATIC
TRANSITION: POST-JASMINE TUNISIA

Of all the countries experiencing the downfall of a political regime in
2011, Tunisia remains the only one on a recognizable, if tenuous, path to
democracy. Most contemporary press accounts of the Arab Spring traced
the Tunisian uprising to the self-immolation of a street vendor, Mohamed
Bouazizi, in December of 2010. Compelling as it was, this popular narrative obscured the fact that Bouazizi's suicide had *followed* a period of
deep social unrest the likes of which Tunisia had not seen since the early
1980s. In 2008 a group of unemployed youth and temporary workers
at the state phosphate mining company in Gafsa (a town located in the
mid-western region of the country) launched a series of strikes to protest
the lack of jobs and unfair hiring practices. Over the next two years,
these protests spread from Gafsa and nearby Sidi Bouzid to the outskirts
of Tunis, and in January 2011 the National Union of Tunisian Workers
(UGTT) called for a national strike. The UGTT's mobilization fueled
the decisive protests of January 14, 2011, which ultimately succeeded in
ousting Ben 'Ali.

Following his departure, the formerly ruling Democratic Constitutional
Rally (RCD) was dissolved and a series of interim governments culminated in the election of a National Constituent Assembly (NCA) on
October 23, 2011. The NCA was tasked with drafting a new constitution and preparing the country for the election of a permanent legislature within one year's time. In a development that would set the regional
trend, Tunisia's formerly banned Islamist movement, Ennahda, emerged
from the October 2011 election in a dominant position, capturing 41
percent of the popular vote and obtaining a plurality of seats in the transitional legislature. The remaining 59 percent of votes went to more than
a dozen non-Islamist parties and independents. Ennahda entered into a
governing coalition with two secular parties, Congress for the Republic
and the Democratic Forum for Labor and Liberties, or Ettakatol, and this
"troika" became Tunisia's new government.

The NCA's one-year mandate was unrealistic from the outset, given
that the elected body also had to assume responsibility for day-to-day
legislating alongside its work on the new constitution and electoral law.
The troika ended up governing for roughly two and a half years, during which time Tunisians enjoyed a broad expansion in their political
rights but the country's economy deteriorated and the security situation
worsened. This period saw increasing violence by radical Islamist groups,

including a September 2012 attack on the US embassy in Tunis, the assassinations of two leftist politicians in February and July of 2013, respectively, and repeated attacks on the part of al-Qaeda-linked groups against military and law enforcement installations along the Algerian border. In the summer of 2013, massive protests brought the NCA to a standstill and the Tunisian transition to the brink of collapse.

A National Dialogue organized under the auspices of the UGTT, the Tunisian League for Human Rights, the Tunisian Union of Industry and Commerce, and the National Bar Association facilitated a series of negotiations between the political factions throughout the fall of 2013. In December, Ennahda yielded to public pressure and agreed to step down, ceding power to an interim government of technocrats. In January 2014 the NCA ratified a new constitution enshrining: freedoms of speech, association, and press; political equality between men and women; and checks and balances between the legislative, executive, and judicial branches. The National Dialogue "Quartet" would go on to win the 2015 Nobel Peace Prize in recognition of its role rescuing the transition.

From January to October 2014, the interim cabinet of Prime Minister Mehdi Jomaa governed to broadly positive reviews as the country's precarious security situation stabilized somewhat,[19] and the NCA adopted the long-awaited electoral law to govern future parliamentary and presidential elections. On October 26, 2014, Tunisians went to the polls to elect a new 217-seat legislature, and the results yielded a parliament dominated by five blocs: the secularist Nida' Tunis ("Tunisian Call") Party with eighty-five seats, the Islamist Ennahda Party with sixty-nine seats, the anti-Islamist Free Patriotic Union (UPL by its French acronym) with sixteen seats, the leftist Popular Front coalition with fifteen seats, and the neo-liberal Afaq Tunis (Tunisian Horizons) Party with eight seats. The remaining twenty-four seats went to independents. On December 21, 2014 Tunisians elected as their new president Beji Caid Essebsi, a veteran statesman and the leader of Nida' Tunis. Both elections, widely

---

[19] A June/July 2014 poll conducted by the International Republican Institute (IRI) found that 67 percent of Tunisians believed the security situation had improved under the Jomaa government. See International Republican Institute, *IRI Poll: Tunisia's Democratic Transition at a Crossroads*, August 19, 2014. Similarly, an October 2014 International Crisis Group (ICG) report noted that the Jomaa government had "practically eradicated" Ansar al-Sharia from the country, although violent confrontations between jihadi groups and security forces continued along the border with Algeria. See International Crisis Group, "Update Briefing," Middle East and North Africa Briefing No. 41 (Tunis/Brussels, October 21, 2014): 2.

praised by international and domestic observers, represented significant achievements, all the more so given the growing chaos next door in Libya and the regional upheaval more generally.

But alongside the political progress embodied in two successful elections and a functioning parliament, Tunisia has struggled to revive a badly damaged economy and contain growing security threats. Perhaps the bleakest aspect of the transition has been economic. For many Tunisians, especially those living in the chronically neglected interior regions, the uprising brought little economic improvement and in some cases made conditions worse. Throughout the governorates where the protests originated, unemployment in 2016 still hovered around 25 percent and had reached 40 percent among young adults. Smuggling across the Libyan and Algerian borders has increased, in part because the state remains reluctant to clamp down for fear of depriving citizens of income – even as these smuggling routes have been used to transport weapons and terrorists alongside goods like oil and food.

Tunisia has also faced ongoing security threats, including spillover from the Libyan civil war, routinely uncovered terrorist cells at home, and the prospect of 3,000–6,000 radicalized Tunisians returning from Syria and Iraq. I have already noted the attack against the US embassy in 2012 and the two political assassinations of 2013. The year 2014 seemed to offer a mild reprieve, but then in March 2015, three gunmen killed nineteen foreign tourists and two Tunisian citizens at the Bardo National Museum, an attack the Tunisian government blamed on a local offshoot of AQIM. Three months later, a Tunisian proclaiming allegiance to IS gunned down thirty-eight, mostly British, tourists on a beach in Sousse. The Sousse attack prompted President Essebsi to impose a state of emergency, and in the ensuing months the government appeared to gain a better handle on the security situation. The calm was shattered on November 24, 2015, when a convoy of Presidential Guard officers was blown up in downtown Tunis, killing twelve. Once again, IS claimed responsibility, and Essebsi reimposed the state of emergency that had expired a month prior. More recently, on March 6, 2016 around sixty militants claiming allegiance to IS attacked police, National Guard, and military sites in Ben Guerdane, a town close to the Libyan border, killing twenty-two law enforcement officials and seven citizens, and injuring seventeen others. As of this writing, the country remains in a state of uneasy calm, its fate very much up for grabs.

What has all of this meant for the state's handling of the religious realm? To answer this question, it is worth assessing more pointedly how developments in Tunisia since the uprising affected the ideological, political, and institutional factors that had dictated the state's regulation of religious institutions up to that point. Let us first consider the matter of ideology. Although Tunisia's government ostensibly has transitioned away from an authoritarian system, the underlying basis of legitimacy for that system remains non-traditionalist insofar as Tunisia's democratically elected leaders do not claim their right to govern on religious grounds, and the new constitution enshrines the notion of a "civil state."

Maintaining the system's non-traditionalism did not come without debate. Shortly after the NCA was constituted in November 2011, disputes broke out in parliament over whether to make Islamic law (sharia) the basis of Tunisia's new constitution. Ennahda's 2011 electoral platform made no mention of sharia, and prior to the elections Ghannouchi stated his party would not seek to insert religious law into the new constitution. After the party's victory in October, however, a group of parliamentarians – including some of Ennahda's more conservative members – proposed adopting sharia as "a source among sources" of the law. While several thousand Salafists rallied in support of the proposal (more on this below), NCA Speaker Mustapha Ben Jaafar, a member of Ettakatol, threatened to resign if the proposal were adopted, and secular parties and nongovernmental organizations pressed Ennahda to clarify its position.

Faced with the prospect of the troika collapsing and growing public demands that Ennahda abide by its self-proclaimed "moderation," the movement's leadership calculated that the costs of pushing for sharia at this stage were too great. On March 26, 2012 the party announced that it would support retaining Article 1 of the 1959 constitution, which declares that "Tunisia is a free, independent, sovereign state; Islam is its religion; Arabic is its language; and the Republic is its form of government." In its official statement, Ennahda explained that the language of Article 1 adequately affirmed Tunisia's Arab-Islamic identity, and reiterated the party's hope that this identity would permeate the rest of the constitution.[20] To some extent, that hope was realized in the final text adopted in 2014. The preamble, for example, acknowledges the Tunisian people's "commitment to the teachings of Islam" and pays tribute to "the foundations of our Islamic-Arab identity." Likewise, and especially relevant for our purposes, Article 39 commits the state to providing an education system for its citizens that "work[s] to consolidate the Arab-Muslim identity and

---

[20] See Ennahda's official statement of March 26, 2012.

national belonging in the youth." Such references to identity notwithstanding, Article 2 enshrines the notion of a "civil state based on citizenship, the will of the people, and the supremacy of law," confirming the non-traditionalist basis of the governing regime.

In contrast to the continuity in legitimating ideology, however, the uprising led to a rupture in the nature of political opposition and in the relative strength of the governing regime's institutional resources. In the months following Ben 'Ali's departure, roughly 8,000 political prisoners were released from prison in a general amnesty, and the Islamists of Ennahda emerged from decades of exclusion to become dominant players in the new political landscape alongside a host of leftist and liberal groups that had opposed the Ben 'Ali regime. Indeed, for a brief period, it seemed there was virtually no organized opposition to the nascent democracy. But the aftermath of the uprising also saw the emergence of ultra-conservative Salafists in Tunisian society, of which jihadi strains – i.e., groups advocating the implementation of an Islamic state through the use of violence – would ultimately oppose the liberalized political system. The presence of jihadists in Tunisia would also carry important implications for the state's regulation of religious institutions and practice.

The Salafist phenomenon in post-Jasmine Tunisia initially encompassed formally recognized political parties such as *Jabhat al-Islah* (The Reform Front) and *Hizb al-Tahrir* (Party of Freedom), and movements such as *Ansar al-Sharia* (Supporters of the Sharia) which refused to participate in the political process but called for the Islamization of Tunisian society. In the two years following the uprising, unofficial estimates of the Salafist presence ranged from 6,000 to 100,000 citizens, and there were reports that Salafists took control of more than 200 mosques throughout Tunisia.[21] Professors at Zaytuna University reported that colleagues with Salafist leanings felt emboldened after the uprising, leading to tense exchanges between professors and students in religion and sociology courses there.[22] A group of Salafist students at Manouba University staged a sit-in that turned violent when the school refused to grant female students the right to attend class fully veiled.

[21] On estimates of Salafists' numerical strength in Tunisia, see Muhammad Al-Jazairy, "Salafism in Tunisia: A Brief History," *Al-Sharq Al-Awsat* (English Edition), August 5, 2012; Noureddin Jebnoun, "Salafi Trouble in Tunisia's Transition," *Jadaliyya*, June 13, 2012; Anna Mahjar-Barducci, "Salafists in Tunisia," *Gatestone Institute International Policy Council*, February 23, 2012.

[22] Interviews with Mongea Suwaihi (Tunis, October 19, 2012) and Iqbal Gharbi (Tunis, October 30, 2012).

Although Salafist groups in the country initially remained largely non-violent, they presented a challenge to the political elites of the nascent democracy, most of whom were intent on liberalizing the political process even as they were cognizant of the undemocratic and illiberal tendencies informing Salafist movements. For Ennahda the challenge was especially acute because, notwithstanding the diversity among Salafist groups, they all advocated the implementation of sharia in Tunisia. (Hizb al-Tahrir also called for reinstating the Caliphate.) When the proposal to insert sharia into the new constitution surfaced in 2012, for example, Salafists staged large demonstrations in support of the plan. Ennahda's ultimate decision to support retaining the original language of Article 1 disappointed the Salafists, but three days after announcing the decision, Jabhat al-Islah was granted a permit to operate as an official political party. The timing of the permit spoke to the delicate balance Ennahda sought in its relations with the Salafists.

Ironically, Ennahda's position vis-à-vis the Salafists initially resembled that of the former regime toward Ennahda in the 1980s, insofar as the Islamist party had to contemplate allowing potentially anti-democratic forces to enter the democratic process. After the 2011 election of the NCA, Ennahda made clear that groups not espousing violence were welcome to participate in the political process, and the party joined the government in announcing the arrest of twelve individuals linked to a violent Salafist cell and busting an arms depot outside Sfax. On the other hand, Ennahda members of the NCA participated in a large gathering of Salafists in Kairouan in May 2012,[23] and Ghannouchi attended Jabhat al-Islah's opening congress later that summer. In granting nonviolent Salafist parties formal recognition, Ennahda initially calculated that excluding them would prompt charges of hypocrisy and fuel further radicalization.

By 2013, however, the inclusive approach to Salafist groups had come under mounting public criticism. Ansar al-Sharia was blamed for the September 2012 attack on the US embassy, and the group was later implicated in the assassinations of Chokri Belaid and Mohamed Brahmi in 2013. In August 2013 the troika government under Ennahda's leadership named Ansar al-Sharia a terrorist organization, a move many Tunisians considered to have come too late. The leadership of Ansar al-Sharia fled to Libya, but the threat of jihadi Salafism remained, as the Bardo and

---

[23] Interview with civil society activists in Kairouan, June 29, 2012.

Sousse attacks in 2015 made clear. Since then, the ongoing activities within Tunisia of groups like Ansar al-Sharia, AQIM, and IS have reinforced the perception for many citizens and government officials that the primary opponent to Tunisia's democratic experiment has emerged in the form of violent Islamism.

Lastly, what of the Tunisian regime's institutional resources? Prior to the Jasmine uprising, the Ben 'Ali regime's relatively robust institutional endowment – reflected in a hegemonic party and a reasonably coherent bureaucracy – had facilitated religious education reforms. One effect of the uprising was to weaken the institutional endowment of the emerging system. To start, the months following Ben 'Ali's departure saw the elimination of the long-time ruling party, the RCD. On February 6, 2011 the Interior Ministry suspended the RCD's operations, and on 9 March the party was formally dissolved in Tunisian courts. In remarkably little time, an institutional pillar of the *ancien regime* was gone, and in its place emerged dozens of political parties of varying strength. Ennahda remains the most well-organized and cohesively structured party, with branches in all twenty-seven provinces and cells in all 264 municipalities. On the non-Islamist side, by contrast, the parties have struggled to cohere, with important implications for the state's management of the religious realm.

The fate of Nida' Tunis, the party Essebsi founded in 2012 to counteract Ennahda, has been especially turbulent. Following Ennahda's strong performance in the 2011 parliamentary election, Essebsi (who had served as a minister under Bourguiba, as Speaker of the Parliament under Ben 'Ali, and as Interim Prime Minister following Ben 'Ali's exit in 2011) created a new party and began rallying Tunisians around a broadly anti-Islamist message. As early as March, Nida' was holding rallies attracting several thousand people, suggesting at least a growing fascination with, if not support for, the emerging rival to Ennahda. By the fall of 2014, Essebsi was pegging the party's membership at 110,000.[24]

Essebsi's rhetoric emphasizing "modernism" (in implied contrast to Islamism), democracy, and the restoration of state prestige (*haybat al-dawla*) attracted three main constituencies to the party: former RCD members, leftists affiliated with a handful of smaller parties that had fared poorly in the 2011 parliamentary election, and secularly oriented academics and other intellectuals who were formerly apolitical but

---

[24] Membership numbers for Nida' Tunis are difficult to independently verify. For Essebsi's remarks, see "L'interview intégrale de Béji Caïd Essebsi à Leaders: J'irai jusqu'au bout!" *Leaders,* September 1, 2014.

gravitated to Nida' out of a desire to stop the Islamists' ascent. The shared determination to counterbalance the Islamists of Ennahda became the glue holding together these otherwise ideologically disparate groups. In Essebsi, they perceived a charismatic leader who could undo the damage of what many had come to view as the troika's lackluster governance, particularly in the economic and security realms.[25]

Taking a page out of Ennahda's playbook, Nida' opened regional offices in twenty-four of the country's twenty-seven governorates and established around 200 municipal cells. Funding for the party's operations reportedly came from four principal sources: donations from business interests, particularly in the tourism and agriculture sectors; private contributions from individual members; public financing during the campaign period; and donations from foreign governments before and during the campaign period. Foreign funding took various forms, including: contributions from the Konrad-Adenauer Stiftung, a foundation affiliated with the German government, which reportedly paid for Nida's headquarters and office materials; and a gift from the government of the United Arab Emirates in the form of two armored cars for Essebsi in July 2014 after he began receiving death threats. The United Arab Emirates' (UAE) gift was controversial, as it fed the narrative that Tunisia's anti-Islamists were being funded by the UAE while Ennahda enjoyed financial support from Islamist-friendly governments in Turkey and Qatar. Public skepticism about foreign funding did little to slow Nida's momentum. Instead, frustration with the troika's (mis)management of the political transition, a growing concern that political Islam posed a threat to the country's future, and Essebsi's charisma propelled Nida' to its parliamentary victory in October 2014 and ultimately carried Essebsi to Carthage Palace in December of that year.

However, the "big tent" of Nida' became one of its greatest liabilities, because beyond the shared – and, by 2014, ostensibly achieved – goal of diminishing Ennahda's clout, the three constituencies drawn to Nida' diverged considerably in their policy preferences. A second liability for Nida' was organizational. The party at one time or another boasted a Founding Committee, consisting of individuals within Essebsi's inner

---

[25] Throughout 2013, polling conducted by the IRI revealed that between 77 percent and 79 percent of Tunisians believed the country was headed in the wrong direction. These percentages would drop to 48 percent with the appointment of Jomaa's interim government in February 2014, and rebound to 67 percent by the eve of the 2014 parliamentary elections. See *IRI Poll: Tunisia's Democratic Transition at a Crossroads*, August 19, 2014.

circle; an Executive Bureau of one hundred members; a National Executive that claimed 400 members but no longer exists; and a thirty-person political bureau that was also short-lived. Nida' members, both among the older generation and younger activists, reported that final decisions were consistently taken by Essebsi himself, who reportedly remained reluctant to authorize decision-making bodies within the party lest they should generate competing power bases. The absence of democratic decision-making apparatuses within the party was partly to blame for a spate of high-level defections in 2014, including the August 2014 resignation of several regional office managers who were angry that they had not been consulted before the dissemination of party lists in anticipation of the parliamentary elections.

In the absence of internal decision-making structures, Nida's fissures only grew following the 2014 elections. One such division concerned the party leadership, with rival factions congregating around then Secretary General, Mohsen Marzouk, and President Essebsi's son, Hafedh. On November 9, 2015 thirty-two members of parliament in Marzouk's camp resigned from Nida', alleging that their opponents within the party had sought to install Hafedh as party leader. The immediate result of the defection was to reduce Nida's seat tally to fifty-four, putting Ennahda in the lead with sixty-nine seats. The implosion of Nida' ultimately led Essebsi to launch a process of negotiations toward a national unity government, putting on hold parliamentary action in multiple policy realms.

Six years into Tunisia's democratic experiment, the governing ideology remains non-traditionalist, the primary political opposition has crystallized in the form of violent Islamism, and the institutional endowment has been severely weakened. These conditions have had a combined effect on religious regulation, and policies concerning religious education specifically. To date, the most dramatic, if short-lived, change has been in the balance between state control and autonomy for institutions of religious learning. By contrast, when it has come to the incorporation of Islamic instruction into the national curricula, and regulations concerning religion instructors, instabilities borne of the democratic transition have produced a stasis. I address each of these developments in turn.

With the transition away from authoritarianism, policy decisions concerning religion and state in Tunisia were for the first time brought into the realm of democratic politics, which in the event came to include an Islamist party seeking (alongside certain non-Islamist allies) to fundamentally change the relationship between religion and state the country had known up to that point. The significance of the prospective change was evident in the constitution-drafting process, during which fierce debates erupted concerning a proposal to make sharia a source of laws (some within Ennahda wanted sharia to become "the" source of laws), and the question of how to define the state's role in the religious realm more generally. On the matter of sharia, Ennahda ultimately dropped its insistence on inserting reference to Islamic law into the text. Delineating the state's role in the religious sphere turned out to be more complicated, for while there was broad support for a close relationship between religion and state, deep disagreements surfaced between those wanting the state to control the religious realm (essentially maintaining the template of the post-independence era) and those wanting the state to govern in accordance with religious rules and precepts.[26]

The resulting compromise was enshrined in Article 6, which committed the state to a robust role in regulating the religious realm while also ensuring a degree of freedom within (and, importantly, from) that realm. Article 6 reads as follows:

The state is the custodian of religion. It guarantees freedom of belief, freedom of conscience, and the freedom of religious worship; it protects the neutrality of mosques and other places of worship from partisan exploitation. The state commits itself to spreading values of moderation and tolerance, protecting sacred [things] and protecting attacks against them, just as it commits itself to prohibiting accusations of apostasy (*takfir*) and incitement to hate and violence, and to confronting them.

Significant as this compromise was, the language of Article 6 did nothing to resolve two central tensions coursing through religion-state dynamics after the Jasmine uprising. The first pits the (non-traditionalist!) state's mandate to protect freedom of thought ("conscience"), which presumably includes the freedom to reject religion, against the state's opposition to "attacks against" sacred things, which theoretically leaves the door open to criminalizing blasphemy. This is not merely an academic debate. In June 2012 a group of Salafists broke into an art gallery outside Tunis and defaced an art exhibit they deemed insulting to Islam. The next day, riots erupted in the capital as protesters angered by the exhibit clashed with police, leading to the arrest of over one hundred individuals and the imposition of a curfew. Ennahda, some of whose members had been among those calling

---

[26] Malika Zeghal, "Constitutionalizing a Democratic Muslim State Without Sharia: The Religious Establishment in the Tunisian 2014 Constitution," in *Sharia Law and Modern Muslim Ethics*, ed. Robert Hefner (Bloomington, IN: Indiana University Press, 2015), 108–9.

for protests, formally denounced the exhibit as a provocation and an insult against religion, while also calling for calm and nonviolence.[27]

The second tension in Article 6 lies between the state's mandate to ensure freedom of religious thought and expression on the one hand – by, for example, protecting mosques and other places of worship from outside interference – and the state's commitment to regulating that expression on the other – by, for example, "spreading values of moderation and tolerance" and "prohibiting accusations of apostasy." This tension has been evident in the state's evolving degree of control over religious institutions. Under the troika government, the state took a largely hands-off approach to the religious realm, eager to allow a greater degree of freedom for Tunisians to practice their faith. (Some critics of Ennahda saw a more sinister intent in the lax environment that permitted radical voices to emerge and thrive.) But when it became clear that an unregulated religious realm was providing spaces for extremists to operate, successor governments changed course and began reasserting control over the mosques. The fate of the Zaytuna Grand Mosque, efforts to evict self-proclaimed preachers from mosques, and the closure of private religious associations have exemplified the swings between autonomy and control for religious institutions in the post-Jasmine environment.

Shortly after the uprising, a group of Tunisian citizens filed a lawsuit calling on the state to reopen the administrative offices, or scientific committee (*al-hay'a al-ʿilmiyya*), of the Zaytuna Grand Mosque after decades of inactivity. The Court of First Instance in Tunis granted the claimants' demand, and in March 2012 the doors to the Zaytuna's offices were unsealed for the first time since 1958, when then-President Bourguiba had largely dismantled a centuries-old system of education centered in the Grand Mosque and its annexes. In May 2012, the Ministers of Education, Higher Education, and Religious Affairs jointly signed a document formally recognizing the reestablishment of the Zaytunian education system and affirming the institution's independence from state regulation.[28]

---

[27] "Scores arrested after Tunis art riots," *Al Jazeera* (online), June 12, 2012.

[28] The document, entitled "Document on the Resumption of Traditional Zaytunian Education," was signed by Minister of Religious Affairs Nourredine Khadmi, Minister of Education Abdellatif Abid, and Minister of Higher Education Moncef Ben Salem on May 12, 2012. See "al-Quda' al-Tunisi Yuqar bi-Istiqlaliat Jamʿa al-Zaytuna ʿan Hukumat al-Jebali [Tunisian judiciary recognizes independence of the Zitouna Mosque under the Jebali government]" *France 24*, August 18, 2012. Malika Zeghal later noted that courses were to be segregated between boys and girls. For Zeghal's account, see Zeghal, "Teaching Again at the Zaytuna Mosque in Tunisia."

This immunity from state interference enabled Hussayn al-ʿAbidi, the man with minimal religious training whom I introduced in Chapter 5, to install himself as Shaykh of the Grand Mosque in the spring of 2012. As I noted earlier, al-ʿAbidi was among those calling for the death of the two artists whose allegedly blasphemous works were being displayed in a gallery outside Tunis. When the Ministry of Religious Affairs attempted to have the locks to the Zaytuna changed in order to keep al-ʿAbidi out, a local court ruled that effort illegal, and al-ʿAbidi filed a criminal complaint against the Ministry for alleged "intimidation." Over the next three years the state repeatedly failed to evict him, largely hamstrung by its own commitment to enshrining the institution's independence. Al-ʿAbidi's case highlights the dilemma facing Tunisian policymakers who remain eager to ease the Ben ʿAli-era restrictions on religious expression but are wary of providing a platform to extremists.

Ultimately, the rise in incitement and religiously motivated violence throughout 2012 and 2013 prompted the post-troika government of Mehdi Jomaa to begin reasserting state control over mosques and religious associations. In the context of a broader campaign to reverse the deteriorating security situation, Jomaa's government ultimately shut down 149 mosques alleged to have been involved in spreading nefarious discourse. At the same time, the Ministry of Religious Affairs began discouraging imams from endorsing political parties or candidates, ostensibly in an effort to enforce the constitution's prohibition against partisan instrumentalization of places of worship. Statements coming out of the Ministry indicated that imams retained full discretion in the subject of their sermons, so long as they displayed a commitment to "realism, wisdom, moderation, and party-neutrality."[29] Jomaa's Minister of Religious Affairs, Munir Tlili, also stressed that the Maliki madhhab should form the basis of all fatwas issued in the country, though the state refrained from centralizing the authority to issue such religious guidelines to the extent seen in Morocco.[30]

Private religious associations similarly came under greater scrutiny after the troika stepped down. Throughout 2012 and 2013 the state had legalized nearly 400 associations engaged in religious instruction and

---

[29] See, for example, the comments of Sadiq al-Arfaoui, an advisor to the Religious Affairs Minister, cited in "al-Awqaf al-Tunisiyya Tanfi Naytiha Tawhid Khutbat al-Jumʿa [Tunisian Ministry of Endowments Denies Intention to Unify Friday Sermons]," *Al-Sharq*, February 3, 2015.

[30] For Tlili's statement on fatwa unification, see "Wazir al-Shuʾun al-Diniyya: Hakadha tam Ikhtiyar al-90 Waʿizan li-Murafaqat al-Hajij [Minister of Religious Affairs: Ninety Preachers Chosen to Accompany Pilgrims]," *al-Sabah*, August 26, 2014.

outreach *(daʿwa)*, and scholars have estimated that around 200 were linked to the terrorist group, Ansar al-Sharia.[31] In July 2014 the Jomaa government announced it was suspending the activities of 157 such associations for "alleged links to terrorism."[32] At the same time, Religious Affairs Minister Tlili was of the view that countering extremism necessitated a deeper reform of the country's religious institutions that could only come through greater state support for Islamic education in the public schools and institutions such as the Zaytuna. In this vein, he looked favorably upon Morocco's ʿatiq system as a model for his own country.[33]

Upon assuming the Religious Affairs portfolio, Tlili undertook a comprehensive evaluation of Tunisia's religious realm. An inter-ministerial committee composed of representatives from the Religious Affairs, Culture, Interior, and Justice Ministries spent most of 2014 interviewing imams and other religious figures around the country, assessing the state of the country's four main institutions of official Islam (the Religious Affairs Ministry, the Zaytuna University, the High Islamic Council, and the largely defunct *Dar al-Ifta*), and issuing recommendations to strengthen these institutions and reform the content of religious instruction. In early 2015, Tlili presented the confidential report to the incoming government of Prime Minister Essid, but the disruptions caused by multiple government turnovers and a series of high-profile terror attacks reduced the bandwidth and appetite for deeper reforms of the religious realm that might have implicated the curricula or the training of future religion instructors. Instead, Tlili's recommendations languished as the state prioritized clamping down on mosques.[34] By March of 2015, fewer than 200 out of the country's 5,500 mosques remained beyond the control of the state, and after the July 2015 terrorist attack in Sousse, Prime Minister Essid announced the state's intention to close an additional eighty mosques that had allegedly been spreading "takfirist" ideology.[35]

[31] Interview with Alaya Allani, Tunis, February 6, 2016.
[32] Ibid. See also Haim Malka, "Tunisia: Confronting Extremism," in *Religious Radicalism after the Arab Uprisings* (Washington, DC: Center for Strategic and International Studies, 2014), 109.
[33] Interview with Munir Tlili, Tunis, February 5, 2016.
[34] Ibid.
[35] Ayman Gharbi, "Tunisie: Mosquées Hors de Contrôle, Radicalisation en Prison et Port du Niqab: Les Mesures de Othman Batikh contre le Terrorisme," *HuffPost Tunisie*, March 31, 2015; Sonia Bahi, "Attaque de Sousse: Les Dix Mesures Prises par le Gouvernement," *Webdo.Tn*, June 27, 2015.

Similarly, the Essid governments continued to close associations sus-
pected of laundering money or otherwise financing terrorist networks.

One result of the democratization process is that such decisions are
now open to contestation in the public domain. When Ennahda came into
power under the troika government, nearly 1,300 imams were reportedly sacked and replaced, provoking a public outcry from the country's
leading imam syndicate. Several years and governments later, it was
Ennahda's turn to protest when Othman Batikh, Essid's first Minister
of Religious Affairs, began firing imams for alleged incitement. A similar
uproar came in early 2016, when the Minister of Women, Children and
the Elderly announced that the government would be shutting down all
Quranic preschools that failed to obtain a license and abide by curricula
sanctioned by the Ministry of Education. After 2011, several dozen such
schools had cropped up, and some were found to be teaching extremist ideas. The Minister's announcement in January 2016 prompted fierce
criticism by the head of Ennahda's parliamentary bloc, who argued that
such measures would prevent instruction of the Quran, thereby violat-
ing the constitution's prohibition against freedom of religion.[36] The tension between preserving freedom of religious expression and reducing
the spaces in which extremist voices can flourish will likely continue to
characterize Tunisia's religious realm in the near to medium term, and
for the moment the state appears unlikely to resume its post-Jasmine
policy of allowing greater autonomy for institutions of religious learning.
Meanwhile, lively debates in the media over the nature of religious education – debates prompted in part by the new constitution's stipulation
that the state must provide an education "consolidating" citizens' Islamic
identity – suggest that policy changes implicating curricula and the training of religion instructors are on the horizon. Just how far that horizon
stretches remains to be seen.

RELIGIOUS REGULATION AND REGIME SURVIVAL

This book has examined the politics of religious education in two Arab
states, with the aim of uncovering the principal factors fueling differential state regulation of religion throughout the region. My central argument has been that Arab states' identification with, endorsement, and

---

[36] Frida Dahmani, "Tunisie: Fermeture des Ecoles Coraniques ne Bénéficiant pas d'Autorisation," *Jeune Afrique*, February 2, 2016.

institutionalization of religion primarily have been by-products of the governing regimes' broader strategies of political survival. But rather than being simply a matter of a leader's rational calculations, or solely the reflection of a ruling elite's ideological inclinations, three key factors interact to produce much of the observed variation in religious regulation, both between states and within states over time: (1) the regime's legitimating ideology, (2) the constellation of political opponents facing the regime, and (3) the regime's institutional endowment, especially the presence or absence of a hegemonic political party and a robust bureaucratic apparatus. If we want to understand how and why Arab states have been regulating religion, this cocktail of ingredients accounts for much of the story. A subsidiary finding has been that state regulation of religion in the Arab world, particularly in the context of political authoritarianism, can become a tool at a regime's disposal when confronting threats to its survival.

These findings take us a step closer to understanding complicated dynamics of religion-state relations in the Arab Middle East, but they also raise questions meriting additional research. One set of questions concerns the transferability of my claims beyond the Arab world. To what extent are regimes and governments in other regions – particularly in countries with formally established religions (or churches, as the case may be) – using the regulation of religious institutions as a mechanism of survival? Another way of phrasing this question might be: how much of the story told in the preceding chapters is uniquely Arab? I suspect the dynamics I have highlighted in two contemporary Arab states can be identified, even in modified form, beyond the Arab world, especially (but not necessarily only) in authoritarian settings where we find formal state establishment of religion. Comparativists and scholars of regions outside the Arab world are well positioned to consider the extent to which the tensions between religious and state authorities at the heart of this book mirror developments in their respective areas of specialization.

A second line of inquiry flowing from the study concerns the relationship between religious regulation and regime survival. This book has focused on the factors motivating and governing a regime's resort to religious regulation in its quest for survival, but I have largely refrained from drawing conclusions about the degree to which state regulation of religion has *accounted for* that survival. The fates of the Moroccan and Tunisia regimes after 2011 raise the question whether differential approaches to regulating religious institutions help to explain why the Moroccan regime emerged from the Spring intact, while the Tunisian

regime crumbled. Is it possible that Tunisia's more forceful consolidation of state control over (and elimination of) religious institutions ultimately contributed to the Ben 'Ali regime's collapse in January 2011?
The absence of robust religious institutions (state or otherwise) probably did handicap the post-Spring regime's efforts to counteract Islamist
extremism, if for no other reason than the Tunisian state could not point
to well-established, institutionalized alternatives to the extremist ideologies then undermining the country's democratic consolidation. But this is
not quite the same as demonstrating that the state's relatively aggressive
approach to regulating religion over the years stripped Ben 'Ali of the
tools needed to survive the protests of 2011. Further research would be
needed to confirm such a hypothesis.

Moving farther west, we might ponder whether Morocco's decision
to leave traditional venues of religious learning alone for decades paved
the way for more favorable conditions facing the regime on February 20,
2011. Perhaps it did, and in that case, the policy decisions chronicled in
the preceding chapters would enhance our understanding of the apparent "monarchical exceptionalism" observed throughout the Arab world
in the last six years. The striking contrast between the survival of all
eight Arab monarchies and the collapse of five Arab republics (Tunisia,
Egypt, Libya, Yemen, and Syria) has brought renewed scholarly attention to the characteristics of the monarchies that may have immunized
them from the latest round of upheavals.[37] I agree with F. Gregory Gause
that the monarchies' remarkable ability to weather the latest storm is
probably "best explained not by monarchy as a regime type but by the
specific portfolios of resources, networks, and strategies of the individual
regime."[38] The storylines traced in this book suggest those "resources,
networks, and strategies" have included policies enacted to regulate religious institutions. To the extent the monarchies have enjoyed a greater
capacity than their republican counterparts to control and steer religious

---

[37] See especially Michael Herb, "Monarchism Matters," *Foreign Policy*, November 26,
2012; Sean L. Yom and F. Gregory Gause III, "Resilient Royals: How Arab Monarchies
Hang On," *Journal of Democracy* 23 (October 2012): 74–88; Andre Bank, Thomas
Richter and Anna Sunik, "Long-term Monarchical Survival in the Middle East: A
Configurational Comparison, 1945–2012," *Democratization* 22 (2015): 179–200;
Maria Josua, "Co-optation Reconsidered: Authoritarian Regime Legitimation Strategies
in the Jordanian 'Arab Spring,'" *Middle East Law and Governance* 8 (2016): 32–56.
[38] F. Gregory Gause III, "Kings for All Seasons: How the Middle East's Monarchies Survived
the Arab Spring," *Brookings Doha Center*, Analysis Paper Number 8 (September 2013), 28.

institutions, religious regulation would appear to be a key tactic of what Steven Heydemann has called "authoritarian upgrading."[39]

Still, we should be cautious about asserting a direct link between these states' varying approaches to regulating religion and their divergent fates in the aftermath of the Arab Spring, not least because any such assertion would also need to account for these regimes' shared success in surviving for decades before the events of 2011, notwithstanding their varied approaches to regulating religion. Additional research is warranted to uncover the connections between state regulation of religion and regime survival, and this book hopefully offers a fruitful starting point in that endeavor.

THE POWER AND THE BURDEN OF REGULATING ISLAM

It was perhaps a historical irony that in their determination to distinguish themselves from the European colonial authorities they replaced, Arab political elites at mid-century adopted a European invention – formal state establishment of religion – in their quest for legitimacy. Declaring Islam to be "the religion of the state" probably did imbue the postcolonial Arab states with a degree of legitimacy, insofar as it signaled the new regimes' intentions to reflect and support the religious identity of the populations they were governing. Beyond the matter of legitimacy, formal establishment of Islam accrued considerable powers to the independent Arab states. In the educational realm, for instance, leaders suddenly found themselves in a position to shape religious knowledge and mold the individuals responsible for imparting that knowledge to a citizenry. The crafting of religious curricula, the balancing of autonomy and state control for institutions of religious learning, and the formation of individuals entrusted to impart knowledge of religious values and rituals to citizens – these are awesome powers, ones the regimes incorporated into their broader strategies of survival.

Still, the trajectories I have traced in this book suggest the enviable power of regulating Islam – of being in a position to define and disseminate religious ideas – has also placed a considerable burden on contemporary Arab states insofar as the imperative to continually regulate religious institutions, discourse, and practice has required the states to

---

[39] Steven Heydemann, "Upgrading Authoritarianism in the Arab World," *Saban Center for Middle East Policy at the Brookings Institution*, Analysis Paper No. 13 (October 2007).

promote religious concepts and principles that are inherently open to contestation and debate. In Tunisia, parliamentarians in 2013 managed to agree on the need to retain a formal link between the state and Islam, but consensus on which or whose "Islam" has been constitutionally enshrined remains elusive as ever. Even in a country such as Morocco, where the regime has arguably managed the religious realm more deftly than elsewhere, the ruling monarch's religious identity has not immunized the regime from religiously motivated opposition groups challenging that identity and the political legitimacy it has been invoked to bolster. The burden of regulating Islam is not likely to diminish anytime soon, given that transnational movements and ideological currents from the Muslim Brotherhood to al-Qaeda to IS are primed to continue challenging the Arab states' approaches to regulating Islam, and in some instances the very notion of a nation-state. How Arab leaders manage the task of regulating religion within their borders amidst such turmoil remains to be seen, but the historical record suggests the relevant regulations they enact will reflect a combination of the ideological, political, and institutional contexts in which decision makers find themselves.

Bibliography

Publications

Abdel Moula, Mahmoud. "L'université zaytounienne et la société tunisienne." Doctoral Dissertation, La Sorbonne: Paris, France, 1967.

Abdesselem, Ahmed. "Tunisia." *Yearbook on Education.* Geneva: International Bureau of Education, 1959.

Abun-Naser, Jamil. "The Salafiyya Movement in Morocco: The Religious Bases of the Moroccan Nationalist Movement." *St. Anthony's Papers* 16 (1963): 90–105.

Adam, André. "Chronique Sociale et Culturelle: Maroc." *Annuaire de l'Afrique du Nord* 3 (1964): 194–219.

"Chronique Sociale et Culturelle: Maroc." *Annuaire de l'Afrique du Nord* 4 (1965): 239–67.

"Chronique Sociale et Culturelle: Maroc." *Annuaire de l'Afrique du Nord* 5 (1966): 322–34.

Al-Ashhab, Muhammad. "al-Maghreb Yuqar Khitat al-Islah al-Ta'lim wa Istratejiyya li-l-Tanmiyya fi-l-Sahra [Morocco Announces an Education Reform Plan and Development Strategy in the Sahara]." *Al-Hayat*, February 8, 2016.

"al-Awqaf al-Tunisiyya Tanfi Naytiha Tawhid Khutbat al-Jum'a [Tunisian Ministry of Endowments Denies Intention to Unify Friday Sermons]." *Al-Sharq*, February 3, 2014.

Al-Jazairy, Muhammad. "Salafism in Tunisia: A Brief History." *Asharq al-Awsat* (English Edition), August 5, 2012.

"al-Quda' al-Tunisi Yuqar bi-Istiqlaliat Jam'a al-Zaytuna 'an Hukumat al-Jebali, [Tunisian Judiciary Recognizes Independence of the Zaytuna Mosque under the Jebali Government]." *France 24*, August 18, 2012.

Anderson, Betty S. "Writing the Nation: Textbooks of the Hashemite Kingdom of Jordan." *Comparative Studies of South Asia, Africa and the Middle East* 21 (2001): 1–14.

Ayachi, Mokhtar. *Écoles et Société en Tunisie 1930–1958*. Tunis: Cahiers du Centre d'Études et de Recherches Economiques et Sociales, 2003.

Bahi, Sonia. "Attaque de Sousse: Les Dix Mesures Prises par le Gouvernement," *Webdo.Tn*, June 27, 2015.

Bank, Andre, Thomas Richter, and Anna Sunik, "Long-term Monarchical Survival in the Middle East: A Configurational Comparison, 1945–2012," *Democratization* 22 (2015): 179–200.

Baskan, Birol. "The State in the Pulpit: State Incorporation of Religious Institutions in the Middle East." *Politics and Religion* 4 (2011): 136–53.

"State Secularization and Religious Resurgence: Diverging Fates of Secularism in Turkey and Iran." *Politics and Religion* 27 (2014): 28–50.

Beck, Colin J. "State Building as a Source of Islamic Political Organization." *Sociological Forum* 24 (2009): 337–56.

Ben Abdeljelil, Moncef. "al-Ta'lim al-Dini bi-Jami'at al-Zaytuna Hadiran [Religious Education in the Modern Zaytuna University]." In *Kayfa Yudarris al-Din al-Yawm? [How Do We Teach Religion Today?]*. Casablanca: King Abdul-Aziz Al Saoud Foundation for Islamic Studies and Human Sciences, 2004.

Ben Bouazza, Bouazza. "Ex-Tunisian Leader Habib Bourguiba Dies," *The Washington Post*, April 7, 2000.

Ben Dhiaf, Issa. "Chronique Politique: Tunisie." *Annuaire de l'Afrique du Nord* 15 (1976): 381–408.

"Chronique Politique: Tunisie." *Annuaire de l'Afrique du Nord* 17 (1978): 411–32.

"Chronique Politique: Tunisie." *Annuaire de l'Afrique du Nord* 19 (1980): 577–601.

"Chronique Politique: Tunisie." *Annuaire de l'Afrique du Nord* 20 (1981): 583–627.

Buehler, Matt. "The Threat to 'Un-moderate': Moroccan Islamists and the Arab Spring." *Middle East Law and Governance* 5, no. 3 (2013): 231–57.

Bouzoubaa, Khadija. "Renover le préscolaire coranique au maroc." In *Tradition et Innovation dans l'Éducation Préscolaire*, edited by Sylvie Rayna and Gilles Brougère. Paris: INRP-CRESAS, 2000, 1–19.

Bras, Jean-Philippe. "Chronique Politique: Tunisie." *Annuaire de l'Afrique du Nord* 23 (1984): 957–92.

Brouksy, Omar. "La fausse réforme de l'éducation islamique enseignée aux enfants marocains," *Le Monde*, July 15, 2016.

"Le Maroc enterre trente ans d'arabisation pour retourner au français," *Le Monde*, February 19, 2016.

Brown, Carl L. "Tunisia: Education, 'Cultural Unity,' and the Future." In *Man, State, and Society in the Contemporary Maghrib*, edited by William I. Zartman. New York: Praeger Publishers, 1973.

Burke III, Edmund. *Prelude to Protectorate in Morocco: Precolonial Protest and Resistance, 1860–1912*. Chicago, IL: University of Chicago Press, 1976.

Camau, Michel. "Le Discours Politique de Légitimité des Elites Tunisiennes." *Annuaire de l'Afrique du Nord* 10 (1971): 25–68.

"Chronique Politique: Tunisie." *Annuaire de l'Afrique du Nord* 12 (1973): 411–36.

Camau, Michel, and Vincent Geisser, eds. *Habib Bourguiba, la Trace et l'Héritage*. Paris: Karthala, 2004.

Casanova, Jose. *Public Religions in the Modern World*. Chicago, IL: Chicago University Press, 1994.

Charfi, Mohamed. "Interview." *Jeune Afrique*, April 30, 1990.

Islam and Liberty: The Historical Misunderstanding. London: Zed Books, 2005.

Charfi, Mohamed, and Hamadi Redissi. "Teaching Tolerance and Open-Minded Approaches to Understanding Sacred Texts." In *International Perspectives on the Goals of Universal Basic and Secondary Education*, edited by Joel E. Cohen and Martin E. Malin. New York: Routledge, 2010.

Charrad, Mounira. "Policy Shifts: State, Islam and Gender in Tunisia, 1930s–1990s." *Social Politics* 4, no. 2 (1997): 284–319.

States and Women's Rights: The Making of Postcolonial Tunisia, Algeria, and Morocco. Berkeley, CA: University of California Press, 2001.

Chekroun, Mohamed. "Système d'Enseignement et Education Religieuse au Maroc," Vol. 22. *Série Colloques et Séminaires*. Rabat: Publications de la Faculté des Lettres et des Sciences Humaines, 1992.

Chennoufi, Ali. "Etudes: l'Enseignement au Maghreb." *Revue Maghreb Machrek* 78 (1977): 61–9.

Cohen, David K., and Susan L. Moffitt, eds. *The Ordeal of Equality: Did Federal Regulation Fix the Schools?* Cambridge, MA: President and Fellows of Harvard College, 2009.

"Communiqué du 'Mouvement de La Tendance Islamique'." *Le Maghreb*, June 13, 1981.

Cremin, Lawrence. *American Education, the National Experience: 1783–1876*. New York: Harper & Row, 1980.

Dahmani, Abdelaziz, and Souhayr Belhassen. "Interview with Mohamed Mzali." *Jeune Afrique*, May 30, 1979.

Dahmani, Frida. "Tunisie: Fermeture des Ecoles Coraniques ne Bénéficiant pas d'Autorisation, " *Jeune Afrique*, February 2, 2016.

Damis, John. "The Origins and Significance of the Free School Movement in Morocco, 1919–1931." *Revue de l'Occident Musulman et de La Méditerranée* 19 (1975): 75–99.

Daoud, Zakya. "Chronique Tunisienne." *Annuaire de l'Afrique du Nord* 28 (1989): 679–712.

De Saenger, Béatrice. "Chronique Politique: Tunisie." *Annuaire de l'Afrique du Nord* 9 (1970): 271–8.

"Chronique Politique: Tunisie." *Annuaire de l'Afrique du Nord* 11 (1972): 331–40.

Eickelman, Dale F. "The Art of Memory: Islamic Education and Its Social Reproduction." *Comparative Studies in Society and History* 20, no. 4 (1978): 485–516.

"Madrassas in Morocco: Their Vanishing Public Role." In *Schooling Islam: The Culture and Politics of Modern Muslim Education*, edited by Robert W.

Hefner and Muhammad Qasim Zaman. Princeton, NJ: Princeton University Press, 2007.

Elahmadi, Mohsine. *La Monarchie et l'Islam*. Casablanca: Ittissalat Salon, 2006.

El Ayadi, Mohammed. "De L'Enseignement Religieux." *Prologues: Revue Maghrébine du Livre* 21 (2001): 32–44.

———. "Entre Islam et Islamisme: La Religion Dans L'école Publique Marocaine." *Revue Internationale d'Éducation de Sèvres* 36 (2004): 111–21.

El Katiri, Mohammed. "The Institutionalisation of Religious Affairs: Religious Reform in Morocco." *Journal of North African Studies* 18, no. 1 (2013): 53–69.

El Mansour, Mohamed. "Salafis and Modernists in the Moroccan Nationalist Movement." In *Islamism and Secularism in North Africa*, edited by John Ruedy, 53–71. New York: St. Martin's Press, 1994.

Ennaji, Moha. *Multilingualism, Cultural Identity, and Education in Morocco*. New York: Springer, 2005.

Entelis, John P. *Comparative Politics of North Africa*. Syracuse, NY: University of Syracuse Press, 1980.

Felk, Abdellatif. "Idéal Éthique et Discours d'Orthodoxie dans l'Enseignement Marocain." *Bulletin Economique et Social du Maroc* 157 (1986): 170–8.

Fetzer, Joel, and J. Christopher Soper. *Muslims and the State in Britain, France and Germany*. Cambridge: Cambridge University Press, 2005.

Fougère, Louis. "La Constitution Marocaine du 7 Décembre 1962." *Annuaire de l'Afrique du Nord* 1 (1962): 155–65.

Fox, Jonathan. *A World Survey of Religion and the State*. Cambridge: Cambridge University Press, 2008.

Frégosi, Franck and Malika Zeghal. "Religion et Politique Au Maghreb: Les Exemples Tunisien et Marocain." *Institut Français Des Relations Internationales*, Policy Paper, 11 (2005): 1–51.

Fuller, Graham. *The Future of Political Islam*. New York: Palgrave, 2003.

Gause III, F. Gregory. "Kings for All Seasons: How the Middle East's Monarchies Survived the Arab Spring." *Brookings Doha Center*, Analysis Paper 8 (2013): 1–33.

Geertz, Clifford. *Islam Observed: Religious Developments in Morocco and Indonesia*. Chicago, IL: University of Chicago Press, 1971.

Geisser, Vincent, and Éric Gobe. "Tunisie: Consolidation Autoritaire et Processus Électoraux." *L'Année du Maghreb 2004*, CNRS Editions, 1 (2006): 323–60.

Gharbi, Ayman. "Tunisie: Mosquées Hors de Contrôle, Radicalisation en Prison et Port du Niqab: Les Mesures de Othman Batikh Contre le Terrorisme," *HuffPost Tunisie*, March 31, 2015.

Gill, Anthony. "Rendering Unto Caesar? Religious Competition and Catholic Political Strategy in Latin America, 1962–79." *American Journal of Political Science* 38 (1994): 403–25.

———. *Rendering Unto Caesar: The Catholic Church and the State in Latin America*. Chicago, IL: University of Chicago Press, 1998.

———. *The Political Origins of Religious Liberty*. Cambridge: Cambridge University Press, 2008.

Gourdon, J. "Chronique Politique: Maroc." *Annuaire de l'Afrique du Nord* 10 (1971): 322–34.

Granai, Georges and André Adam. "Chronique Sociale et Culturelle, Algerie-Maroc-Tunisie." *Annuaire de l'Afrique du Nord* 1 (1962): 539–85.

Haykel, Bernard, Thomas Hegghammer, and Stephane Lacroix. *Saudi Arabia in Transition: Insights on Social, Political, Economic and Religious Change.* Cambridge: Cambridge University Press, 2015.

Hefner, Robert W. and Muhammad Qasim Zaman, eds. *Schooling Islam: The Culture and Politics of Modern Muslim Education.* Princeton, NJ: Princeton University Press, 2007.

Herb, Michael. "Monarchism Matters." *Foreign Policy*, November 26, 2012.

Hermassi, Abdelbaki (Elbaki). *Leadership and National Development in North Africa.* Berkeley, CA: University of California Press, 1972.

"L'État Tunisien et Le Mouvement Islamiste [The Tunisian State and the Islamist Movement]." *Annuaire de l'Afrique du Nord* 28 (1989): 297–308.

"The Political and the Religious in the Modern History of the Maghreb." In *Islamism and Secularism in North Africa*, edited by John Ruedy, 87–99. New York: St. Martin's Press, 1994.

Heydemann, Steven. "Upgrading Authoritarianism in the Arab World," *Saban Center for Middle East Policy at the Brookings Institution*, Analysis Paper No. 13 (2007): 1–35.

Hibou, Béatrice. *The Force of Obedience: The Political Economy of Repression in Tunisia.* Cambridge: Polity Press, 2011.

Howe, Marvine. *Morocco: The Islamist Awakening and Other Challenges.* New York: Oxford University Press, 2005.

Human Rights Watch. *Morocco: Human Rights at a Crossroads.* 2004. www.hrw.org/reports/2004/morocco1004/morocco1004.pdf.

International Bureau of Education. *Rapport Présenté à la 43ème Session de la Conférence Internationale de l'Éducation Genève* Rabat/Geneva: UNESCO, 1994.

"Maroc," *Données Mondiales de l'Education* 7e édition, (2010/2011), 1–35.

International Crisis Group, "La Tunisie des frontières (II): terrorisme et polarization régionale," Briefing Moyen-Orient et Afrique du Nord N. 41 (Tunis/Brussels, 21 October 2014), pp. 1–19.

International Republican Institute. *IRI Poll: Tunisia's Democratic Transition at a Crossroads*, August 19, 2014.

Jean-Claude Santucci and Maurice Flory. "Documents: Tunisie." *Annuaire de l'Afrique du Nord* 11 (1972): 817–54.

Jebnoun, Noureddin. "Salafi Trouble in Tunisia's Transition," *Jadaliyya*, June 13, 2012.

Josua, Maria. "Co-optation Reconsidered: Authoritarian Regime Legitimation Strategies in the Jordanian 'Arab Spring'," *Middle East Law and Governance* 8 (2016): 32–56.

Juergensmeyer, Mark. *The New Cold War? Religious Nationalism Confronts the Secular State.* Berkeley, CA: University of California Press, 1993.

Kaestle, Carl F. *Pillars of the Republic: Common Schools and American Society, 1780–1860.* New York: Hill and Wang, 1983.

Kalyvas, Stathis. *The Rise of Christian Democracy in Europe*. Ithaca, NY: Cornell University Press, 1996.

Kaplan, Sam. *The Pedagogical State: Education and the Politics of National Culture in Post-1980 Turkey*. Stanford, CA: Stanford University Press, 2006.

Keddie, Nikki R. "Secularism and the State: Towards Clarity and Global Comparison." *New Left Review* 1, no. 226 (1997): 21–40.

"The New Religious Politics: Where, When, and Why Do 'Fundamentalisms' Appear?" *Comparative Studies in Society and History* 40, no. 4 (1998): 696–723.

Khtou, Hssein. *Reforms in the Religious Sphere and Their Educational Repercussions Vis-À-Vis Islamic Schools: The Case of Dar El Hadith El Hassania Institution in Morocco*. Unpublished report. Rabat: Dar al-Hadith al-Hassaniyya, 2012.

Koenig, Matthias. "Politics and Religion in European Nation-States: Institutional Varieties and Contemporary Transformations." In *Religion and Politics: Cultural Perspectives*, edited by Bernhard Giesen and Daniel Suber, 291–315. Leiden: Brill, 2005.

Kuru, Ahmet. *Secularism and State Policies toward Religion: The United States, France and Turkey*. Cambridge: Cambridge University Press, 2009.

Essebsi, Béji Caid. "J'irai jusqu'au bout!" *Leaders*. September 1, 2014.

Ladjili-Mouchette, Jeanne. "Le Kuttab et le Jardin d'Enfants en Tunisie." In *Les Institutions Traditionnelles dans le Monde Arabe*, edited by Hervé Bleuchot, 125–49. Paris: Karthala, 1996.

Larif-Béatrix, Asma. "Chronique Tunisienne." *Annuaire de l'Afrique du Nord* 27 (1988): 743–57.

"Changement dans la Symbolique du Pouvoir en Tunisie." *Annuaire de l'Afrique du Nord* 28 (1989): 141–51.

Le Tourneau, Roger. "Chronique Politique." *Annuaire de l'Afrique du Nord* 2 (1963): 219–53.

"Chronique Politique." *Annuaire de l'Afrique du Nord* 3 (1964): 111–41.

"Chronique Politique." *Annuaire de l'Afrique du Nord* 4 (1965): 165–90.

"Chronique Politique." *Annuaire de l'Afrique du Nord* 5 (1966): 237–57.

"Chronique Politique." *Annuaire de l'Afrique du Nord* 6 (1967): 298–318.

"Chronique Politique." *Annuaire de l'Afrique du Nord* 7 (1968): 177–99.

Lelong, Michel. "Le Patrimoine Musulman dans l'Enseignement Tunisien Après l'Indépendance." PhD Dissertation, Université de Provence I: Lille, France, 1971.

"Les Évolutions Récentes de l'Enseignement Islamique en Tunisie." *Communiqué*. Paris, 1973.

Lindsey, Ursula. "Private Universities in Morocco Aim to Fill Gap between Higher Education and Job Market," *Financial Times*, November 23, 2015.

"Mashru' Wizarat al-Awqaf wa-l-Shu'un al-Islamiyya hawl al-Waqf . . . Tamuh Kabir Yahtaj ila Irada Siyasiyya li-l-Tafil [The Ministry of Pious Endowments and Islamic Affairs' Project for the Endowments: A Big Ambition that Will Need the Political Will to Implement]." *al-Tajdid*, January 20, 2004. Accessible at www.maghress.com/attajdid/15243.

Madani, Mohamed, Driss Maghraoui, and Saloua Zerhouni. *The 2011 Moroccan Constitution: A Critical Analysis.* Stockholm: International IDEA, 2012.

Maghraoui, Driss. "The Dynamics of Civil Society in Morocco." In *Political Participation in the Middle East,* edited by Ellen Lust-Okar and Saloua Zerhouni. Boulder, CO: Lynne Rienner Publishers, 2008.

"The Strengths and Limits of Religious Reforms in Morocco." *Mediterranean Politics* 14, no. 2 (2009): 195–211.

Mahjar-Barducci, Anna. "Salafists in Tunisia," *Gatestone Institute International Policy Council,* February 23, 2012.

Mahjoubi, Ali. "La Réforme de l'Enseignement en Tunisie (1989–1994) [Education reforms in Tunisia (1989–1994)]." *Attariq Aljadid,* June 5, 2010.

Malka, Haim. "Tunisia: Confronting Extremism," in *Religious Radicalism after the Arab Uprisings.* Washington, DC: Center for Strategic and International Studies, 2014.

Mandaville, Peter. *Global Political Islam.* London: Routledge, 2007.

Mann, Michael. "The Autonomous Power of the State: Its Origins, Mechanisms and Results." *Archives Européennes de Sociologie [European Journal of Sociology]* 25 (1984): 185–213.

Marais, Octave. "L'élection de la Chambre de Représentants du Maroc." *Annuaire de l'Afrique du Nord* 2 (1963): 85–106.

Maurice Flory and Jean-Louis Miège. "Discours prononcé par sa majesté le Roi Hassan II le 3 Mars 1962." *Annuaire de l'Afrique du Nord* 1 (1962): 755–63.

McCarthy, Rory. "Re-thinking Secularism in Post-Independence Tunisia." *The Journal of North African Studies* 19 (2014): 733–50.

Meijer, Roel, ed. *Global Salafism: Islam's New Religious Movement.* Oxford: Oxford University Press, 2013.

Menashri, David. *Education and the Making of Modern Iran.* Ithaca, NY: Cornell University Press, 1992.

Messadi, Mahmoud. *Nouvelle Conception de l'Enseignement en Tunisie.* Tunis: Tunisian Ministry of Education, October 1958. File 1666. Tunisian National Archives.

Michel Camau, Jean-Claude Santucci and Maurice Flory. "Documents: Tunisie." *Annuaire de l'Afrique du Nord* 8 (1970): 849–86.

Migdal, Joel. *State in Society: Studying How States and Societies Transform and Constitute One Another.* Cambridge: Cambridge University Press, 2001.

Miller, Susan Gilson. "Studying the State." In *Comparative Politics: Rationality, Culture, and Structure,* edited by Mark Lichbach and Alan Zuckerman. Cambridge: Cambridge University Press, 1997.

Miller, Susan Gilson. *A History of Modern Morocco.* Cambridge: Cambridge University Press, 2013.

Monastiri, Taoufik. "Chronique Sociale et Culturelle: Tunisie." *Annuaire de l'Afrique du Nord* 10 (1971): 424–43.

Monsma, Stephen V. and J. Christopher Soper. *The Challenge of Pluralism: Church and State in Five Democracies.* Lanham: Rowman & Littlefield Publishers, Inc., 1997.

Moore, Clement Henry. "The Neo-Destour Party of Tunisia: A Structure for Democracy?" *World Politics* 14, no. 3 (1962): 461–82.

Tunisia since Independence: The Dynamics of One-Party Government. Berkeley, CA: University of California Press, 1965.

"Political Parties." In *Polity and Society in Contemporary North Africa*, edited by William I. Zartman and William Mark Habeeb, 42–67. Boulder, CO: Westview Press, 1993.

Moroccan Ministry of Education. *al-Madrassa al-Maghrebiyya: As'ila wa Ruhanat [The Moroccan School: Questions and Stakes].* Rabat: Moroccan High Council of Education, 2009.

Le Mouvement Educatif au Maroc, 1973–1974 et 1974–1975. Rabat: Moroccan High Council of Education, 1975.

Le Mouvement Educatif au Maroc, 1975–1976 et 1976–1977. Rabat: Moroccan High Council of Education, 1977.

Le Mouvement Educatif au Maroc, 1978–1979 et 1979–1980. Rabat: Moroccan High Council of Education, 1981.

Harakat al-Ta'lim fi-l-Maghreb Khilal al-Fatra ma Bayna 1980–1981, 1983–1984 [The Progression of Education in Morocco during 1980–1981 and 1983–1984]. Rabat: Moroccan High Council of Education, 1985.

Le Mouvement Educatif au Maroc Durant La Periode 1980–1981/1983–1984. Rabat: Moroccan High Council of Education, 1985.

Le Mouvement Educatif au Maroc Durant la Période 1990–1991 et 1991–1992. Rabat: Moroccan High Council of Education, 1994.

al-Wathiqa al-'Itar al-Ikhtiyarat wa-l-Tawjihat al-Tarbawiyya [Document on the Framework of Educational Choices and Orientations]. Rabat: Moroccan High Council of Education, 2002.

Aperçu Sur le Système Éducatif Marocain. Rabat: Moroccan High Council of Education, 2004.

Daftir al-Tahamulat al-Khassa al-Muta'alaq bi-Ta'lif wa Intaj al-Kutub al-Madrassiyya: Kitab al-Talmidh wa Dalil al-Ustadh [Specifications for the Writing and Production of School Textbooks: Student's Workbook and Teacher's Manual]. Rabat: Moroccan High Council of Education, 2004.

Daftir al-Tahamulat al-Khassa al-Muta'alaq bi-Ta'lif wa Intaj al-Kutub al-Madrassiyya [Specifications for the Writing and Production of School Textbooks]. Rabat: Moroccan High Council of Education, 2006.

al-Tawjihat al-Tarbawiyya wa-l-Baramij al-Khassa bi-Tadris Mada al-Tarbiyya al-Islamiyya bi-Suluk al-Ta'lim al-Thanawi al-Ta'hili [Educational Orientations and Curricula for Islamic Education at the Secondary School Level]. Rabat: Moroccan High Council of Education, 2007.

Rapport National Sur Le Developpement de l'Education, Préparé Pour La Conférence Internationale de l'Education 2008. Rabat: Moroccan High Council of Education, 2008.

L'évaluation de l'Impact des Programmes de l'Éducation aux Droits Humains et à la Citoyenneté du Ministère de l'Education Nationale. Rabat: Moroccan High Council of Education, 2011.

Moroccan Ministry of Higher Education, *Rapport National sur le Developpement de l'Education, Préparé Pour la Conférence Internationale de l'Education de 2008.* Rabat: Moroccan Ministry of Higher Education, 2008.

Moroccan Ministry of Pious Endowments and Islamic Affairs. *'Ashar Sanawat min al-'Ahad al-Muhammadi al-Zahir: I'Adah Haykalat al-Haql al-Dini wa Tatwir al-Waqf [Ten Years of the Glorious Reign, 1999–2009: Reorganization of the Religious Realm and the Development of Pious Endowments]*. Rabat: Moroccan Ministry of Pious Endowments and Islamic Affairs, 2012.

al-Ta'lim al-'Atiq [Traditional Education] (Rabat, 2013).

Mashru' al-Mayzaniyya al-Far'iyya li-Sanat 2016 [Draft Budget for 2016] (Rabat, 2016).

Moroccan Special Commission on Education and Training. *Charte Nationale d'Éducation et de Formation* Rabat: Moroccan Special Commission on Education and Training, 2000.

Mouline, Nabil. *The Clerics of Islam: Religious Authority and Political Power in Saudi Arabia*. New Haven, CT: Yale University Press, 2014.

Munson Jr., Henry. *Religion and Power in Morocco*. New Haven, CT: Yale University Press, 1993.

Mzali, Mohamed. "Les Nouvelles Options de Notre Enseignement [The New Choices for our Education]." Tunis: Tunisian Ministry of Education, 1970.

Un Premier Ministre de Bourguiba Témoigne. Paris: Jean Picollec, 2004.

Nasr, Sayyed Vali Reza. *Islamic Leviathan: Islam and the Making of State Power*. New York: Oxford University Press, 2001.

Norris, Pippa and Ronald Inglehart. *Sacred and Secular: Religion and Politics Worldwide*. Cambridge: Cambridge University Press, 2004.

Nouira, Asma. "al-Mu'asasat al-Islamiyya al-Rasmiyya fi Tunis min 1956 ila al-Yawm [Institutions of Official Islam in Tunisia from 1956 to the Present]." PhD Dissertation, University of Tunis, Tunis, 2008.

Ozgur, Iren. *Islamic Schools in Modern Turkey: Faith, Politics, and Education*. Cambridge: Cambridge University Press, 2015.

Perkins, Kenneth. *A History of Modern Tunisia*. Cambridge: Cambridge University Press, 2004.

Pierret, Thomas. *Religion and State in Syria: The Sunni Ulama from Coup to Revolution*. Cambridge: Cambridge University Press, 2013.

Rahmouni, Hassan, ed. *La Grande Encyclopédie du Maroc*. Rabat: 1988.

Sadiki, Larbi. "Ben Ali's Tunisia: Democracy by Non-Democratic Means." *British Journal of Middle Eastern Studies* 29, no. 1 (2002): 57–78.

Santucci, Jean-Claude. "Chronique Politique: Maroc." *Annuaire de l'Afrique Du Nord* 20 (1981): 567–82.

"Chronique Politique: Maroc." *Annuaire de l'Afrique du Nord* 23 (1984): 899–942.

Sater, James. "The Dynamics of State and Civil Society in Morocco." *The Journal of North African Studies* 7, no. 3 (2002): 101–18.

"Scores Arrested after Tunis Art Riots," *Al-Jazeera*. June 12, 2012.

Scott, James C. *Seeing Like a State: How Certain Schemes to Improve the Human Condition Have Failed*. New Haven, CT: Yale University Press, 1998.

Scott, Rachel M. "Managing Religion and Renegotiating the Secular: The Muslim Brotherhood and Defining the Religious Sphere." *Politics and Religion* 7 (2014): 51–78.

Segalla, Spencer D. "French Colonial Education and Elite Moroccan Muslim Resistance, from the Treaty of Fes to the Berber Dahir." *The Journal of North African Studies* 11, no. 1 (2006): 85–106.

The Moroccan Soul: French Education, Colonial Ethnology, and Muslim Resistance, 1912–1956. Lincoln: University of Nebraska Press, 2009.

Shahin, Emad Eldin. "Secularism and Nationalism: The Political Discourse of 'Abd Al-Salam Yassin." In *Islamism and Secularism in North Africa*, edited by John Ruedy, 167–86. New York: St. Martin's Press, 1994.

Skocpol, Theda. "Bringing the State Back In: Strategies of Analysis in Current Research." In *Bringing the State Back In*, edited by Theda Skocpol, Dietrich Rueschemeyer, and Peter Evans. Cambridge: Cambridge University Press, 1985.

Souali, Mohamed, and Mekki Merrouni. "Question de L'enseignement Au Maroc." *Bulletin Economique et Social du Maroc* 143–4 (1981): 1–465.

Souriau, Christiane. "Quelques Données Comparatives Sur les Institutions Islamiques Actuelles du Maghreb." *Annuaire de l'Afrique du Nord* 18 (1979): 341–79.

Sraieb, Noureddine. "Mutations et réformes de structures de l'enseignement en Tunisie." *Annuaire de l'Afrique du Nord* 6 (1967): 45–114.

"Chronique Sociale et Culturelle: Tunisie." *Annuaire de l'Afrique du Nord* 9 (1970): 400–32.

"Politiques Culturelles Nationales et Unité Maghrébine." *Annuaire de l'Afrique du Nord* 9 (1970): 101–27.

Colonisation, Décolonisation et Enseignement: l'Exemple Tunisien. Tunis: Publications de l'Institut National des Sciences de l'Education de Tunis, 1974.

"l'Idéologie de l'école en Tunisie Coloniale (1881–1945)." *Revue du Monde Musulman et de la Méditerranée* 68–69 (1993): 239–54.

Stacher, Joshua. *Adaptable Autocrats: Regime Power in Egypt and Syria.* Stanford, CA: Stanford University Press, 2012.

Starrett, Gregory. *Putting Islam to Work: Education, Politics and Religious Transformation in Egypt.* Berkeley, CA: University of California Press, 1998.

Storm, Lise. *Party Politics and the Prospects for Democracy in North Africa.* Boulder, CO: Lynne Rienner Publishers, 2014.

Talmoudi, Aida. "Min al-Katatib ila Riyad al-Aftal: Tatawur Mu'asasat Tarbawiyya ma Qabl al-Madrasiyya [From Kuttabs to Daycare Centers: The Development of Preschool Education in Tunisia]." Master's Thesis, University of Tunis, Tunis, 2013.

Tamer, Bashir. "al-Nizam al-Ta'limi al-Maghrebi Khilal al-Qarn al-'Ashrin: Ishkaliyyat al-Islah wa-l-Tatawur al-Kronologi [The Moroccan Educational System Throughout the Twentieth Century: Reforms and Chronology]." *Al-Madrassa Al-Maghribiya*, 1, 161–92. Rabat: Moroccan High Council of Education, 2009.

Tepe, Sultan. *Beyond Sacred and Secular: Politics of Religion in Israel and Turkey.* Palo Alto, CA: Stanford University Press, 2008.

The World Bank. *Education Development in Morocco: Enhancing Educating Quality and Governance*, April 15, 2014 www.worldbank.org/en/results/2014/04/15/education-development-in-morocco.

Tozy, Mohamed. "Islam et État au Maghreb." *Maghreb Machrek* 126 (1989): 25–46.
Tunisian Ministry of Education. "Statistique au 15 Novembre 1956: Tableau récapitulatif général." *Tunis*, 1956. File OPF 46(1). Archives of the Tunisian Museum of National Education.
Programmes Officiels de l'Enseignement Secondaire Fascicule VI: Instruction Civique et Religieuse. Tunis: Tunisian Ministry of Education, 1959.
Programmes Officiels de l'Enseignement Secondaire, Fascicule XIV: Philosophie et Etude de la Pensée Islamique. Tunis: Tunisian Ministry of Education, 1963.
Al-Ahdaf al-'Ama li-l-Tarbiyya al-Islamiyya [General Goals of Islamic Education]. Tunis: Tunisian Ministry of Education, 1968.
Programmes Officiels de l'Enseignement Du Second Cycle, Fascicule No. 6: Philosophie et Pensée Islamique. Tunis: Tunisian Ministry of Education, 1969.
Al-Baramij al-Rasmiyya li-l-Ta'lim al-Thanawi: al-Tarbiyya al-Islamiyya wa-l-Wataniyya [Official High School Curricula: Islamic and Civic Education]. Curriculum. Tunis: Tunisian Ministry of Education, 1970a.
Programmes Officiels de l'Enseignement, Fascicule No. 13: Philosophie et Pensée Islamique [Official Curricula, Part 13: Philosophy and Islamic Thought]. Tunis: Tunisian Ministry of Education, 1970b.
Al-Taqrir al-Niha'i 'an I'mal al-Lajna al-Qarah li-l-Falsafa al-'Ama wa-l-Falsafa al-Islamiyya [Final Report of the Working Group on General and Islamic Philosophy]. Tunis: Tunisian Ministry of Education, 1972.
Rapport Sur Le Mouvement Éducatif En Tunisie. Tunis: Tunisian Ministry of Education, 1977.
Tyack, David B. *The One Best System: A History of American Urban Education.* Cambridge, MA: Harvard University Press, 1974.
Vermeren, Pierre. "Une Si Difficile Réforme: La Réforme de L'université Qarawiyyin de Fès Sous Le Protectorat Français Au Maroc, 1912–1956." *Cahiers de La Méditerranée* 75 (2007): 119–32.
Wagner, Daniel A., and Abdelhamid Lotfi. "Traditional Islamic Education in Morocco: Sociohistorical and Psychological Perspectives." *Comparative Education Review* 24, no. 2 (1980): 238–51.
Waltz, Susan. "Islamist Appeal in Tunisia." *Middle East Journal* 40, no. 4 (1986): 651–70.
Human Rights and Reform: Changing the Face of North African Politics. Berkeley, CA: University of California Press, 1995.
Warner, Carolyn. *Confessions of an Interest Group: The Catholic Church and Political Parties in Europe.* Princeton, NJ: Princeton University Press, 2000.
Waterbury, John. *The Commander of the Faithful: The Moroccan Political Elite – A Study in Segmented Politics.* New York: Columbia University Press, 1970.
"Wazir al-Shu'un al-Diniyya: Hakadha tam Ikhtiyar al-90 Wa'izan li-Murafaqat al-Hajij [Minister of Religious Affairs: Ninety Preachers Chosen to Accompany Pilgrims]." *Al-Sabah*, August 26, 2014.
Weber, Eugen. *Peasants into Frenchmen: The Modernization of Rural France, 1870–1914.* Stanford, CA: Stanford University Press, 1976.

Weber, Max. "Politics as a Vocation." In *Max Weber: Essays in Sociology*, edited by H.H. Gerth and C. Wright Mills. New York: Oxford University Press, 1946.

Economy and Society: An Interpretive Sociology. 4th ed. Berkeley, CA: University of California Press, 1978.

Wegner, Eva. *Islamist Opposition in Authoritarian Regimes: The Party of Justice and Development in Morocco*. Syracuse, NY: Syracuse University Press, 2011.

Willis, Michael. "Between Alternance and the Makhzen: At-Tawhid wa Al-Islah's Entry into Moroccan Politics," *The Journal of North African Studies* 4, no.3 (1999): 45–80.

"Political Parties in the Maghrib: Ideology and Identification. A Suggested Typology." *The Journal of North African Studies* 7, no.3 (2002): 1–28.

"Political Parties in the Maghrib: The Illusion of Significance?" *The Journal of North African Studies* 7, no. 2 (2002): 1–22.

"Wizarat al-Awqaf: Tarfa' Mayzaniat al-Ta'lim al-'Atiq min Thalathat Milayeen ila 300 Milayun Dirham," [Ministry of Endowments: Increase in the budget for traditional education from 3 million to 300 million dirhams] *PJD.ma*, December 15, 2015.

Yom, Sean L. and F. Gregory Gause III, "Resilient Royals: How Arab Monarchies Hang On," *Journal of Democracy* 23 (2012): 74–88.

Zeghal, Malika. "Religion et Politique au Maroc Aujourd'hui." *Institut Français des Relations Internationales*, Working Paper, 2003.

Islamism in Morocco: Religion, Authoritarianism, and Electoral Politics. Princeton, NJ: Markus Wiener Publishers, 2008.

"Public Institutions of Religious Education in Egypt and Tunisia: Contrasting the Post Colonial Reforms of Al-Azhar and the Zaytuna." In *Trajectories of Education in the Arab World: Legacies and Challenges*, edited by Osama Abi-Mershed, 111–24. New York: Routledge, 2010.

"Teaching Again at the Zaytuna Mosque in Tunisia," *On Islam and Politics*, May 17, 2012.

"Constitutionalizing a Democratic Muslim State without Sharia: The Religious Establishment in the Tunisian 2014 Constitution," In *Sharia Law and Modern Muslim Ethics*, edited by Robert Hefner. Bloomington, IN: Indiana University Press, 2015.

Zghal, Abdelkader. "Le Retour du Sacré et la Nouvelle Demande Idéologique des Jeunes Scolarisés." *Annuaire de l'Afrique du Nord* 18 (1979): 41–64.

"Le Concept de Société Civile et La Transition Vers Le Multipartisme." *Annuaire de l'Afrique du Nord* 28 (1989): 207–28.

Regulations

Kingdom of Morocco. Dahir 1.15.71 of June 24, 2015. *In* Bulletin Officiel du Royaume du Maroc of July 2, 2015, no. 6374, 3710–14.

Dahir 1.14.103 of May 20, 2014. *In* Bulletin Officiel du Royaume du Maroc of June 26, 2014, no. 6268, 5470–73.

Decree 1.13.50 of May 2, 2013. *In* Bulletin Officiel du Royaume du Maroc of May 20, 2013, no. 6153, 4196–98.

Dahir 1.11.19 of March 1, 2011. *In* Bulletin Officiel du Royaume du Maroc of March 3, 2011, no. 5922, 260–66.

Ministerial Order 2836-09 of January 18, 2010. *In* Bulletin Officiel du Royaume du Maroc of March 18, 2010, no. 5822, 258–9.

Ministerial Decision 877.06 of May 3, 2006. *In* Bulletin Officiel du Royaume du Maroc of August 21, 2006, no. 5449, 2086–7.

Royal Decree 1-05-159 of August 24, 2005. *In* Bulletin Officiel du Royaume du Maroc of September 15, 2005, no. 5352, 643–7.

Royal Decree 1-03-300 of April 22, 2004. *In* Bulletin Officiel du Royaume du Maroc of May 6, 2004, no. 5210, 698.

Ordinance 763-04 of April 13, 2004. *In* Bulletin Officiel du Royaume du Maroc of June 17, 2004, no. 5222, 916.

Ordinance 1051 of March 3, 2004. *In* Bulletin Officiel du Royaume du Maroc of May 6, 2004, no. 5210, 704.

Royal Decree 1-03-193 of December 4, 2003. *In* Bulletin Officiel du Royaume du Maroc of January 1, 2004, no. 5174, 105–10.

Ordinance 950-03 of May 8, 2003. *In* Bulletin Officiel du Royaume du Maroc of October 2, 2003, no. 5148, 1213.

Law 13.01 of January 29, 2002. *In* Bulletin Officiel du Royaume du Maroc of February 21, 2002, no. 4980, 108–12.

Ordinance 2070 of November 23, 2001. *In* Bulletin Officiel du Royaume du Maroc of April 4, 2002, no. 4992, 259.

Ordinance 1082 of June 20, 1997. *In* Bulletin Officiel du Royaume du Maroc of August 7, 1997, no. 4506, 755.

Ordinance 18-96 of January 12, 1996. *In* Bulletin Officiel du Royaume du Maroc of February 15, 1996, no. 4352, 55.

Ordinance 55-95 of June 20, 1995. *In* Bulletin Officiel du Royaume du Maroc of August 2, 1995, no. 4318, 559.

Decree 1-93-164 of November 8, 1993. *In* Bulletin Officiel du Royaume du Maroc of November 2, 1994, no. 4279, 530.

Ministerial Order 1643-92 of November 5, 1992. *In* Bulletin Officiel du Royaume du Maroc of January 6, 1993, no. 4148, 8.

Royal Decree 2-88-293 of August 3, 1989. *In* Bulletin Officiel du Royaume du Maroc of November 15, 1989, no. 4020, 1448–53.

Ordinance 1446 of November 17, 1987. *In* Bulletin Officiel du Royaume du Maroc of November 18, 1987, no. 3916, 370.

Royal Decree 2-84-142 of February 15, 1985. *In* Bulletin Officiel du Royaume du Maroc of March 20, 1985, no. 3777, 161.

Decree 1-84-150 of October 2, 1984. *In* Bulletin Officiel du Royaume du Maroc of October 3, 1984, no. 3753, 386.

Royal Decree 2-82-319 of January 31, 1983. *In* Bulletin Officiel du Royaume du Maroc of February 2, 1983, no. 3666, 158–64.

Royal Decree 1-80-270 of April 8, 1981. *In* Bulletin Officiel du Royaume du Maroc of May 6, 1981, no. 3575, 231–2.

Royal Decree 2-79-637 of May 12, 1980. *In* Bulletin Officiel du Royaume du Maroc of June 4, 1980, no. 3527, 380–2.

Ministerial Order 1180-79 of January 11, 1980. *In* Bulletin Officiel du Royaume du Maroc of April 30, 1980, no. 3522, 285.

Ordinance 182-79 of February 1, 1979. *In* Bulletin Officiel du Royaume du Maroc of March 21, 1979, no. 3464, 160.

Royal Decree 2-78-608 of January 25, 1979. *In* Bulletin Officiel du Royaume du Maroc of January 31, 1979, no. 3457, 68–70.

Royal Decree 2-78-455 of September 28, 1978. *In* Bulletin Officiel du Royaume du Maroc of October 4, 1978, no. 3440, 1099–101.

Decree 2-76-313 of June 11, 1976. *In* Bulletin Officiel du Royaume du Maroc of June 16, 1976, no. 3320, 718–20.

Decree 1-75-300 of April 12, 1976. *In* Bulletin Officiel du Royaume du Maroc of April 28, 1976, no. 3313, 529–30.

Ministerial Order 633-75 of May 7, 1975. *In* Bulletin Officiel du Royaume du Maroc of June 25, 1975, no. 3269, 824–5.

Ordinance 26-74 of February 1, 1974. *In* Bulletin Officiel du Royaume du Maroc of March 20, 1974, no. 3203, 376.

Ministerial Order 332-72 of March 7, 1972. *In* Bulletin Officiel du Royaume du Maroc of April 12, 1972, no. 3102, 604–5.

Ordinance 500-71 of June 23, 1971. *In* Bulletin Officiel du Royaume du Maroc of June 30, 1971, no. 3061, 732.

Decree 2-70-455 of October 7, 1970. *In* Bulletin Officiel du Royaume du Maroc of November 4, 1970, no. 3027, 1509–11.

Decree 2-70-454 of October 7, 1970. *In* Bulletin Officiel du Royaume du Maroc of November 4, 1970, no. 3027, 1507–9.

Ministerial Order 326-64 of June 22, 1964. *In* Bulletin Officiel du Royaume du Maroc of July 29, 1964, no. 2700, 908–10.

Ordinance 315-64 of May 29, 1964. *In* Bulletin Officiel du Royaume du Maroc of July 8, 1964, no. 2697, 841.

Ministerial Orders of June 8, 1963. *In* Bulletin Officiel du Royaume du Maroc of June 14, 1963, no. 2642, 949–53.

Decree 2-62-621 of June 7, 1963. *In* Bulletin Officiel du Royaume du Maroc of June 14, 1963, no. 2642, 949–53.

Ordinance 219-63 of May 7, 1963. *In* Bulletin Officiel du Royaume du Maroc of May 24, 1963, no. 2693, 750.

Royal Decree 1-62-249 of February 6, 1963. *In* Bulletin Officiel du Royaume du Maroc of February 22, 1963, no. 2626, 260–1.

Ordinance 039-63 of December 26, 1962. *In* Bulletin Officiel du Royaume du Maroc of February 1, 1963, no. 2623, 178.

Royal Decree 2-60-374 of July 2, 1960. *In* Bulletin Officiel du Royaume du Maroc of July 22, 1960, no. 2491, 1425.

Royal Decree 1-58-390 of July 21, 1959. *In* Bulletin Officiel du Royaume du Maroc of August 7, 1959, no. 2441, 1326–7.

Royal Decree 1-59-049 of June 1, 1959. *In* Bulletin Officiel du Royaume du Maroc of June 12, 1959, no. 2433, 987.

Royal Decree 2-57-1947 of January 15, 1958. *In* Bulletin Officiel du Royaume du Maroc of March 14, 1958, no. 2368, 475–6.

Royal Decree 1-57-214 of December 16, 1957. *In* Bulletin Officiel du Royaume du Maroc of January 10, 1958, no. 2359, 63–4.

Royal Decree 2-57-0084 of March 14, 1957. *In* Bulletin Officiel du Royaume du Maroc of March 29, 1957, no. 2318, 417.

Republic of Tunisia. Decree 2008-3542 of November 22, 2008. *In* Journal Officiel de la République Tunisienne of November 28, 2008, no. 96, 4001–2.

Decree 2003-2411 of November 17, 2003. *In* Journal Officiel de la République Tunisienne of December 2, 2003, no. 96, 3489.

Decree 2003-2082 of October 14, 2003. *In* Journal Officiel de la République Tunisienne of October 21, 2003, no. 84, 3146–50.

Ministerial Order of February 6, 1996. *In* Journal Officiel de la République Tunisienne of February 13, 1996, no. 13, 331–4.

Ministerial Order of November 3, 1995. *In* Journal Officiel de la République Tunisienne of November 17, 1995, no. 92, 2150–4.

Decree 95-993 of June 5, 1995. *In* Journal Officiel de la République Tunisienne of June 9, 1995, no. 46, 1264–5.

Decree 95-865 of May 8, 1995. *In* Journal Officiel de la République Tunisienne of May 19, 1995, no. 40, 1136–7.

Decree 94-558 of March 17, 1994. *In* Journal Officiel de la République Tunisienne of March 25, 1994, no. 23, 494–5.

Decree 93-1952 of August 31, 1993. *In* Journal Officiel de la République Tunisienne of October 1, 1993, no. 74, 1645–7.

Decree 92-1180 of June 22, 1992. *In* Journal Officiel de la République Tunisienne of June 26, 1992, no. 41, 810.

Law 91-65 of July 29, 1991. *In* Journal Officiel de la République Tunisienne of August 6, 1991, no. 55, 1398.

Decree 92-1183 of June 22, 1991. *In* Journal Officiel de la République Tunisienne of June 26, 1992, no. 41, 813.

Decree 90-578 of March 30, 1990. *In* Journal Officiel de la République Tunisienne of April 17, 1990, no. 26, 515–17.

Decree 89-1690 of November 8, 1989. *In* Journal Officiel de la République Tunisienne of November 17–21, 1989, no. 77, 1805–6.

Law 87-83 of December 31, 1987. *In* Journal Officiel de la République Tunisienne of December 29–31, 1987, no. 91, 1637.

Decree 87-664 of April 22, 1987. *In* Journal Officiel de la République Tunisienne of April 28–May 1, 1987, no. 31, 575–6.

Decree 86-532 of May 6, 1986. *In* Journal Officiel de la République Tunisienne of May 9, 1986, no. 30, 580.

Ministerial Order of April 21, 1981. *In* Journal Officiel de la République Tunisienne of April 28 – May 1, 1981, no. 29, 941–3.

Ordinance of April 16, 1981. *In* Journal Officiel de la République Tunisienne of April 24, 1981, no. 28, 904–9.

Order of the Prime Minister of September 6, 1980. *In* Journal Officiel de la République Tunisienne of September 16, 1980, no. 51, 2237–8.

Decree 77-938 of November 17, 1977. *In* Journal Officiel de la République Tunisienne of November 22–25, 1977, no. 77, 3224–5.

Ministerial Order of October 30, 1976. *In* Journal Officiel de la République Tunisienne of November 5, 1976, no. 67, 2656–7.

Ministerial Order of June 6, 1973. *In* Journal Officiel de la République Tunisienne of June 8–12, 1973, no. 116, 918–20.

Decree 67-345 of October 5, 1967. *In* Journal Officiel de la République Tunisienne of October 6–10, 1967, no. 43, 1252–3.

Decree 66-151 of April 8, 1966. *In* Journal Officiel de la République Tunisienne of April 8–12, 1966, no. 17, 602–4.

Ministerial Order of August 9, 1965. *In* Journal Officiel de la République Tunisienne of August 6–10, 1965, no. 41, 986–7.

Ministerial Order of March 25, 1963. *In* Journal Officiel de la République Tunisienne of March 26–29, 1963, no. 15, 370–2.

Decree 62-107 of April 6, 1962. *In* Journal Officiel de la République Tunisienne of April 6–10, 1962, no. 19, 390.

Decree 61-357 of October 27, 1961. *In* Journal Officiel de la République Tunisienne of October 27–31, 1961, no. 46, 1388–9.

Decree 61-110 of March 1, 1961. *In* Journal Officiel de la République Tunisienne of March 3–7, 1961, no. 9, 354.

Law 58-118 of November 4, 1958. *In* Journal Officiel de la République Tunisienne of November 7, 1958, no. 89–102, 1056.

Decree of April 26, 1956. *In* Journal Officiel de la République Tunisienne of April 27, 1956, no. 34, 592.

Decree of March 29, 1956. *In* Journal Officiel de la République Tunisienne of April 3, 1956, no. 27, 497–8.

Interviews (positions listed were at the time of interview)

Morocco

Ahmed Abbadi, Secretary General of the League of Moroccan Ulama. Washington, DC, May 8, 2015.

Samir Abu Kacem, Office of Curricula at the Ministry of Education, former member of Islamic Education reform committee. Rabat, December 18, 2012.

Hassan Al Zahir, Dean of Sharia College, Qarawiyyin University. Fes, December 31, 2012.

Anonymous, Student at Dar al-Hadith al-Hassaniyya. Rabat, January 6, 2016, October 7, 2015, and December 1, 2016.

Mokhtar Benabdallaoui, Professor at Hassan II University and former member of Islamic education reform committee. Casablanca, December 15, 2012.

Abdelwahab Bendaoud, Director of Traditional Education at the Ministry of Pious Endowments and Islamic Affairs. Rabat, January 16, 2013 and February 11, 2015.

Mohammed Bennis, Professor of English, Sidi Ben Abdellah University. Fes, June 21, 2011.

Mohammed Boutarboush, Head of Salé Regional Council of Ulama, Salé, January 3, 2013.

Aziz Chbani, Director of Literacy and Professional Training Program/Consultant with the Millennium Challenge Corporation. Rabat, June 24, 2011.

Mohsine Elahmadi, Professor at Cadi Ayyad University. Rabat, January 7, 2013.

Imad Elarbi, Director of the Moroccan Center for Civic Education. Casablanca, January 8, 2013.

Rached Elamrani, Director of the Office of Textbooks at the Ministry of Education. Rabat, December 18, 2012.

Abdelkader Ezzaki, Consultant with Project ITQANE (Improving Training for Quality Advancement in National Education). Rabat, June 10, 2011.

Lahcen Haddad, Education consultant with MSI Morocco. Rabat, June 10, 2011.

Abdellatif Hakim, Professor of English, Sidi Mohamed Ben Abdellah University. Fes, June 21, 2011.

Abdelali Hami el-Din, member of PJD's executive council. Rabat, February 12, 2015.

Jaafar Kansoussi, Member of Islamic Affairs Minister Ahmed Toufiq's cabinet, former director of the ministry's Islamic Affairs Directorate for the Marrakesh region. Rabat, January 17 and 25, 2013; Marrakesh, February 8, 2015.

Hssein Khtou, Professor of English at Dar al-Hadith al-Hassaniyya. Rabat, December 9, 2013.

Brahim Machrouh, Assistant Director of Dar al-Hadith al-Hassaniyya. Rabat, October 7, 2015.

Mohamed Melouk, Professor of Education at Mohamed V University. Rabat, June 15, 2011 and December 18, 2012.

Nizar Messari, Dean of the School of Humanities and Social Sciences, Al-Akhawayn University. Ifrane, January 10, 2013.

Mohammed Moubtassime, Professor of English at Sidi Mohamed Ben Abdellah University. Fes, June 21, 2011.

Connell Monette, Coordinator of imam training program at Al-Akhawayn University. Rabat, December 26, 2012.

Kristen Potter, Director of USAID Education office, U.S. Embassy. Rabat, June 15, 2011.

Sadik Rddad, Professor of English and Sociology at Sidi Mohamed Ben Abdellah University, Fes, June 21, 2011.

Mohamed Ramh, Vice-Dean for Sciences and Cooperation at Sharia College, Qarawiyyin University. Fes, December 31, 2012.

Abderrahmane Rami, Former Director of Pedagogy at the Ministry of Education. Rabat, June 14, 2011.

Khalid Saqi, Assistant Director of Dar al-Hadith al-Hassaniyya. Rabat, December 9, 2013.

Director of Mohamed VI Insititute for Quranic Readings and Studies. Rabat, October 6, 2015.

Fouad Shafiki, Director of Office of Curricula, Moroccan Ministry of Education. Rabat, January 3, 2013.

Students in the Muhammad VI Institute for the Training of Imams. Rabat, October 8, 2015.

Bilal Talidi, member of PJD's executive council. Rabat, October 7, 2015.

Tunisia

Mohamed Nejbi Abd El-Moula, Mayor of Sfax. Sfax, July 3, 2012.

Rafik Abdessalem, former Foreign Affairs Minister and member of Ennahda's Shura Council. Tunis, February 2, 2015.

Hussayn al-ʿAbidi, Shaykh of the Zaytuna Grand Mosque. Tunis, February 5, 2015.

Alaya Allani, Professor at Manouba University. Tunis, February 6, 2016.

Chiraz Arbi, staff person in the National Democratic Institute's Tunisia office. February 6, 2015.

Mokhtar Ayachi, Director of the Tunisian Museum of National Education. Tunis, October 18, 2012.

Bochra Belhaj Hmida, former President of l'Association Tunisienne des Femmes Democrates. Tunis, June 28, 2012.

Moncef Ben Abdeljelil, Professor and former member of Education Minister Mohamed Charfi's cabinet. Sousse, October 23, 2012.

Hatem Ben Salem, Director of Tunisian Institute for Strategic Studies and former Minister of Education. Tunis, September 23, 2016.

Faouzia Charfi, Minister Mohamed Charfi's widow. Tunis, September 17, 2012.

Hamadi Ben Jaballah, former high school philosophy teacher. Tunis, October 12, 2012.

Mahmoud Ben Romdhane, founding member of Nida' Tunis Party. Tunis, February 3, 2015.

Civil society activists, Kairouan, June 29, 2012.

Hmida Ennaifer, former member of Education Minister Mohamed Charfi's cabinet. Tunis, September 19, 2012, October 11, 2012, and February 2, 2015.

Ridha Ferchiou, President of l'Institut Tunis-Dauphine. Tunis, September 4, 2012.

Said Ferjani, Member of Ennahda's Shura Council. Tunis, February 5, 2015.

Iqbal Gharbi, Professor at Zaytuna University. Tunis, October 30, 2012.

Tarek Kahlaoui, Director of the Tunisian Institute for Strategic Studies. Tunis, June 29, 2012.

Habib Kazdaghli, Dean of the Manouba University Faculty of Humanities. Tunis, February 3, 2016.

Riadh Moakhar, Member of Parliament with the Afaq Tunis Party. Tunis, February 4, 2016.

Asma Nouira, Professor of Political Science at the University of Tunis. Tunis, June 26, 2012.

Habib Sayah, Security sector consultant. Tunis, February 4, 2016.

Oussama Sghaier, Member of Parliament with Ennahda and member of Ennahda's Shura Council. Tunis, September 23, 2016.

Mongea Suwaihi, Professor at Zaytuna University. Tunis, October 19, 2012 and February 2, 2016.

Munir Tlili, Professor at Zaytuna University. Tunis, October 10, 2012.
    Former Minister of Religious Affairs. Tunis, February 5, 2016.

Sami Triki, member of Ennahda's Shura Council. Tunis, February 5, 2015.

Amira Yahyaoui, Founder of al-Bawsala. Tunis, February 5, 2016.

Index

Abbadi, Ahmed, 182
al-'Abidi, Hussayn, 128, 129, 196
Afaq Tunis Party, 186
agricultural collectivization (Tunisia), 114,
    115, 120, 121, 140, 141, 156, 166
Alaouites, 8, 28, 40, 42, 43, 49, 55, 82,
    83, 104, 134, 173
  in the nationalist struggle, 32, 92
  political opponents of, 27, 29, 31–33,
    34, 39, 69, 75, 86, 93, 97, 101, 102,
    179
  religious legitimacy of, 19, 28–31, 54,
    59, 68, 81, 83, 99
  stance toward religious institutions, 20,
    76, 77, 79, 81, 91, 92
al-Fikr (magazine), 144
Algeria, 14, 15, 39, 41, 186, 187
Amir al-Mu'minin. *See* Commander of the
    Faithful
Ansar al-Sharia, 189, 190, 197
Arab Spring, 7–8, 28, 49, 128, 129, 173,
    174, 175, 181, 184, 185, 201
Ash'arism, 184
authoritarianism, 2, 4, 8, 13, 15, 17,
    18, 19, 49, 50, 173, 174, 188, 193,
    199, 201
Authority of Pious Endowments
    (Tunisia), 132

Ba'ath Party (Syria), 113
bachelor's degree, 91, 95, 96, 100,
    101, 168
Bardo National Museum, 187, 190

Batikh, Othman, 198
bay'a. *See* Investiture ritual
Belaid, Chokri, 190
Belmokhtar, Rached, 182
Ben Abbes, Youssef, 60
Ben Abdeljelil, Moncef, 147, 169, 170
Ben 'Achour, Fadhl, 154, 155
Ben 'Ali, Zine el-'Abidine, 8, 109, 111,
    123, 124, 126, 130, 159, 191,
    196, 200
  and political liberalization, 117,
    121–23, 148
  education policies of, 158, 160, 167
  opponents of, 111, 117, 118, 148–49,
    159, 169, 170, 171, 172, 189
  ouster of, 5, 8, 173, 185, 189, 191,
    200
  views on religion, 19, 106, 109,
    110–11, 159
Ben Barka, Mehdi, 35, 59
Ben Guerdane (town in Tunisia), 187
Ben Jaafar, Mustapha, 188
Ben Jaballah, Hamadi, 138
Ben Salah, Ahmed, 114, 141
Ben Youssef, Salah, 111–12, 134, 152,
    153, 162, 163, 171
  partisans of (Youssefists), 113, 142,
    152, 153, 155, 171
Bendaoud, Abdelwahab, 102, 103
Benhima, Mohamed, 60–63
Benjelloun, Omar, 35, 61
Benkirane, Abdelilah, 36, 38, 175, 177,
    178, 180, 182